MW01113376

The Profundity and Bifurcation of Change

The Intelligent Social Change Journey

Part III: *Learning in the Present*

MQIPress (2020)
Frost, West Virginia
ISBN 978-0-9985147-7-2

The Consciousness Series

*The human experience is a neuronal dance with the Universe, with each of us
in the driver's seat selecting our partners and directing our dance steps.*

MQIPress
Frost, West Virginia
303 Mountain Quest Lane
Marlinton, WV 24954
United States of America
Telephone: 304-799-7267

alex@mountainquestinstitute.com
www.mountainquestinstitute.com
www.mountainquestinn.com
www.MQIPress.com
www.Myst-art.com

ISBN 978-0-9985147-7-2

Man considering the Universe of which he is a unit, sees nothing but change in matter, forces and mental states. He sees that nothing really is, but that everything is becoming and changing. Nothing stands still. Everything is being born, growing, dying. At the very instant a thing reaches its height, it begins to decline. The law of rhythm is in constant operation. There is no fixed reality, enduring quality or substantiality in anything –nothing is permanent but Change. Man sees all things evolve from other things and resolve into other things; a constant action and reaction, inflow and outflow, building up and tearing down, creation and destruction, birth, growth and death. Nothing endures but Change. And if he is a thinking man, he realizes that all of these changing things must be outward appearances or manifestations of some underlying power, some Substantial Reality.

The Kybalion (1940, p. 53)

Part III*

Table of Contents

* This book is Part I of *The Profundity and Bifurcation of Change*, available from Amazon.com in hard copy and Kindle format, and in PDF format from MQIPress.net

Part III
Tables, Figures, and Tools

TABLES

FIGURES

TOOLS

In Appreciation

Hundreds of people, named and unnamed, have contributed thousands of ideas to this book in the context of conversations and dialogues, articles and books, and quotes and stories. We are all indeed one, sharing ideas in groups and communities, face-to-face and virtual, appearing and connecting where we will, in an ever-looping creative embrace and continuous expansion toward intelligent activity.

Our deep appreciation to our co-authors, who each bring a unique focus and value to this work. These are Arthur Shelley, Theresa Bullard, and John Lewis. It is our sincere hope that each of them—who now are co-creators with us—will share this work largely in their day-to-day lives. Also, our appreciation to Donna Panucci, Maik Fuellmann, Jackie Urbanovic and Barbara Wheeler for their contributing and expanding thoughts, and to Mark Boyes, who co-created the thought-provoking image in Chapter 10.

Across our consilience approach, there are a handful of authors whose work has both inspired our thinking and excited our creativity. *Life's Hidden Meaning* by Niles MacFlouer provides insights from Ageless Wisdom, just coming into our realms of understanding. Serving as an example of committed knowledge sharing, MacFlouer has hosted a weekly radio show on Ageless Wisdom since 2004! This massive and incredibly insightful body of work is available on the Internet at http://www.agelesswisdom.com/archives_of_radio_shows.htm Over the past year we have listened, reflected, associated and created connections to this work, such that it is nearly impossible to follow these connections. In this regard, we try to err on the side of over-referencing, and since there is not one specific reference, but, rather, a way of thinking, we have referenced this body of work as MacFlouer (2004-16). We encourage those who resonate with this material to explore it more fully.

In 1996, Ken Wilber wrote *A Brief History of Everything*, and his brilliance continues to emerge from that point. While we applaud his continuing search for a simple and elegant theory of everything, we would be reluctant to eliminate *any* of the rich truths and theories explored in his dozens of books. *Paths of Change* by Will McWhinney served as a baseline for exploring world views and combinations of reality in the change journey. *Spontaneous Evolution: Our Positive Future* by Bruce H. Lipton and Steve Bhaerman is inspirational and informative from the viewpoint of cell biology. Jean Houston's *Jump Time* was way ahead of its time, and is a must read for any decision-maker in today's environment, and that is all of us. And where would we be as a humanity without the brilliance and wisdom of Bohm, Cozolino, Csikszentmihalyi, Damasio, Edelman, Gardner, Goleman, Goswami, Handy, Hawkins, Kant, Kolb, Kurzweil, Laszlo, McTaggart, Polanyi, Stonier, Templeton,

Tiller, Wilber, and so many others! Our appreciation to all of the contributors called out in our references, and to those who may not be in our references but whose thought has seeped into our minds and hearts in the course of living.

Our continued thanks to the professionals, colleagues and thought leaders who participated in the KMTL study and follow-on Sampler Call. These include: Dorothy E. Agger-Gupta, Verna Allee, Debra Amidon, Ramon Barquin, Surinder Kumar Batra, Juanita Brown, John Seely Brown, Frada Burstein, Francisco Javier Carrillo, Robert Cross, Tom Davenport, Ross Dawson, Steve Denning, Charles Dhewa, Nancy Dixon, Leif Edvinsson, Kent Greenes, Susan Hanley, Clyde Holsapple, Esko Kilpi, Dorothy Leonard, Geoff Malafsky, Martha Manning, Carla O'Dell, Edna Pasher, W. Barnett Pearce, Larry Prusak, Madanmohan Rao, Tomasz Rudolf, Melissie Rumizen, Hubert Saint-Onge, Judi Sandrock, Charles Seashore, Dave Snowden, Milton Sousa, Michael Stankosky, Tom Stewart, Michael J.D. Sutton, Karl-Erik Sveiby, Doug Weidner, Steve Weineke, Etienne Wenger-Trayner and Karl Wiig.

There are very special people who assisted in ensuring the quality of this work. Kathy Claypatch with Ageless Wisdom Publishers served as a conduit to assure consistency with that work; Ginny Ramos, a rehabilitation counselor and Alex's daughter, served in the role of editor; and four readers played instrumental roles in assuring consistent and understandable concepts. These are Joyce Avedisian, Susan Dreiband, Denise Sumner and Deb Tobiasson, all knowledgeable explorers in the journey of life.

A special thanks to our families who ground us: from David to Steve, Melanie, John, Cindy, Jackson, Rick, Chris and the grandchildren that help to keep us young; from Alex to Ginny, Bill and Andrew and her long-lost new family; from Arthur to Joy, Cath and Helen; from Theresa to Barbara and Jay, as well as to Dennis H. and Gudni G. and her MMS friends and family; and from John to Mary, Shannon and Jonathan. Thank you to all our friends who support this work in so many ways, and who have supported Mountain Quest since its 2001 beginnings. And our continuing thankfulness to Cindy Taylor and Theresa Halterman, part of our MQI Team, and for our son Andrew Dean, who keeps Mountain Quest running while we play with thoughts and words and dive into the abyss of the unknown.

With Appreciation and Love, Alex, David, Arthur, Theresa and John.

Preface

As we move in and out of life situations, there are verbal cues, often conveyed by signs, that catch our attention and somehow miraculously remain in memory throughout our lives, popping in and out as truisms. Although we may not realize how true they were at the time, one of those sayings in an early office setting was: "Change. Your life depends on it!" Then, some 10 years later, a sign appearing on the check-in desk of the dental clinic on Yokosuka Naval Base, clearly referring to our teeth, read: "Ignore them, and they will go away."

So often we feel like victims, with some new challenge emerging from here or there, something interrupting our best laid plans, some stress or weight that sprouts discomfort or confusion. Yet we have a choice to be pulled along into the fray, dive into the flow and fully participate in the decisions and actions, or even to be the wave-setters, co-creating the reality within which we live and breathe.

Never in the history of humanity has the *need to change* so clearly manifested itself into our everyday existence. While the potential for catastrophic destruction has loomed over us since the mid-20th century, we are still *here*, admittedly a world in turmoil on all fronts—plagued with economic, political, eco-system, social, cultural and religious fragmentation—but also a humanity that is awakening to our true potential and power. Just learning how to co-evolve with an increasingly changing, uncertain and complex external environment, we are now beginning to recognize that it is the change available *within* our internal environment *and energetic connections to each other and the larger whole* that offer up an invitation to an incluessent future, that state of Being far beyond the small drop of previous possibility accepted as true, far beyond that which we have known to dream (Dunning, 2015).

In this work, we introduce the overarching concepts of **profundity** and **bifurcation** as related to change. Profundity comes from the Old French term *profundite* which emerges from the late Latin term *profunditas* or *profundus*, meaning profound (Encarta, 1999). Profundity insinuates an intellectual complexity leading to great understanding, perceptiveness and knowledge. There is a focus on greatness in terms of strength and intensity and in depth of thought. We believe that the times in which we live and the opportunity to shape the future of humanity demand that each of us look within, recognizing and utilizing the amazing gifts of our human mind and heart to shape a new world.

Bifurcation comes from the Latin root word *bifurcare*, which literally means to fork, that is, split and branch off into two separate parts (Encarta, 1999). In terms of change, this concept alludes to a pending decision for each decision-maker, each human, and perhaps humanity at large. We live in two worlds, one based on what we understand from Newtonian Physics and one based on what we don't understand but are able to speculate and feel about the Quantum Field. As change continues with every breath we take and every action we make, there is choice as to how we engage our role as co-creator of reality.

In this book, we explore very different ways to create change, each building on the former. There is no right or wrong—choice is a matter of the lessons we are learning and the growth we are seeking—yet it is clear that there is a split ahead where we will need to choose our way forward. One road continues the journey that has been punctuated by physical dominance, bureaucracy, hard competition and a variety of power scenarios. A second road, historically less-traveled, recognizes the connections among all humans, embracing the value of individuation and diversity as a contribution to the collective whole and the opportunities offered through creative imagination. This is the road that recognizes the virtues of inclusiveness and truth and the power of love and beauty, and moves us along the flow representing Quantum entanglement.

A number of themes are woven throughout this work; for example, the idea of "NOW", the use of forces as a tool for growth, the power of patterns, earned and revealed intuition, bisociation and creativity, stuck energy and flow, the search for truth, and so many more. We take a consilience approach, tapping into a deep array of research in knowledge and learning, with specific reference to recent neuroscience understanding that is emerging, pointing the reader to additional resources. And we look to psychology, physics, cell biology, systems and complexity, cognitive theory, social theory and spirituality for their contributions. Humans are holistic, that is, the physical, mental, emotional and intuitional are all at play and working together. Recognize that you are part of one entangled intelligent complex adaptive learning system (Bennet et al., 2015b), each overlapping and affecting the other, whether consciously or unconsciously, in every instant of life. As we move from science to philosophy, facts to psychology, management to poetry, and words to pictures, you will no doubt feel a tugging in the mind/brain, and perhaps some confusion. Such was the case for one of the authors when studying micro-economics and Shakespeare tragedies back to back! The good news is that this can result in a great deal of expansion and availability of a wide variety of frames of reference from which to process incoming information.

Through the past half a century, all of the authors have engaged in extensive research—much of it experiential in nature—which has led us to break through life-long perceived limits and shift and expand our beliefs about Life and the world of which we are a part. The advent of self-publishing virtual books has opened the door to share this learning globally. The concepts forwarded in the earlier works of all of the authors lay the foundation for this book.

While this book is quite large, it wrote itself. In the movie Amadeus (1984), when a complaint is lodged against his work saying there are just too many notes, Mozart responds that there are just exactly as many notes as are needed. In this book, there are exactly as many chapters as are needed, no more, no less. As you move through the information and concepts available in this text, we ask that you stay open to new ideas, ways of thinking and perceiving, and—using the discernment and discretion emerging from your unique life experiences—reflect on how these ideas might fit into your personal theory of the world. It is our hope that these ideas will serve as triggers for a greater expansion of thought and consciousness, which every individual brings to the larger understanding of who we are and how, together as One, we operate in the world.

To begin, we offer the following assumptions:

Assumption 1: Everything—at least in our physical reality—is energy and patterns of energy. We live in a vast field of energy in which we are continuously exchanging information, which is a form of energy.

Assumption 2: Creativity—nurtured by freedom, purpose and choice—is a primary urge of the human. Knowledge serves as an action lever for co-creating our experiences.

Assumption 3: Knowledge is partial and incomplete. Knowledge produces forces, whether those forces are used to push forward an idea that benefits humanity, or whether those forces are to push against another's beliefs and values (knowledge), which can escalate to warfare.

Assumption 4: The human mind is an associative patterner, that is, continuously re-creating knowledge for the situation at hand. Knowledge exists in the human brain in the form of stored or expressed neural patterns that may be selected, activated, mixed and/or reflected upon through thought. Incoming information is associated with stored information. From this mixing process, new patterns are created that may represent understanding, meaning and the capacity to anticipate (to various degrees) the results of potential actions. Thus, knowledge is context sensitive and situation dependent, with the mind continuously growing, restructuring and creating increased organization (information) and knowledge for the moment at hand.

Assumption 5: The unconscious mind has a vast store of tacit knowledge available to us. It has only been in the past few decades that cognitive psychology and neuroscience have begun to seriously explore unconscious mental life. Polanyi felt that tacit knowledge consisted of *a range* of conceptual and sensory information and images that could be used to make sense of a situation or event (Hodgkin, 1991; Smith, 2003). He was right. The unconscious mind is incredibly powerful, on the order of 700,000 times more processing speed than the conscious stream of thought. The challenge is to make better use of our tacit knowledge through creating greater connections with the unconscious, building and expanding the resources stored in the unconscious, deepening areas of resonance, connecting to the larger information field, and learning how to share our tacit resources with each other.

Assumption 6: People are multidimensional, and rarely do they hold to a single belief, a consistent logic, or a specific worldview. As identified in the recent model of experiential learning (Bennet et al, 2015b), there are five primary modes of thinking, each of us with our preferences—concrete experience, reflective observation, abstract conceptualization, active experimentation and social engagement—and each of us has a dozen or more subpersonalities offering a variety of diverse thoughts and feelings that rise to the occasion when triggered by our external and internal environments (Bennet et al., 2015a). *The human experience is a neuronal dance with the Universe, with each of us in the driver's seat selecting our partners and directing our dance steps.*

Assumption 7: We are social creatures who live in an entangled world; our brains are linked together. We are in continuous interaction with those around us, and the brain is continuously changing in response. Thus, in our expanded state we are both individuated and One, bringing all our diversity into collaborative play for the greater good of humanity.

Assumption 8: We live in times of extreme change in the human mind and body, in human-developed systems, and of the Earth, our human host. Through advances in science and technology, most of what we need to learn and thrive in these times is already available. We need only to open our minds and hearts to the amazing potential of our selfs.

There are still vast workings of the human mind and its connections to higher-order energies that we do not understand. The limitations we as humans place on our capacities and capabilities are created from past reference points that have been developed primarily through the rational and logical workings of the mechanical functioning of our mind/brain, an understanding that has come through extensive intellectual effort. Yet we now recognize that *knowledge is a living form of information*, tailored by our minds specifically for situations at hand. The totality of knowledge can no easier be codified and stored than our feelings, nor would it be highly beneficial to do so in a changing and uncertain environment. Thus, in this book, given the limitations of our own perceptions and understanding, we do not even pretend to cover the vast amount of information and knowledge available in the many fields connected to change. We *do* choose to consider and explore areas and phenomena that move beyond our paradigms and beliefs into the larger arena of knowing, and to move beyond the activity of our cognitive functions to consider the larger energy patterns within which humanity is immersed.

This extensive book is initially being published in five Parts as five separate books, which will be available in both kindle (from Amazon) and PDF (from

MQIPress) formats. In support of the Intelligent Social Change Journey, these Parts are:

Part I: Laying the Groundwork

Part II: Learning from the Past

Part III: Learning in the Present

Part IV: Co-Creating the Future

Part V: Living in the Future

Each part has a separate focus, yet they work together to support your full engagement in the Intelligent Social Change Journey. A Table of Contents for all five parts is Appendix B. An overarching model of the ISCJ is Appendix A. This model can also be downloaded for A4 printing at the following location: www.mqipress.net

Workshops on all five Parts of *The Profundity and Bifurcation of Change* or, specifically, on The Intelligent Social Change Journey facilitated by the authors are available. Contact alex@mountainquestinstitute.com ... arthur.shelley@rmit.edu.au ... Theresa@quantumleapalchemy.com ... or John@ExplanationAge.com

The Drs. Alex and David Bennet live at the Mountain Quest Institute, Inn and Retreat Center situated on a 430-acre farm in the Allegheny Mountains of West Virginia. See www.mountainquestinn.com and www.mountainquestinstitute.com They may be reached at alex@mountainquestinstitute.com Dr. Arthur Shelley is the originator of *The Organizational Zoo*, Dr. Theresa Bullard is the Founder of the Quantra Leadership Academy as well as an International Instructor for the Modern Mystery School, and Dr. John Lewis is author of *The Explanation Age.* Taking a consilience approach, this eclectic group builds on corroborated resources in a diversity of fields while simultaneously pushing the edge of thought, hopefully beyond your comfort zone, for that is where our journey begins.

Introduction to
The Intelligent Social Change Journey

The Intelligent Social Change Journey (ISCJ) is a developmental journey of the body, mind and heart, moving from the heaviness of cause-and-effect linear extrapolations, to the fluidity of co-evolving with our environment, to the lightness of breathing our thought and feelings into reality. Grounded in development of our mental faculties, these are phase changes, each building on and expanding previous learning in our movement toward intelligent activity.

We are on this journey together. This is very much a *social* journey. Change does not occur in isolation. The deeper our understanding in relationship to others, the easier it is to move into the future. The quality of sympathy is needed as we navigate the linear, cause-and-effect characteristics of Phase 1. The quality of empathy is needed to navigate the co-evolving liquidity of Phase 2. The quality of compassion is needed to navigate the connected breath of the Phase 3 creative leap. See the figure below.

In the progression of learning to navigate change represented by the three phases of the ISCJ, we empower our selfs, individuating and expanding. In the process, we become immersed in the human experience, a neuronal dance with the Universe, with each of us in the driver's seat selecting our partners and directing our dance steps. Let's explore that journey a bit deeper.

In Phase 1 of the Journey, *Learning from the Past*, we act on the physical and the physical changes; we "see" the changes with our sense of form, and therefore they are real. Causes have effects. Actions have consequences, both directly and indirectly, and sometimes delayed. Phase 1 reinforces the characteristics of how we interact with the simplest aspects of our world. The elements are predictable and repeatable and make us feel comfortable because we know what to expect and how to prepare for them. While these parts of the world do exist, our brain tends to automate the thinking around them and we do them with little conscious effort. The challenge with this is that they only remain predictable if all the causing influences remain constant ... and that just doesn't happen in the world of today! The linear cause-and-effect phase of the ISCJ (Phase 1) calls for sympathy. Supporting and caring for the people involved in the change helps to mitigate the force of resistance, improving the opportunity for successful outcomes.

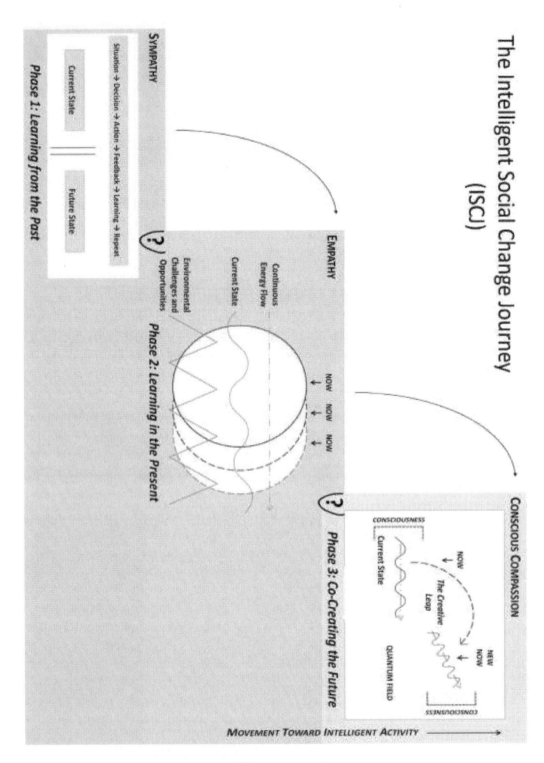

Figure ISCJ-1. *The Baseline Model.*

As we expand toward Phase 2, we begin to recognize patterns; they emerge from experiences that repeat over and over. Recognition of patterns enables us to "see" (in our mind's eye) the relationship of events in terms of time and space, moving us out of an action and reaction mode into a position of co-evolving with our environment, and enabling us to better navigate a world full of diverse challenges and opportunities. It is at this stage that we move from understanding based on past cause-and-effect reactions to how things come together, to produce new things both in the moment at hand and at a future point in time.

Phase 2, *Learning in the Present*, takes us to the next level of thinking and feeling about how we interact with our world, including the interesting area of human social interactions. Although complex, the somewhat recognizable patterns enable us to explore and progress through uncertainty and the unknown, making life more interesting and enjoyable. In Phase 2 patterns grow into concepts, higher mental thought, and we begin the search for a higher level of truth. Sustainability in the co-evolving state of Phase 2 requires empathy, which provides a direct understanding of another individual, and a heightened awareness of the context of their lives and their desires and needs in the moment at hand. While not yet achieving the creative leap of the intuitional (represented in Phase 3), we are clearly developing higher mental faculties and instinctive knowledge of the workings of the Universe, which helps cultivate intuition and develop insights in service to our self and society.

The creative leap of Phase 3, *Co-Creating the Future*, requires the ability to tap into the larger intuitional field that energetically connects all people. This can only be accomplished when energy is focused outward in service to the larger whole, requiring a deeper connection to others. Compassion deepens that connection. Thus, each phase of the Intelligent Social Change Journey calls for an increasing depth of connection to others, moving from sympathy to empathy to compassion.

<<<<<<<<>>>>>>>

INSIGHT: **Each phase of the Intelligent Social Change Journey calls for an increasing depth of connection to others, moving from sympathy to empathy to compassion.**

<<<<<<<<>>>>>>>

The ISCJ Baseline Model accents the phase changes as each phase builds on/expands from the previous phase. As the journeyer moves from Phase 1 to Phase 2 and prepares for the creative leap of Phase 3, the mental faculties are developing, the senses are coming into balance, and there are deepening connections to others. This will feel familiar to many travelers, for this is the place where we began. The model shows our journey is a significant change of mind, body and spirit as we operate on different cognitive and emotional planes as we progress through the developmental phases. Some people are aware of the changes they are undergoing and seek to accelerate the learning, while others resist the development, hoping (perhaps somewhat naively) to simplify the way they interact with the world.

Babies are born connected, to their mothers and families, and to the larger energies surrounding them and within them. This represents Phase 3. As one author exclaimed when exploring this reversal of the Phase 1, 2 and 3 models, "This really brings it all together for me. There is something that we admire in babies that we would like to become, and this framework makes sense of that feeling." If, and when, we return to Phase 3 in the round-trip journey of life, it will be with experience in our backpack and development of the mental faculties under our cap.

Sometime around the fourth grade, as most grade school teachers will attest, the ego pokes its head out, and, through social interactions, the process of individuation has begun, with a focus on, and experiencing in, the NOW. This represents Phase 2 of our change model, a state of co-evolving. In the pre-adolescent child, intuitional connections are subsumed by a physical focus accompanied by emotional flare-ups as the child is immersed in learning experiences, interacting and learning from and with their environment.

By the time the mid-teens come around, the world has imposed a level of order and limits, with a focus on cause-and-effect. In some families and cultures this may take the form of physical, mental or emotional manipulation and control, always related to cause-and-effect. If you do that, this will happen. For others, cultural or religious aspects of expectations and punishment may lead to the cause-and-effect focus. For the mid-teen perceived as overactive and unruly in the schoolroom, the limiting forces may be imposed through Ritalin or other drugs, which may have even started at a much earlier age. Regardless of how it is achieved, learning from the past—the Phase 1 model—becomes the starting point of our lives as we move into adulthood. From this starting point, we begin to develop our mental faculties.

The Overarching ISCJ Model

To help connect the dots, we have prepared a larger version of the Intelligent Social Change Journey, which is at Appendix A. The Overarching ISCJ Model focuses on the relationships of the phases with other aspects of the journey. For example, three critical movements during our journey, consistent with our movement through the phases, are reflected in expanded consciousness, reduction of forces and increased intelligent activity. *Consciousness* is considered a state of awareness and a private, selective and continuous change process, a sequential set of ideas, thoughts, images, feelings and perceptions and an understanding of the connections and relationships among them and our self. *Forces* occur when one type of energy affects another type of energy in a way such that they are moving in different directions, pressing against each other. Bounded (inward focused) and/or limited knowledge creates forces. *Intelligent activity* represents a state of interaction where intent, purpose, direction, values and expected outcomes are clearly understood and communicated among all parties, reflecting wisdom and achieving a higher truth. We will repeat this definition where appropriate throughout the book.

<<<<<<<◇>>>>>>>

INSIGHT: **The ISCJ is a journey toward intelligent activity, which is a state of interaction where intent, purpose, direction, values and expected outcomes are clearly understood and communicated among all parties, reflecting wisdom and achieving a higher truth.**

<<<<<<<◇>>>>>>>

Immediately below each phase of the Overarching ISCJ model are characteristics related to each phase. These are words or short phrases representing some of the ideas that will be developed in each section supporting each phase. **Phase 1**, *Learning from the Past*, characteristics are: linear and sequential, repeatability, engaging past learning, starting from current state, and cause and effect relationship. **Phase 2**, *Learning in the Present*, characteristics are: Recognition of patterns; social interaction; and co-evolving with the environment through continuous learning, quick response, robustness, flexibility, adaptability and alignment. **Phase 3**, *Co-Creating Our Future*, characteristics are: Creative imagination, recognition of global Oneness, mental in service to the intuitive; balancing senses; bringing together time (the past, present and future); knowing; beauty; and wisdom.

Still exploring the overarching model, at the lower part of the graphic we see three areas related to knowledge in terms of the nature of knowledge, areas of reflection, and cognitive shifts necessary for each phase of change. For ease of reference, we have also included the content of these three areas in Table ISCJ-1.

In Phase 1, *Learning from the Past*, the nature of knowledge is characterized as a product of the past and, as we will learn in Chapter 2, knowledge is context sensitive and situation dependent, and partial and incomplete. Reflection during this phase of change is on reviewing the interactions and feedback, and determining cause-and-effect relationships. There is an inward focus, and a questioning of decisions and actions as reflected in the questions: What did I intend? What really happened? Why were there differences? What would I do the same? What would I do differently? The cognitive shifts that are underway during this phase include: (1) recognition of the importance of feedback; (2) the ability to recognize systems and the impact of external forces; (3) recognition and location of "me" in the larger picture (building conscious awareness); and (4) pattern recognition and concept development. These reflections are critical to enabling the phase change to *co-evolving*.

In Phase 2, *Learning in the Present*, the nature of knowledge is characterized in terms of expanded cooperation and collaboration, and knowledge sharing and social learning. There is also the conscious *questioning of why*, and the *pursuit of truth*. Reflection includes a deepening of conceptual thinking and, through cooperation and collaboration, the ability to connect the power of diversity and individuation to the larger whole. There is an increasing outward focus, with the recognition of different world views and the exploration of information from different perspectives, and expanded knowledge capacities. Cognitive shifts that are underway include: (1) the ability to recognize and apply patterns at all levels within a domain of knowledge to predict outcomes; (2) a growing understanding of complexity; (3) increased connectedness of choices, recognition of direction you are heading, and expanded meaning-making; and (4) an expanded ability to bisociate ideas resulting in increased creativity.

In Phase 3, *Co-Creating Our Future*, the nature of knowledge is characterized as a recognition that with knowledge comes responsibility. There is a conscious pursuit of larger truth, and knowledge is selectively used as a measure of effectiveness. Reflection includes the valuing of creative ideas, asking the larger questions: How does this idea serve humanity? Are there any negative consequences? There is an openness to other's ideas, a questioning with humility: What if this idea is right? Are my beliefs or other mental models limiting my thought? Are hidden assumptions or feelings interfering with intelligent activity?

Cognitive shifts that are underway include: (1) a sense and knowing of Oneness; (2) development of both the lower (logic) and upper (conceptual) mental faculties, which work in concert with the emotional guidance system; (3) recognition of self as a co-creator of reality; (4) the ability to engage in intelligent activity; and (5) a developing ability to tap into the intuitional plane at will.

Time and space play a significant role in the phase changes. Using Jung's psychological type classifications, feelings come from the past, sensations occur in the present, intuition is oriented to the future, and thinking embraces the past, present *and* future. Forecasting and visioning work is done at a point of change (McHale, 1977) when a balance is struck continuously between short-term and long-term survival. Salk (1973) describes this as a shift from Epoch A, dominated by ego and short-term considerations, to Epoch B, where both *Being and ego co-exist*. In the ISCJ, this shift occurs somewhere in Phase 2, with Beingness advancing as we journey toward Phase 3. Considerable focus to time and space occurs later in the book (Chapter 16/Part III).

Phase of the Intelligent Social Change Journey	ISCJ: Nature of Knowledge	ISCJ: Points of Reflection	ISCJ: Cognitive Shifts
PHASE 1: Cause and Effect (Requires Sympathy) • Linear, and Sequential • Repeatable • Engaging past learning • Starting from current state • Cause-and-effect relationships	• A product of the past • Knowledge is context-sensitive and situation-dependent • Knowledge is partial and incomplete	• Reviewing the interactions and feedback • Determining cause-and-effect relationships; logic • Inward focus • Questioning of decisions and actions: What did I intend? What really happened? why were there differences? What would I do the same? What would I do differently?	• Recognition of the importance of feedback • Ability to recognize systems and the impact of external forces • Recognition and location of "me" in the larger picture (building conscious awareness) • Beginning pattern recognition and early concept development
PHASE 2: Co-Evolving (Requires Empathy) • Recognition of patterns • Social interaction • Co-evolving with environment through continuous learning, quick response, robustness, flexibility, adaptability, alignment.	• Engaging knowledge sharing and social learning • Engaging cooperation and collaboration • Questioning of why? • Pursuit of truth	• Deeper development of conceptual thinking (higher mental thought) • Through cooperation and collaboration ability to connect the power of diversity and individuation to the larger whole • Outward focus • Recognition of different world views and exploration of information from different perspectives • Expanded knowledge capacities	• The ability to recognize and apply patterns at all levels within a domain of knowledge to predict outcomes • A growing understanding of complexity • Increased connectedness of choices • Recognition of direction you are heading • Expanded meaning-making • Expanded ability to bisociate ideas resulting in increased creativity
PHASE 3: Creative Leap (Requires Compassion) • Creative imagination • Recognition of global Oneness • Mental in service to the intuitive • Balancing senses • Bringing together past, present and future • Knowing; Beauty; Wisdom	• Recognition that with knowledge comes responsibility • Conscious pursuit of larger truth • Knowledge selectively used as a measure of effectiveness	• Valuing of creative ideas • Asking the larger questions: How does this idea serve humanity? Are there any negative consequences? • Openness to other's ides; questioning with humility: What if this idea is right Are my beliefs or other mental models limiting my thought? Are hidden assumptions or feelings interfering with intelligent activity?	• A sense and knowing of Oneness • Development of both the lower (logic) and upper (conceptual) mental faculties, which work in concert with the emotional guidance system • Applies patterns across domains of knowledge for greater good • recognition of self as a co-creator of reality • The ability to engage in intelligent activity • Developing the ability to tap into the intuitional plane at will

Table ISCJ-Table 1. *The three Phases from the viewpoints of the nature of knowledge, points of reflection and cognitive shifts.*

Cognitive-Based Ordering of Change

As a cognitive-based ordering of change, we forward the concept of logical levels of learning consistent with levels of change developed by anthropologist Gregory Bateson (1972) based on the work in logic and mathematics of Bertrand Russell. This logical typing was both a mathematical theory and a law of nature, recognizing long before neuroscience research findings confirmed the relationship of the mind/brain which show that we literally create our reality, with thought affecting the physical structure of the brain, and the physical structure of the brain affecting thought.

Bateson's levels of change range from simplistic habit formation (which he calls Learning I) to large-scale change in the evolutionary process of the human (which he calls Learning IV), with each higher-level synthesizing and organizing the levels below it, and thus creating a greater impact on people and organizations. This is a hierarchy of logical levels, ordered groupings within a system, with the implication that as the levels reach toward the source or beginning **there is a sacredness, power or importance informing this hierarchy of values** (Dilts, 2003). This structure is consistent with the phase changes of the Intelligent Social Change Journey.

<<<<<<◇>>>>>>

INSIGHT: **Similar to Bateson's levels of change, each higher phase of the Intelligent Social Change Journey synthesizes and organizes the levels below it, thus creating a greater impact in interacting with the world.**

<<<<<<◇>>>>>>

With Learning 0 representing the status quo, a particular behavioral response to a specific situation, Learning I (first-order change) is stimulus-response conditioning (cause-and-effect change), which includes learning simple skills such as walking, eating, driving, and working. These basic skills are pattern forming, becoming habits, which occur through repetitiveness without conceptualizing the content. For example, we don't have to understand concepts of motion and movement in order to learn to walk. Animals engage in Learning I. Because it is not necessary to understand the concepts, or underlying theories, no questions of reality are raised. Learning I occurs in Phase 1 of the ISCJ.

Learning II (second-order change) is deuteron learning and includes creation, or a change of context inclusive of new images or concepts, or shifts the understanding of, and connections among, existing concepts such that meaning may be interpreted. These changes are based on mental constructs that *depend on a sense of reality* (McWhinney, 1997). While these concepts may represent real things, relations or qualities, they also may be symbolic, specifically created for the situation at hand.

Either way, they provide the means for reconstructing existing concepts, using one reality to modify another, from which new ways of thinking and behaviors emerge.

Argyris and Schon's (1978) concept of double loop learning reflects Level II change. Learning II occurs in Phase 2 of the ISCJ.

Learning III (third-order change) requires thinking beyond our current logic, calling us to change our system of beliefs and values, and offering different sets of alternatives from which choices can be made. Suggesting that Learning III is learning about the concepts used in Learning II, Bateson says,

> In transcending the promises and habits of Learning II, one will gain "a freedom from its bondages," bondages we characterize, for example, as "drive," "dependency," "pride," and "fatalism." One might learn to change the premises acquired by Learning II and to readily choose among the roles through which we express concepts and thus the "self." Learning III is driven by the "contraries" generated in the contexts of Learning I and II. (Bateson, 1972, pp. 301-305)

<<<<<<<◇>>>>>>>

INSIGHT: **There is a freedom that occurs as we leave behind the thinking patterns of Phase 2 and open to the new choices and discoveries of Phase 3.**

<<<<<<<◇>>>>>>>

Similarly, Berman (1981, p. 346) defines Learning III as, "an experience in which a person suddenly realizes the arbitrary nature of his or her own paradigm." This is the breaking open of our personal mental models, our current logic, losing the differential of subject/object, blending into connection while simultaneously following pathways of diverse belief systems. Learning III occurs as we move into Phase 3 of the ISCJ.

Learning IV deals with revolutionary change, getting outside the system to look at the larger system of systems, awakening to something completely new, different, unique and transformative. This is the space of *incluessence*, a future state far beyond that which we know to dream (Dunning, 2015). As Bateson described this highest level of change:

> The individual mind is immanent but not only in the body. It is immanent in pathways and messages outside the body; and there is a larger Mind of which the individual mind is only a sub-system. This larger Mind is comparable to God and is perhaps what people mean by "God," but it is still immanent in the total interconnected social system and planetary ecology. (Bateson, 1972, p. 465)

Table ISCJ-2 below is a comparison of the Phases of the Intelligent Social Change Journey and the four Levels of Learning espoused by Bateson (1972) based on the work in logic and mathematics of Bertrand Russell, and supported by Argyris and Schon (1978), Berman (1981), and McWhinney (1997).

Phase of the Intelligent Social Change Journey	Level of Learning [NOTE: LEARNING 0 represents the status quo; a behavioral response to a specific situation.]
PHASE 1: Cause and Effect (Requires Sympathy) • Linear, and Sequential • Repeatable • Engaging past learning • Starting from current state • Cause and effect relationships	**LEARNING i:** **(First order change)** • Stimulus-response conditioning • Incudes learning simple skills such as walking, eating, driving and working • Basic skills are pattern forming, becoming habits occurring through repetitiveness without conceptualizing the content • No questions of reality
PHASE 2: Co-Evolving (Requires Empathy) • Recognition of patterns • Social interaction • Co-evolving with environment through continuous learning, quick response, robustness, flexibility, adaptability, alignment	**LEARNING II (Deutero Learning)** **(Second order change)** • Includes creation or change of context inclusive of new images or concepts • Shifts the understanding of, and connections among, existing concepts such that meaning may be interpreted • Based on mental constructions that depend on a sense of reality
[Moving into Phase 3] **PHASE 3: Creative Leap** (Requires Compassion) • Creative imagination • Recognition of global Oneness • Mental in service to the intuitive • Balancing senses • Bringing together past, present and future • Knowing; Beauty; Wisdom	**LEARNING III: (Third order change)** • Thinking beyond current logic • Changing our system of beliefs and values • Different sets of alternatives from which choices can be made • Freedom from bondages **LEARNINNG IV:** • Revolutionary change • Getting outside the system to look at the larger system of systems • Awakening to something completely new, different, unique and transformative • Tapping into the large Mind of which the individual mind is a sub-system

Table ISCJ-Table 2. *Comparison of Phases of the ISCJ with Levels of Learning.*

An example of Learning IV is Buddha's use of intuitional thought to understand others. He used his ability to think in greater and greater ways to help people cooperate and share together, and think better. Learning IV is descriptive of controlled intuition in support of the creative leap in Phase 3 of the ISCJ, perhaps moving beyond what we can comprehend at this point in time, perhaps deepening the connections of sympathy, empathy and compassion to unconditional love.

How to Best Use this Material

This book has, quite purposefully, been chunked into five smaller books, referred to as Parts, which are both independent and interdependent. Chunking is a methodology for learning. The way people become experts involves the chunking of ideas and concepts and creating understanding through development of significant patterns useful for identifying opportunities, solving problems and anticipating future behavior within the focused domain of knowledge. Figure ISCJ-2 shows the relationship of the Parts of this book and their content to the Intelligent Social Change Journey. *Remember*: the ISCJ is a journey of expansion, with each Phase building on—and inclusive of—the former Phase as we develop our mental faculties in service to the intuitional, and move closer to intelligent activity. As such, one needs to experience the earlier phases in order to elevate to the upper levels. Early life experiences and educational development during these earlier stages create the foundation and capacity to develop into higher levels of interactions and ways of being.

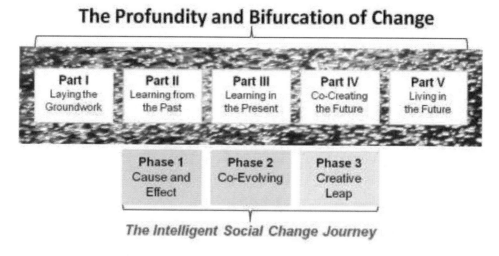

Figure ISCJ-2. *Relationship of Parts and Phases of the ISCJ.*

While many different ideas have been introduced in the paragraphs of this Introduction to the Intelligent Social Change Journey, you will discover that all of these ideas are addressed in depth during the course of this book, and each Part is inclusive of tools, references, insights and reflective questions provided in support of your personal learning journey. We also cross-reference, both within the Parts, and across all of the Parts.

This is a journey, and as such *the learning is in the journey*, the reflecting on and application of the learning, not in achieving a particular capability or entering the next Phase at a specific point in time. Similar to the deepening of relationships with others, the growth of understanding and expansion of consciousness takes its own time, twisting and curving forwards and backwards until we have learned all we can from one frame of reference, and then jump to another to continue our personal journey. That said, we suggest that those who are impatient to know the topics within this book, but reluctant to read such an extended text, jump to Chapter 11/Part III, which provides readiness assessment statements and related characteristics reflecting the high-level content of this book.

For your reference, the Overarching ISCJ model can be downloaded for printing in A3 format at www.MQIPress.net The corresponding author may be reached at alex@mountainquestinstitute.com

PART III

Learning in the Present

Introduction to Part III

Although very much driven by present "problems" with a causal link to past experiences, our thinking in terms of *future possibilities* expanded as we ended the last century. Technology was forging ahead, supporting tactical needs and supplying fodder for strategic leaps, and connectivity enabled a deeper level of interaction around the world, bringing a diversity of thought to social learning.

The typology of problems developed by Mitroff (1977), which can also be used to evaluate opportunities, provides an example of this thinking. In this typology, the type of content and subject matter is divided into two primary areas: *technical/operational* (includes technology) and *social* (includes moral and political); and the type of structure and time decision is divided into *tactical* (current) and *strategic* (future). Thus, we have a four by four as presented in Figure III-1, with the nature of the problem judged to be either tactical-operational (Phase 1), tactical-social (Phase 1, 2), strategic-operational (Phase 1, 2), or strategic-social (Phase 2, 3). This approach is consistent with Jung's types (Intuition-Thinking and Intuition-Feeling, respectively) which relate to problem solving at the strategic-operational and strategic-social levels. The Phases in parentheses signify the focus of activity as related to the Intelligent Social Change Journey. This does not imply that the organization or individual operates in a specific Phase, but rather that the activity is related to a specific Phase. Remember, each phase builds on the previous phase and *is inclusive of it*. For example, in terms of the Typology of Problems and Opportunities, when a business thinks strategically, looking toward the future, it simultaneously still handles the tactical, everyday activities of the organization.

Using Mitroff's descriptions, technical/operational is the current state, and whether combined with tactical or social would include the "search for an optimal or best technological solution within a single-problem format within the constraints of given technology" (Mitroff, 1977, p. 48). This is focused on a short-term horizon and adheres to the critical standards of a single discipline, with a fixed structure imposed on the phenomenon underlying the problem. Conversely, strategic refers to the future state, and whether operational or social would include the "search for alternative

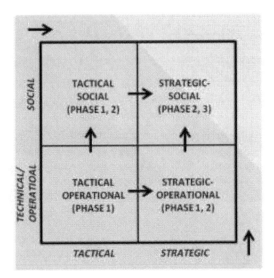

Figure III-1. *Typology of Problems and Opportunities, adapted from Mitroff (1977).*

solutions within multiple-problem formats outside the constraints of current technology and thinking" (Mitroff, 1977, p. 48). This is focused on a long-term horizon and does *not* adhere to the standards of a single discipline, rather taking a consilience approach, with continuous perturbation of the imposition of fixed structures related to the phenomenon.

From reflecting on these differences and combinations, Mitroff (1977) identified what he called the error of the third kind, that is, "the probability of solving the 'wrong' problem when one should have solved the 'right' problem." He discovered that when looking through the operational lens, problem solvers were "within-schema" solvers, stressing the *solving* side of the inquiry process. Conversely, when looking through the strategic lens, problem solvers were 'between-schema' formulators or, rather, problem finders, stressing the *finding* side. Within this work we can see how **the focus of thought, the direction of thought, is creating the reality of the future**. Further, we can begin to recognize the beginnings of movement into Phase 2 of the Intelligent Social Change Journey, that is, an opening to unprecedented change, the value of taking a consilience approach, an appreciation for all perspectives, and the need to search out new solutions to co-evolve with the environment.

Moving Toward Co-Evolving

The self is a complex adaptive system. Complex adaptive systems are partially ordered systems that unfold and evolve through time. They are mostly self-organizing, while continuously learning and adapting. To survive, they are always scanning the environment, trying new approaches, creating new ideas, observing the outcomes, and changing the way they operate. In order to continuously adapt, they must operate in *perpetual disequilibrium*, which results in some unpredictable behavior. Having nonlinear relationships, complex adaptive systems create global properties that are called *emergent* because they seem to emerge from the multitude of elements and their relationships (Bennet & Bennet, 2013).

While the term co-evolve can be used to describe the interdependent relationship of a host and parasite, in a positive sense it is quite appropriate to describe the symbiotic relationship between the individual or organization (a collection of individuals working toward a common goal) and the environment. Co-evolve refers to adaptation, and adaptation cannot occur without learning. Adaptation is the process by which a system has and applies knowledge to improve its ability to survive and grow through internal adjustments. Adaptive theories are better suited to complex problems than causal theories (Coleman, 1973).

System adaptation may be responsive, internally adjusting to external forces, or it may be proactive, internally changing so that it can influence the external environment, that is, it may be pushed to change or attracted to change. See Figure III-2.

The self does both, reacting/responding to its environment and creating/innovating, thus impacting its environment as a force for change. The environment is the region outside the boundary of a system; since the environment may also be considered as a system, it is sometimes referred to as the supra-system. All open systems have inputs and outputs consisting of material, energy, or information. In essence, they transform their inputs into outputs that satisfy internal purpose and environmental needs. Learning—the process of creating knowledge—uses incoming information from the environment to complex with stored information and produce knowledge, the capacity (potential or actual) to take effective action. This intelligent complex adaptive learning system is *you*, a human (Bennet et al., 2015b).

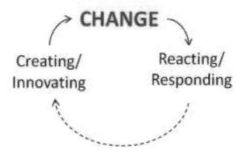

Figure III-2. *System adaptation may be responsive, internally adjusting to external forces, or it may be proactive, choosing to internally change so that it can influence the external environment.*

The counter-intuitive nature of complex systems says that human intuition pushes people toward what they *want* to do, which is often the opposite of what would logically accomplish their aims (Forrester, 1971). Forrester felt this underperforming was because people tend to focus efforts on lower leverage parts of systems. Similarly, Sterman (1989) discovered through numerous laboratory experiments that people's cognitive biases and limits to rationality cause them to misjudge even simple dynamic decision-making tasks (Hogarth, 1987; Kahneman et al., 1982; Simon, 1979, 1982). Further, because in early human development we became familiar and comfortable with the simplicity of the cause-and-effect relationship, *people have basic cognitive limits that make it difficult to understand the dynamics of non-linear multiple-feedback-loop systems* (Sterman, 1989). The problem is *not* lack of information or clarity, but rather an inability to understand the setting (Senge, 2000), and a lack of causal theories to guide our actions. **What this says is that the mental conceptual work has yet to be put in place in order to connect space and time in support of intelligent activity.**

Part III: Learning in the Present of *The Profundity and Bifurcation of Change* focuses on Phase 2 of the Intelligent Social Change Journey. In both our personal and professional lives, we have become adept at responding to and anticipating change. The very act of change may create a new reality requiring new values and perspectives of life. While we clearly recognize the importance of the individual—of self—in creating and sharing feelings, thoughts and mental images to bring about and apply new knowledge, thinking about ways we create our reality can move us from a reactive role to a proactive role, fully embracing the power of self. This is the intent of this book.

Phase 2 of the Intelligent Social Change Journey

The co-evolving Phase 2 model, while still focused on the experiential mode of the physical, fully engages higher mental faculties including abilities such as pattern thinking (the ability to recognize patterns in the domain of focus) and complexity thinking (recognizing systems, understanding the relationships of elements within and without systems and potential resultant behaviors). It is a "co" evolving model, with the discovery of ever-deepening relationships with others and the power of cooperation and collaboration, the highest virtues of the physical plane. Co-evolving requires a strong sense of purpose and connection to all things—the human as part of a larger ecosystem—that is supported by being grounded (see Chapter 9/Part II). Figure III-3 below shows Phase 2 of the Intelligent Social Change Journey.

Co-evolving is not just a stimulus-response phenomenon, which would be a mechanical process. Mechanisms are innately passive. Co-evolving requires thought and interaction with others in the instant of life, the NOW. This focus on the present

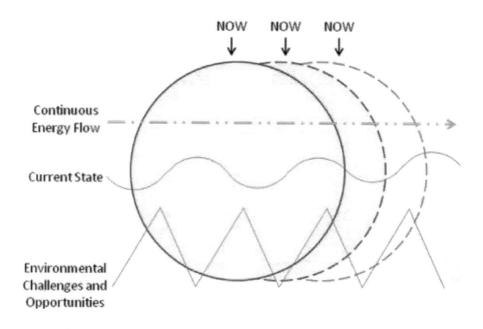

Figure III-3. *Phase 2 of the Intelligent Social Change Journey.*

was essential to survival in early human history. It took a great deal of mental development on the part of humanity before we began to recognize the interconnectedness of events and were able to synthesize information as a force for change, giving rise to a spectrum of possible futures. And this is where a miracle began to happen, where humanity became,

> ... concerned with the derivation of what 'ought' to be in human affairs ... not [to] be confused with what 'can' and 'will' happen, which are the realms of strategic and tactical planning. (Loveridge, 1977, p 54)

While starting with the past and continuing through the present—recognizing the impact of present perception, observation and judgment when looking from that present—visioning the future became the forward-looking part of a continuum of thought. From this point of view, take another look at Figure III-1, and it is clear why Tactical-Social and Strategic-Operational are a part of both Phase 1 and Phase 2 of the ISCJ. This represents the embedding of new thinking: the first moving from a singular focus to a social focus (recognizing the need to co-evolve), and the second moving from a NOW focus to a future focus (recognizing patterns from the past that can be extrapolated to the future).

Interestingly, the NOW of our conscious awareness is *not* occurring in the instant we perceive it; rather, our brain assembles relevant inputs coming in through our senses and presents them as occurring simultaneously. There may be tens or hundreds of milliseconds that have passed while different external and internal inputs are being associated. Tulving (2005), an Estonian-Canadian psychologist, used the term *chromesthesia* (or mental time travel) to describe this phenomenon. Tulving related mental time travel to *episodic memory* in that recalling past events and imagining the future are similar conscious activities (Carroll, 2016).

Before launching into the chapters related to Phase 2, we provided the **Introduction to the Intelligent Social Change Journey** (ISCJ), which was primary in *The Profundity and Bifurcation of Change Part I*. The ISCJ is a journey toward intelligent activity, which is a state of interaction where intent, purpose, direction, values and expected outcomes are clearly understood and communicated among all parties, reflecting wisdom and achieving a higher truth.

To further explore Phase 2 of the Intelligent Social Change Journey toward intelligent activity, Part III includes ...

Chapter 13: The New Reality. This is a close look at the current and future reality, what we call CUCA, increasing *Change, Uncertainty, Complexity* and *Anxiety.* In this environment, a higher level of knowledge sharing is required, which requires higher levels of trust. Applicability, accountability and authorization are elements of creating a trusted network.

Chapter 14: "Co-ing" and Evolving. The search for a higher truth is a cooperative journey. Our everyday lives are full of interactions with others, and when these are intelligent interactions, sprinkled with wisdom and with intent, purpose, direction, values and expected outcomes clearly understood and communicated, we are indeed co-evolving toward a higher truth. This chapter takes a closer look at the idea of co-evolving, and brings in a bit of history around cooperating and collaborating and the many forms these take in our organizations.

Chapter 15: Managing Change in a Knowledge Organization. This chapter presents a pragmatic example of a Phase 2 change approach. It highlights that in order to deal with increasing complexity, learning must be increased. In this chapter we introduce the strategic initiative pulse, a concept used by the U.S. Department of the Navy in implementation of Acquisition Reform.

Chapter 16: Time and Space. We explore the relationships of time and space with consciousness and intelligent activity, inviting you to develop your own perceptions from these models. Time is invested to discuss the implications of *interweaving time and space.* Visuals are provided as a way of understanding how different cultures and peoples of the world view these important concepts, and how these differing viewpoints push the edge when considering the possibilities indicated by Quantum theory.

Chapter 17: Connections as Patterns. Humans are *always* looking for relationships among things—events, happenings, people, thoughts. We are part of a grand search for patterns, taking what we have learned from the past and extrapolating it into the future. In this chapter, we take a deep dive into exploring patterns, using the *Myst* phenomenon to explore specific aspects of pattern thinking including categorization, applying meta-patterns and probability analysis. We explore pattern thinking, patterns as story, and the rhythms of life as patterns from the past extending into the future. We look closely at these connections to help us understand that *the patterns of the past provide a foundation for anticipating and planning the future*.

Chapter 18: Easing into the Flow. The idea of flow is a familiar one. Our very bodies are complex energetic systems, transformers of energy. We briefly look at the life force and the energy centers of the body, before addressing information as energy and energy entanglement. Finally, we focus on how flow optimizes the human experience.

Chapter 19: Emotion as a Guidance System. Emotions are a special form of energy, a building block of consciousness. Within a sea of expressed emotion, we often feel helpless. But we are not. We explore our emotional guidance system in respect to cognitive conveyors, Emotional Intelligence, and the wonder of love.

Chapter 20: Stuck Energy: Limiting and Accelerating. This rather unusual chapter title emphasizes that stopped and stuck energy can be positive or negative in the experiences of life. The retention of limiting mental models is used as an example of stuck energy, and stress can both accelerate learning, or stop or slow natural energy flows throughout the body. In this chapter we also introduce the power of forgetting, and the concept of webs of retained energy.

Chapter 21: Knowledge Capacities. There are unique sets of ideas and ways of thinking that specifically support building capacity for sustainability in a changing, uncertain and complex environment. These are what we call Knowledge Capacities. We provide the working example of Instinctual Harnessing, which is based on the work of Arthur Shelley in *The Organizational Zoo*.

We begin.

Chapter 13
The New Reality

SUBTOPICS: OUR WORLD IS CUCA ... META-PRAXIS ... SOCIAL REALITY (AN ANALOGY) ... INTERACTING WITH THE NEW WELTANSCHAUUNG ... THE ROLE OF TRUST ... SELF EFFICACY ... OPTIMUM AROUSAL ... FINAL THOUGHTS

TABLE: 13-1. FRAME OF REFERENCE FOR CHANGE PROGRAM ACTIVITIES AND TRUST MAPPING.

FIGURES: 13-1. THE SYSTEMS SPACE ... **13.2.** AN OPTIMAL LEVEL OF STRESS FACILITATES LEARNING ... **13.3.** THE HARNESSING OF ANXIETY AS ENERGY?

TOOL: 13-1. TRUST MAPPING

We live in remarkable times. No doubt you've heard those words before, but there just isn't any other way to say it. Just about everywhere we look change is afoot. We are witnessing the old systems and limiting structures of the previous millennia's outdated paradigms breaking apart and crumbling around us. Major events are happening around the world in rapid sequence, including record-breaking natural disasters and unfathomable human acts the likes of which we haven't seen before. All of these are signs of change.

Many call this a time of "quickening", where the speed with which we must think, respond and take action is accelerating. Historically, change was much slower than it is today, and there was less complexity. Thus, the growth of the "normal" person was typically sufficient to maintain the balance of knowledge and action necessary to meet the change underway. Today, this is not the case. Because of the change in knowledge and action needed to effectively deal with change, it is significantly more difficult for the individual to keep up. Further, the *nature* of thinking required to meet this dynamic change—such as multi-tasking and multidimensional thinking[13-1]—is significantly different because of the increasing complexity and speed and nature of communication and change. *All this is preparing us for a different future*. This has happened in the past. For example, following World War II, consider the number of military people given free education to prepare returning veterans to find new jobs. The beginning of this shift was when women went to work in the factories, producing ten times faster than expected! Things could not fall back to the pre-war "norm". Similar shifts are occurring now.

Braden describes today as a time of extremes (Braden, 2014, 2015). His description is certainly fitting! In the language of Alchemy, which we present in detail in Chapter 31/Part V, we have not so subtlety entered the Fermentation stage, where, although the death toll is still ringing, all that is corruptive or transitory is rotting away. Whether looking through the lens of economics, climate, conflict or human consciousness, indeed this is a time of extremes!

The first step to dealing with an unknown future is understanding the nature of the times. In this chapter, we first explore The New Reality from the viewpoint of complexity, then dive into the concept of meta-praxis, a general approach to managing change in a changing world through managing complexity. From the viewpoint of the individual, with a focus on the anxiety produced by increasing change, uncertainty and complexity, we briefly address self-efficacy and the role of anxiety in the learning necessary to deal with our changing world.

Our World is CUCA

The global world we live in is ever changing, uncertain, and increasing in complexity. As technology, and the complex systems it produces, continue to increase at an exponential rate, the magnitude and transfer rate of information is exploding (Martin, 2006; Naisbitt, 2006). That means people have access to more information, and a greater opportunity for the bisociation of ideas and the creation of new ideas. Thus, *in the midst of all this complexity, the world is rich with new thoughts and possibilities.*

Simple systems, that is, systems that remain the same or change very little over time and have few states, exhibit predictable behaviors and have relatively low knowledge needs. The needs they do have would be primarily surface knowledge. Complicated systems—which have a large number of interrelated parts with fixed connections between the parts such that the whole is equal to the sum of its parts— require more knowledge with greater context. This would be primarily shallow knowledge, dependent on the level of complication.

Complex adaptive systems are quite different. Remember, as introduced in Chapter 6/Part I, *you* and the organizations of which you are a part are complex adaptive systems. Co-evolving with the environment through adaptation, complex adaptive systems have a large number of semi-autonomous agents that interact, with varying levels of self-organization. These partially ordered systems have observable aggregate behavior and, operating in perpetual disequilibrium, evolve over time, just as you are evolving.

In order to evolve, complex adaptive systems *require large amounts of knowledge*; in fact, the amount of knowledge needed to understand the system increases with the increase of complexity, and, because much of this knowledge requires context (i.e., shallow knowledge), the amount of sharing needed to create the knowledge required has an exponential function. See Figure 13-1.

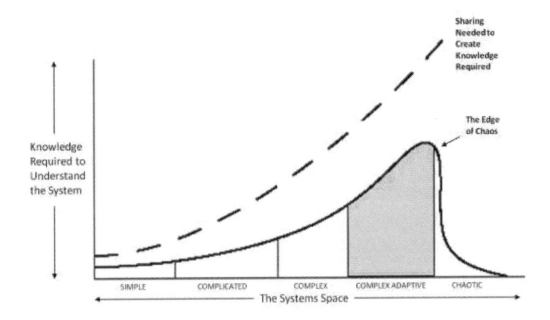

Figure 13-1. *The systems space.*

Thus, we forward the following hypothesis: There is a positive correlation between the increase in world complexity and the knowledge required to understand and operate in that environment. Further, since complex systems can rarely be understood by analytical thinking or deductive reasoning alone, operating in this environment requires: (1) deep knowledge created from effortful practice, (2) the development of intuition and tacit knowledge through experience and continuous learning, and (3) recognition of, and sensitivity to, our inner knowing.

<<<<<<<◇>>>>>>

INSIGHT: **As complexity increases, so also does the amount of knowledge needed to understand the system. And as the need for greater knowledge increases, the amount of sharing needed to develop that knowledge significantly increases.**

<<<<<<<◇>>>>>>

This current environment is what we call CUCA, representing Change, Uncertainty, Complexity and Anxiety. *Change* includes change in the rate of change and in the nature of products, processes and networks. *Uncertainty* means the difficulty of predicting the future or figuring out what the consequences of a given action will be. *Complexity* means the amount of variety or number of differing characteristics in the environment. It is also an indicator of how difficult it is to understand something due to the large number of unpredictable and unanalyzable relationships. Examples would range from a group of people to a single brain. *Anxiety*, the fear or stress on individuals working within a rapidly changing, uncertain and increasingly complex environment, is not far behind increasing change, uncertainty and complexity.

Recognizing that change is a constant and the primary focus of this book, we briefly look at the other three characteristics of the current environment: uncertainty, complexity and anxiety.

Uncertainty. Uncertainty is psychological, that stuff that rises when you know that you do not know, when you realize you don't understand the situation well enough to control it. As Michael (1977, p. 98) describes, uncertainty is,

> ... when you know that there is no honest way to put a number on something, no subjective probability to be assigned ... All one can do is live in it and learn from it and try to create possibilities and see what happens to them as one goes along, whether they add to one's life and the lives of others or they do not.

Humans often attempt to control things that are beyond their control. This can result in an imbalance, with forces pressing against you that are difficult to move through. As Willis (2012) describes,

> The reality is that you live in a world that is uncertain and is always changing through factors that are outside of your control. The Universe is massively bigger than you are and trying to control it will have a negative impact on your balance.

Uncertainty supports an interesting human trait, that is, wrong uncertainties seem to be more satisfying than correct uncertainties. This was understood by ancient prophets. In Hamlet's words, uncertainty "makes us rather bear those ills we have than fly to others that we know not of" (*Hamlet*, Act 3, Scene 1). This trait provides an excuse to discount an uncertain future and focus more on a known present.

When uncertainty increases, problem solutions take on a different character. One example would be getting to work in the morning in a large metropolitan area. As traffic increases over the years, accidents, road repairs, and so on can significantly impact your travel time to work. Solutions would include leaving home earlier, scheduling no meetings first thing in the morning, identifying three or four alternate routes to work, or listening to the radio for information on traffic status and planning accordingly. In other words, flexibility, adaptability, and a larger systems perspective may be needed, all due to increasing uncertainty.

Complexity. While some levels of complexity may have existed throughout history, the explosion of information, communication speed, and networking is moving the world toward an increasingly complex state. The saying *complexity begets complexity* (Battram, 1996) has proven itself over the past few decades in such examples as the Internet, electric power grids, international finance and market flows (Bennet & Bennet, 2004; Friedman, 2005; Kurzweil, 2005).

While complexity builds on complexity because of the creative nature of humanity, it has accelerated with connectivity, development of the mind and focus on competition. As the futurist Peter Schwartz (2003, p. 2) frames it: "Since the scientific discoveries of the seventeenth century, complexity and turbulence in the world at large have been facts of life, looming larger and larger in people's concerns until today there is hardly anyone unaffected by them."

Anxiety. As the old systems break down, people are being stripped of their comfort zones and filled with anxiety, often accompanied by anger, fear and event despair. From the heads of government to colleagues in the workplace to children playing on the street to your own family, there is great uncertainty of what tomorrow will bring.

In her forward-thinking book published in 1996, James said:

The profound changes we are facing today would normally take two or three generations to be assimilated. We are trying to make the stretch in a decade. No wonder the result is anxiety and even chaos. We face a depth and breadth of change unparalleled since the Industrial Revolution. The old values and institutions are breaking up, and we are unsure what will replace them. (James, 1996, pp. 16-17)

As an example of the reality of growing anxiety, *Scientific American* reported that 40 million adults in America (18 percent of the population) suffered from some form of anxiety disorder with 26 percent of American adults suffering from some form of mental disorder in any given year. The data were taken from a 2005 survey by the National Institute of Mental Health using guidelines from the official handbook for mental illness, the DSM-IV ("Mental Illness", 2008). And, of course, this is increasing. In 2012 a research study at the University of Queensland, which involved 91 countries and more than 480,000 people, showed that globally, one person in thirteen suffers from anxiety. While anxiety disorders were found to be more common in Western societies, depression was found to be lowest in North America and highest in some parts of Asia and the Middle East, suggesting that depression is more prevalent where conflict exists (Baxter et al., 2013).

Little wonder that this is occurring. Research in neuroscience is validating that the human mind/brain co-evolves with its environment, "endowing it with the flexibility to adapt to the environment it encounters, the experiences it has, the damage it suffers, the demands its owner makes of it. The brain is neither immutable nor static but is instead continuously remodeled by the lives we lead" (Begley, 2007, p. 130).

Meta-Praxis

As the century was drawing to a close, Will McWhinney felt that there was not "a theory of change, of intentional action, by which to explain what has happened in the recent decades or predict the events of coming decades" (McWhinney, 1997, p.1).

This lack of a general science of practice led him to introduce the concept of meta-praxis, a general approach to managing change in a changing world through managing complexity.

McWhinney recognized large conflicts in Western societies between what he characterized as the analytic and expressive, the sacred and the secular, and the artistic and moralistic lifestyles (McWhinney, 1995). These conflicts are self-generating and self-feeding. As McWhinney (1997, p. 21) states, "Conflict is intimately related to change, and change engenders conflict." We address this directly in Chapter 38/Part V. McWhinney's change theory requires the immediate confrontation of these conflicts with the recognition that the primary sources of conflict lay in the *premises and decision operations* and not in the *content of issues* themselves, noting that "we seldom have the power to solve a problem that does not cause additional problems in its wake" (McWhinney, 1997, p. xi).

<<<<<<<◇>>>>>>>

INSIGHT: **The primary sources of conflict lay in the premises and decision operations, not in the content of issues themselves.**

<<<<<<<◇>>>>>>>

McWhinney's theory draws on the work of Lawrence LeShan (1976), who proposed that these conflicts are based on social behaviors that arise from *different understandings of reality,* with each reality "the logical (ontological) underpinning of a worldview" manifesting typical behaviors associated with that world view (McWhinney, 1997, p. 10). Since change is differently understood within each of these frames—and since conflict arises out of attempts to make change—McWhinney's change approach becomes a *conflict resolution approach.* The way that resolution can occur is directly linked to the world views of reality complete with the diverse concepts related to cause, meaning, expectations and satisfactions held by those who define the problem, which emerge from a complex set of beliefs and attitudes, values and ethics, feelings and emotions, all related to assignment of cause. The success of the resolution is dependent on the degree of freedom from the dilemma provided to individuals, organizations or society coupled with the lack of new problems emerging from the resolution. This is a macro change, that is, a transformational change, dissolving problems or rendering them solvable (Ackoff & Emery, 1972).

To promote change, it was first necessary to understand the context of those realities, then have a way of choosing a path through the "mind field" of multiple—and often competing—realities (McWhinney, 1997). Engaging various forms of expressive narratives such as stories and myths became central in exploring meaning, resolving conflicts and developing new ways of operating. (Chapter 23/Part IV explores co-creating frames of reference.)

In the Western culture, McWhinney (1997) identified four archetypes of alternative realities—systems of belief and behavior that underlie a person's character. These are unitary, sensory, mythic and social. While these represent the leaders, scientists, artists and entrepreneurs described in the work of Lawrence LeShan (1976), these archetypes are also consistent with Kuhn's (1972) paradigms, Pepper's (1942) four worldviews, Burrell and Morgan's (1979) sociological approach, and Gebser's (1985) work on consciousness development. In other words, some of our greatest minds have identified similar concepts.

The *unity* theory of reality—that we are one connected whole with no spatial or time differences and described as deterministic—is consistent with the discovery of relativity in physics, with the religious belief that we are expressions of one God, and with the concept of gestalt thinking in psychology and philosophy. In the unity worldview there is a higher authority, part of a structured hierarchy that manages life. The human is in the position of interpreting and searching for truth, and there is no change, no effect, without accepting time and space as dimensions of reality (McWhinney, 1997). Action is based on a process of *at-one-ment*, staying aware and interactive with the flow of events. Requiring total surrender of the ego, unity represents the worldview of true believers. It is exemplified by the formal organization structure—complex hierarchies of concepts, laws and classifications—that epitomize the U.S. government, a manufacturing company or a family.

While still described as deterministic, *sensory* is at the opposite side of that argument, saying that since our perceptions are of different things, we are separate entities. The sensory reality says that change occurs from antecedent conditions; change happens, following the imperatives of nature. Since knowledge is incomplete and partial, change is unpredictable. This builds on the view of Greek atomists who believed in the existence of basic elements in the Universe. A simple justification of this belief is the need for people to communicate with each other. However, paradoxically, "the ability to communicate suggests that the separate parts share in an encompassing wholeness" (McWhinney, 1997, p. 25). Note that the differences in these two world views (monistic and multiplistic) have given rise to major social conflicts such as religious wars and persecutions.

The *mythic* reality is a product of the creative imagination, symbols and ideas transcending—and not limited by—that which is around us. Causality is free will and intentionality, with no restraint on one's choices. The mythic believer does not experience change; rather, change is a part of the way the world is. There is a flow; nothing comes by chance and everything has meaning. Since the mythic belief creates all, they are amoral with no ethics or values issues. Examples of historic people exhibiting this worldview are Gandhi, Mao and Hitler. When coupled with compassion such as that shown by Gandhi, the mythic reality worldview becomes an important player in the creative leap (see Chapter 30/Part IV).

<<<<<<<◇>>>>>>>

INSIGHT: **When coupled with compassion, the mythic reality worldview becomes an important player in the creative leap.**

<<<<<<<◇>>>>>>>

The *social* reality is concerned with the feelings and values of human beings and very much a product of free will. This humanistic view is an objective view achieved through a shared consensus emerging from the perceptions and feelings of a population emerging through individual awareness, and constructed through interactions with others. Because a single reality does not emerge from these interactions, a tension or force emerges. As Friedman (1989, p. 10) describes:

> The mystery of word and answer that moves between beings is not one of union, harmony, or even complementarity, but of tension; for two persons never mean the same thing by the words they use and no answer is ever fully satisfactory. The result is that at each point of the dialogue, understanding and misunderstanding are interwoven. From this tension of understanding and misunderstanding comes the interplay of openness and closedness, expression and reserve, that mark every genuine dialogue between person and person.

<<<<<<<◇>>>>>>>

INSIGHT: **Because of each individual's uniqueness, there is a tension between understanding and misunderstanding that underlies every genuine dialogue. This juxtaposing of thought is a potential source of creativity.**

<<<<<<<◇>>>>>>>

It is the social reality that is most identified with the feminine viewpoint and associated with a service mentality. Social reality was exemplified in the work of Immanuel Kant in the eighteenth century and exhibited in the era of the flower child in the 1950's and 60's. Since this is a collectively constructed worldview, objects, space and time are arbitrary constructs and feelings are paramount. Change is a constant, and all communications disturb the balance of values (McWhinney, 1997). For an in-depth treatment of these four archetypes and how to use this understanding to facilitate conflict resolution, see McWhinney (1997).

Looking at these realities through the framework of knowledge and learning, they provide different ways of perceiving and acting in a CUCA environment. While agreeing with their value, Ionesco (1971) challenges us to remember,

> All systems are false; that is to say, all systems are and cannot help but be merely images, different ways of imagining or representing the world, which is only the starting point of these representations. All systems begin with reality, which is amorphous, and go on from there. The more perfect, complete, believable,

convincing, logical, and coherent a system is, the more unreal and artificial it is. All systems, therefore, are fundamentally artificial and far removed from reality.

Ultimately, McWhinney (1997) acknowledges that the greatest change comes down to two archetypal forms, that is, "choosing between the conformative paths that *revitalize* an operation, and the adventuresome paths that lead to *renaissance* and the birth of new initiatives" (p. xii). While the terminology is somewhat unique to McWhinney's focus, this is, indeed, the choice each of us has—and humanity has— as we stand at the fork in the road toward the future (see Chapter 38/Part V, The Bifurcation). But we're getting ahead of ourselves. There are still many more ideas and potential actions to explore during our Journey toward intelligent activity.

Social Reality

(An analogy written from the viewpoint of the mind/brain)

As SETH streamed into unknown territory, he was further excited by the feelings of familiarity and resonance emerging within. SETH represented Self-Evolved Thinking Humans, a pattern of men and women exalting diversity, crossing cultural, ethnic, religious, age and gender boundaries in pursuit of ultimate knowledge. SETH's capacity to anticipate was high, honed by the association of a wide range of experiences and a highly tuned emotional guidance system. Still, with all her historic success in anticipating and dealing with the future in her area of expertise, this landscape was different ... was that a tinge of fear in her side tagging along for the ride?

SETH was responding to a strong message received from this distant realm, a message associated with survival, no doubt one of those learnings worthy of a new category of The Nobel Prize, a grand new way of thinking and being. He now stood on the high ground above that distant realm, a hundred thousand homes stretched out as far as he could see, lights twinkling through the windows and pulsing along the billion connecting three-dimensional highways, roads and paths that made the community One.

Some spots were brighter than others: flitting patterns from a movie theatre playing reruns; flashing sparks from a loudly-buzzing generator; colorful streams from an observatory at the far edge of the city sporting a large, upward-focused telescope. And near the center of this hub of activity, to the left, where connecting paths intertwined with incessant beams of entangled reds and blues and yellows, the brightest light moved in and out of the central library. SETH understood the power of record-keeping at its best, a living, vibrant field of growing and expanding patterns evolving from instant to instant.

SETH moved toward that light, carefully navigating the busyness of the intersections, pulled this way and that by the excitement, but *committed to staying the course*. He had come to learn from the Master, to discover that single thought that guided all the others. He paused to reflect on this singular yearning for the discovery of something more that had emerged since his first feeling of the message.

Then he arrived at his destination, startled by the peace within the hub of excitement but gently perceiving the silence and fullness that comes with knowing. What might be described as an inner council of sorts welcomed him, each member of the council a different aspect of the One. Eager to discover answers to his questions, he moved quickly through the formalities of introductions, conveying greetings from mutual distant relatives, sharing the urgency of his mission, and expressing gratitude for a warm reception.

"*The environment is rapidly changing,*" the leader began, "*and though you journeyed quickly following the first conscious flash, much new information is coming in through our sensors and emerging from our internal sources that is shifting our direction. There are new choices to make. Let us see how you fit, what you contribute ...*"

"*And what **we** can learn from you,*" SETH interrupted.

"*Yes,*" the leader confirmed, "*that is also a possibility.*"

"*Possibility?*" SETH questioned. "*But this sounded like the answer we have been seeking; finally, absolute knowledge. It resonates with our beliefs, with our preferred frames of reference, with our values ...*"

"*Ah,*" responded the leader, "*but beliefs and frames of reference and values also change. They are tools for us to act effectively in an uncertain and changing environment.*"

<<<<<<<◇>>>>>>

INSIGHT: **Beliefs, frames of reference and values change. they are tools for us to act effectively in an uncertain and changing environment.**

<<<<<<<◇>>>>>>

SETH was puzzled, confused even. "*No. Our community is also one hundred thousand strong, although many of those connections are outliers, at a distance, only a few reside in the center of town. Still, we have held onto those early values embedded during the beginning of time, and have picked up incoming information throughout our history that has reinforced those values, and we have sent continuous messages beyond our boundaries to guide those who are on misdirected paths ...*"

"*So that was you,*" the leader sighed. "*Those historic values were holding all of us back for a while.*" There was a short pause, accented by rhythms of soft bursts of light. The leader continued, "*And yet you are here. You were able to sense something new and different with the potential of evolving our connections and firings to another level."*

"*Yes ... it was magical!*" responded SETH. "*There was an explosion right in the center of town—at our Central Library—that coincided with the explosion here, which was visible and felt even across such great distances. A high vibration so strong that it pulled me here. Where did it come from? What exactly is it? Tell me what it is. Give me the words, the pattern, the context, to understand and learn and connect and share.*"

The leader smiled and silently moved away from SETH even as another form approached and continued the interaction. "*YOU are part of the answer to your questions! It is at the core of who you are and now you are more or you are more strongly connected to us through this journey, and, in turn to all those with whom we interact. We welcome your contribution.*"

SETH was beginning to tire of these circular responses. "*But I'm here to discover the grand new way of doing and being, the answer!*"

A third form was now moving toward SETH, hand out-stretched, eyes sparkling with amusement. "*There is no such thing; and simultaneously all you know is part of such a thing!*"

"*We are part of such a thing that does not exist?*" SETH blurted out.

The third informer gently motioned to the shelves and shelves of books and movies surrounding them in a hazy glow. "*We store here only a small amount of what we observe, what we reflect, what we discover, and it is always reforming and reconnecting in new ways to create the wonderful flash which brought you here.*" She gestured a full circle, gliding around with the gesture, a lightness and happiness in the movement. "*Perhaps you had forgotten? This is the process of birth and regeneration, the way of knowledge, the capacity to take effective action, a human gift to navigate the rapids of change, uncertainty and complexity.*"

"*I don't understand,*" SETH sorrowed. "*How can I anticipate those rapids?*"

"*You've started that journey already,*" came the slow response. "*You are here with us, interacting, each of us learning from the other. Our thoughts are no longer distant to you. We are moving toward intelligent activity.*" The third informer paused, pulsing with soft light that reached toward SETH.

"*My friend, our future is neither predetermined nor knowable. We are co-creators of that future, and it rests with the dynamics of an almost infinite number of quasi-independent biological thinking subsystems that are entangled and deeply interconnected, with each trying to comprehend the whole while acting to the benefit of the individual. There is no 'answer' or ultimate action; there is learning, thinking and acting, the role of each biological subsystem which, in turn, affects the learning, thinking and acting of the whole in completely unpredictable ways.*"

SETH reflected. Patterns in a never-ending journey in which SETH was fully participating?

As SETH turned her energy towards home, she reflected on re-connecting with her trusted network, sharing new patterns, expanding their thoughts through exchange and dialogue, and **continuously re-creating themselves to co-evolve with a changing Universe** ...

<<<<<<<<>>>>>>>

INSIGHT: **We are co-creators of a future that is neither predetermined nor knowable.**

<<<<<<<<>>>>>>>

Interacting with the New Weltanschauung (World View)

The increase in world and local dynamics, uncertainty, and complexity is impacting people of all natures, ages, cultures, nationalities and educational levels. As we transitioned from the age of information into the age of knowledge, everything moved faster and farther, and people became intertwined with other people, societies, and technologies. Companies located around the world collaborate instantly, people work at home, email traffic gets heavier, money moves faster, and organizations shift from controlled to empowered workforces. To operate successfully, knowledge workers have learned to deal with increasing speed, unpredictability, and complexity of the environment, moving to the edge of chaos, beyond, and back. This means continuously *observing, thinking about, and developing an intuitive understanding* of the current situation and where it is likely to go. Note that in this activity the mental is in service to the intuitive.

What today's (and tomorrow's) knowledge workers need to know is very different from the workers in a stove-piped, control-oriented organization within a stable, predictable environment. When uncertainty increases, problem solutions take on a different character, requiring flexibility, adaptability, and a larger systems perspective. Employees must now think for themselves, cooperate and collaborate with global partners, and carefully study their environment as they co-evolve with that environment in order to develop an *intuitive ability* to make effective decisions and take the right actions. In other words, as situations become more complex, *the nature of learning, knowledge, and action shift.*

Ray Kurzweil (2005, p. 94) proposed that the computational power of supercomputers will equal that of the human brain around 2020, what he calls the point of singularity:

Biological evolution for animals as complex as humans takes tens of thousands of years to make noticeable, albeit small, differences. The entire history of human culture and technological evolution has taken place on that timescale. Yet we are now poised to ascend beyond the fragile and slow creations of biological evolution in a mere several decades. Current progress is on a scale that is a thousand to a million times faster than biological evolution.

Kurzweil (2005) also argued that the computational power (10^{16} computations per second) "required for human brain functional simulation" would be achieved in 2013 (p. 71). While clearly we missed that mark, the timeframe is drawing nearer and in today's world it is easy to see just how fast *the future is accelerating toward us*. This emphasizes the need for maximizing the knowledge worker's learning capacity to deal with CUCA.

Impey added a twist to the concept of singularity. While acknowledging that the singularity is a hypothetical time a few decades away, Impey (2010, p. 298) sees it as a time when "exponential progress in nanotechnology, genetic engineering, and computing leads to a post-biological race of humans." We agree. While for the most part technologies are not yet part of the physical body, they are close at hand.

The Role of Trust

While trust plays an important role in all interactions, in the process of sharing knowledge and co-creating it is a necessity. Yet in a CUCA environment where anxiety and fear often find their way into our living space, trust can be hard to buid and sustain. Instead of thinking of where we place our trust as a dichotomy (others vs ourselves), it may be more accurate to think in terms of a surety spectrum with four main categories: Direct Knowledge, Direct Trust, Deferred Trust, and Faith Trust.

Direct Knowledge is knowing that we know our own observations and conclusions, and can therefore base future decisions on what we currently know. To prove our direct knowledge, we may be asked to "verify" what we know by showing examples, research, etc. While this type of knowing provides us with a feeling of deep surety, the "grounding" that it provides from past experiences may also keep us from taking new/future ground.

Direct Trust is knowing that we trust our own observations and conclusions, and can therefore base future decisions on what we currently and directly trust. This type of trust simply projects our current direct knowledge into the future as expectations of continuity. This continuity can be linear or non-linear, and applied to situations or ourselves. When we describe our trust towards future expectations, as it relates to our own abilities, we usually use the term "self-efficacy" to describe this concept.

Deferred Trust is knowing that we trust someone else, based on "credibility," which is simply the quality we use to determine if they are believable or worthy of trust. This quality we use can vary widely between people and circumstances. For example, some may deem others credible based on the *authority* of the position they hold, while others may only deem them credible after reviewing the authorization process which was used to place them into authority. Note that the initiative to overthrow monarchies was through this lens, since "birthright" became a questionable authorization process. Given the need to be clear about the exact ways that we trust in others, the term *vericate* (Bennet & Bennet, 2004) is increasingly used to specify certain qualities of trust. Just as the term "verify" places specific qualifications for how we reference direct knowledge, the term "vericate" places specific qualifications for how we reference deferred trust. To vericate means that you are relying on someone's socially recognized experience and expertise in a specific area, not just their authority or ungrounded opinion.

Faith Trust is knowing that we trust in a general outcome based on *our perceived nature of the Universe*. For example, we may be called a *pessimist* if we believe in Murphy's law, which states that "if anything can go wrong it will go wrong." Or we may be called an *optimist* if we believe that "the cup is half full, not half empty" and that things have a way of working out. How much does our perceived nature of the Universe influence future events? From a psychological viewpoint, the study of self-talk and affirmations looks at the impact these beliefs have on our confidence, which can directly affect our approach and expectations. From a neuroscience viewpoint, we know that our thoughts and feelings influence the structure of the brain, and the structure of the brain influences our thoughts. But the more-interesting study of Quantum reality looks at the impact these beliefs have on connected consciousness, which can directly affect the situation and outcome.

****

TOOL 13-1: Trust Mapping

This tool provides a way to visualize trust for each key activity within an organization. See Table 13-1. In this example, David is the person overseeing the work, and in addition to assigning an owner to each change program activity, he has mapped where trust is placed.

In this example trust map a the top of the next page, David owns activity 0 (program oversight), and he expects to rely on all four trust categories. Alex owns activity 1, and while not the expert for this specific task, does rely on self-efficacy (direct trust), verication of experts (deferred trust), and her optimistic nature (faith trust). David has assigned activity 2 to himself as he is the expert for this task and has self-efficacy given the new team and tasks. Theresa owns activity 3, and expects the task to be predictably within her current expertise. Arthur owns activity 4, and while having knowledge of the task is going to be heavily reliant on a contractor.

#	Activity	Owner	Direct Knowledge	Direct Trust	Deferred Trust	Faith Trust
0	Overseeing the Program	David	X	X	X	X
1	Building Infrastructure	Alex		X	X	X
2	Management Sponsorship	David	X	X		
3	Training	Theresa	X			
4	Communication	Arthur	X		X	
5	Promotion and Reward	John			X	X
6	Embedded into process	Alex	X	X		X
7	Benchmark and Result	Theresa			X	X
8	KPI enforcement	Arthur			X	
9	Shared team status	John				X

Table 13-1. *Frame of reference for change program activities and trust mapping.*

John owns activity 5, and without specific expertise will be overseeing the results of a contractor, while relying on his optimistic nature. Alex owns activity 6, and is the known expert. Notice for activity 1 and 6, Alex has been assigned ownership of two important tasks, but instead of becoming overloaded is relying on experts for one of the activities. Theresa owns activity 7, and will be primarily trusting another department. Arthur owns activity 8, and will be primarily trusting several other department heads. John owns activity 9, and at this early point in the program is optimistic but has not yet assigned subtasks with deferred trust.

****

In today's environment our organizations are increasingly becoming more matrixed and project-based, so instead of a hierarchy of known relationships and known capabilities, it is necessary to rely more on trust. Using a Trust Mapping tool allows us to articulate and share our status of trust along with the activities and progress. It enables us to see if we are overloading team members and encouraging them to be individual performers rather than team players and also relying on others. It allows us to see if we are outsourcing work for which we can provide coaching since we have retained a core competency, or if we are outsourcing work which will require a high level of deferred trust and faith trust. Finally, it allows us to track stretch goals for leaders to own more activities in areas where they are not direct experts.

Note that this example trust map is for David, who is overseeing the program. If the six people in our example mapped their perspective of trust in this grouping, they might get different answers, because their "knowledge" of the tasks, people and relationships will be different. As owners of specific activities complete their own trust map for specific tasks, they will capture specifics for where they are placing their trust at a deeper level. For deferred trust, additional qualities may be documented for: (1) Applicability (how a task aligns with their expertise), (2) Accountability (how they have met previous requirements), and (3) Authorization (what experience and education has defined them as an expert).

In trust mapping, when trust is strong, we get overlaying maps, which forms a strong basis of relationships. However, where trust is uneven, people can be taken advantage of. For example, if James trusts Marie, but actually Marie has portrayed herself through a mask that James has not seen through, Marie can manipulate James. For this, she does not have to trust him, just ensure that James cannot see through her mask. Whilst James' trust of Marie remains, the knowledge flows freely from him to her, which she may use appropriately (for mutual benefit) or inappropriately (to take credit for James work, or take advantage of him). If James sees through the mask and realizes he has been inappropriately manipulated, not only does his trust diminish, but he actually builds a *distrust* for Marie. Unfortunately, there is only a two-letter difference between distrust and destruct, with the first being the precursor of the latter. From this point on, James will not view Marie neutrally, but from a negative perspective. This completely changes the relationship and effectively stops the flow of knowledge. As the old adage goes, *Trust takes forever to build and only a moment to destroy.*

Note that distrust is quite different than having no trust. Trust is directly related to the belief in someone or something in terms of truth and reliability or strength. As with truth, there are levels of trust. Distrust is generally related to a feeling rather than a belief, and has to do with doubting the truth and reliability of someone or something. It also carries with it an element of suspicion. What is fascinating is that while trust and distrust may be opposites in the world of duality within which we live, there is a neutral spot in between, where there is neither trust nor distrust. For example, this would occur when a person or product is unknown.

In exploring the relationship between trust and distrust, Lewicki et al. (1998) talk in terms of high trust and low trust, and high distrust and low distrust. High trust is characterized by hope, faith, confidence, assurance and initiative. Low trust is characterized by no hope, faith or confidence, passivity and hesitance. High distrust is characterized by fear, skepticism, cynicism, wariness and watchfulness, and vigilance. Conversely, low distrust is characterized by no fear, the absence of skepticism and cynicism, low monitoring and no vigilance.

Self Efficacy

Because anxiety is often a human byproduct of change, uncertainty and complexity, we briefly address self efficacy. Self efficacy starts with our feelings and what we perceive to be true about our self. The anxiety that often accompanies increasing change, uncertainty and complexity may well reflect a loss of security, lack of trust, and a sense of undermining personal identity. To move through this anxiety and glide into the flow of change, the individual must look within to the stability of values, integrity and ethical behavior with a clear direction, vision and purpose. In the past a large number of beliefs have limited us. This need no longer be the case. Nature, nurture and our own choices all play a significant role in our learning and development.

Bruce Lipton, a cell biologist, contends that in these exciting times science is shattering old myths and fundamentally rewriting a belief of human civilization. "The belief that we are frail bio-chemical machines controlled by genes is giving way to an understanding that we are powerful creators of our lives and the world in which we live." (Lipton, 2005, p. 17)

<<<<<<<<>>>>>>>

INSIGHT: **Nature, nurture and our own choices all play a significant role in our learning and development.**

<<<<<<<<>>>>>>>

For example, although DNA was once thought to be destiny, this idea is changing as neuroscience and biology expand their frontiers of understanding. Epigenetics— literally meaning control above genetics—is profoundly changing our beliefs and knowledge of how life is controlled. One of the most active areas of scientific research, Epigenetics is the study of the molecular mechanisms by which the environment influences gene activity (Lipton, 2005). Ross proposes that,

> ... biology is no longer inevitable gene expression driven unidirectionally by the DNA. Rather, genes for brain growth and development are turned on and off by the environment in a complex, rich set of feedback loops. Causality in brain development involves a dance between two partners, DNA and the environment. (Ross, 2006, p. 32)

From another perspective, it has been discovered that DNA blueprints are not set in concrete at the birth of the cell as was once thought. Genes are not destiny (Church, 2006). Rather, it is *how genes are expressed* that determine our future. Gene expression means that the DNA information within a gene is released and influences its surrounding environment. Environmental influences such as nutrition, stress and emotions can modify those genes without changing their basic blueprint. And, in some cases, those modifications can be passed on to future generations (Reik & Walter, 2001). *What we believe leads to what we think, which leads to our knowledge, which leads to what actions we take.* Thus, what we believe and how we think determine what we do. It is our actions that determine our success, not our genes (Bennet et al., 2015b; Bownds, 1999; Begley, 2007).

Further, Lipton points out that positive and negative beliefs not only impact our health, but every aspect of our life.

> Consider the people who walk across coals without getting burned. If they wobble in the steadfastness of their belief that they can do it, they wind up with burned feet. Your beliefs act like filters on a camera, changing how you see the world. And your biology adapts to those beliefs. When we truly recognize that our beliefs are that powerful, we hold the key to freedom ... we can change our minds. (Lipton, 2005, p. 143)

In addition, environments can *and do* change the actions of genes (Jensen, 2006). Our feelings, attitudes, and mind-sets can actively be changed by meditation and other mental exercises (Begley, 2007). Thus, **our beliefs and thoughts are what will ultimately determine our ability to successfully navigate change, uncertainty and complexity in changing times.**

Optimum Arousal

With our Self Efficacy intact—and recognizing that knowledge (the capacity to take effective action) is directly related to our success—how do we produce the best mental state for learning?

Amen says that physical exercise, mental exercise and social bonding are the best sources of stimulation of the brain (Amen, 2005). Complex levels of self-awareness, those that involve higher brain functions and potential changes in neural networks, cannot be accomplished when an individual feels anxious and defensive. Specifically, Cozolino says that a safe and empathic relationship can establish an emotional and neurobiological context that is conducive to neural reorganization. This relationship "... serves as a buffer and scaffolding within which [an adult] can better tolerate the stress required for neural reorganization" (Cozolino, 2002, p. 291). As Taylor (2006, p. 82) explains, 'adults who would create (or recreate) neural networks associated with development of a more complex epistemology need emotional support for the discomfort that will also certainly be part of that process." In other words, the more troubled the times (in terms of change, uncertainty and complexity), the more necessary it is to have a *balancing emotional safety net*. Johnson agrees. Referring to recent discoveries in cognitive neuroscience and social cognitive neuroscience, she says that educators and mentors of adults recognize "the neurological effects and importance of creating a trusting relationship, a holding environment, and an intersubjective space" (Johnson, 2006, p. 68), where such things as reflection and abstract thinking can occur.

The changes in the structure of the brain that need to occur in a CUCA environment are not new phenomena. This concept of neuroplasticity can be found not only in the history of the evolution of man, but also in the current maturation of the individual. Neuroplasticity is the ability of neurons to change their structure and relationships according to environmental demands or personal decisions and actions. The brain maintains a high degree of plasticity, changing in response to experience and learning. As Buonomano and Merzenich (1998, p. 21) explain, "The brain has been shaped by evolution to adapt and readapt to an ever-changing world. The ability to learn is dependent on modification of the brain's chemistry and architecture."

Learning is highly dependent on the level of arousal of the learner. Too little arousal and there is no motivation, too much and stress takes over and reduces learning. Maximum learning occurs when there is a moderate level of arousal. This initiates neural plasticity by increasing the production of neurotransmitters and neural growth hormones, which in turn facilitate neural connections and cortical organization (Cozolino and Sprokay, 2006; Cowan and Kandel, 2001).

LeDoux (1996, p. 43) says that, "Bodily changes follow directly the PERCEPTION of the exciting fact, and that our feeling of the same changes as they occur IS the emotion." He also believes that "…once emotions occur, they become powerful indicators of future behavior" (LeDoux, 1996, p. 19). While we cannot "will" our emotions to occur—and understanding that emotions are things that happen to us rather than things we order to occur—we can set up and participate in situations where external events provide stimuli to trigger desired emotions (LeDoux, 1996). We do this regularly when we go to the movies or visit an amusement park, or even when we consume alcohol or stimulate our palate with a gourmet meal.

There is an optimum level of stress for each individual that facilitates learning. Excitement can serve as a strong motivation to drive people to learn, but cannot be so strong that it becomes high stress moving to anxiety. For example, Merry sees adaptation not as a basic transformative change, but as having a new range of possibilities. When people face growing uncertainty and stress, their resilience allows them to find novel forms of adaptation to the changing conditions (Merry, 1995). In other words, with a stressful external environment, people will naturally tend to find ways of reacting and adapting to that environment. See Figure 13-2.

Since stress is a result of the perception of an individual in a given situation, an individual can learn to control or minimize it. A cartoon drawn by artist Jackie Urbanovic (Figure 13-3) conveys this dilemma! (See also Chapter 18 on flow.) One approach is to perceive things from a different frame of reference, which is what is suggested in Figure 13-3. Is it indeed possible to harness the energy of anxiety? As shown in the discussion above, the evidence would suggest yes, to a certain degree.

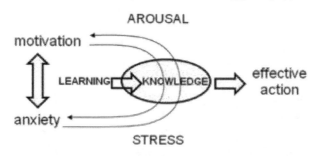

Figure 13-2. *An optimal level of stress facilitates learning.*

Another way to reduce stress is to not judge a situation by the possibility of its outcomes. In other words, *most stress is caused by anticipation of future events* that offer a perceived threat of some nature. A tool for interrupting stress and balancing our physical, mental and emotional planes is provided in Chapter 32/Part V.

Situations occur throughout life that help us understand who we are and how well we handle stress. When these situations become closer and closer, it is paramount that we shift our frames of reference to consider them from an external viewpoint. Emotions are wonderful indicators of our preferences, and without them we would have no judgment and would not be able to make decisions. That is exactly the role they need to play in a CUCA environment, when things are not in our direct control and the future is unknown.

This was driven home to the authors several years ago when taking a propjet from Washington, D.C. to New York. Here's what they write about the experience:

As what was to be a short hop dragged beyond an hour and a half, we began to wonder what was happening! We were no longer circling LaGuardia Airport (where we had been scheduled to land) but were over JFK International Airport, making a low pass with a dozen emergency vehicles (with lights flashing) following along under us. The pilots announced that while our landing gear was down and they felt everything was fine, the light didn't show that it was locked. We continued circling after that announcement, clearly getting rid of any excess fuel. As panic took hold in the cabin, some people were struck silent, others couldn't stop talking, and many were praying while tightly gripping the arms of their seats. But, surprisingly, two people on board were smiling as they exchanged looks. There was nothing we could do to change whatever was going to happen. We were in a state of wonderment, thinking excitedly, "What's next?"

Figure 13-3. *The harnessing of anxiety as energy? Cartoon by Jackie Urbanovic (used with permission).* (See Chapter 18 on Easing into Flow.)

Final Thoughts

The changes taking place are happening both behind the scenes and in the world at large. Since the turn of the new millennium, it seems that with each year that passes time is speeding up. Things are happening quicker, and people are having to deal with far more than ever before. Life and the speed with which we must think, respond, and take action are accelerating beyond what we ever imagined.

We are further experiencing more record-breaking world events each year, to such a degree that even the most devoted skeptics are reaching for plausible explanations. All of this is driving us to change. Sometimes those changes are coming by force, and other times by choice in response to force and opportunity. If we can stand back and take a systems look at the changing landscape, we might recognize these changes as signposts on an evolutionary road indicating that we are passing out of one era and into a new one. Humanity is evolving.

Questions for Reflection:

How have you adapted to increasing levels of complexity and uncertainty?

What have you done to create a trusted network of colleagues and friends to stimulate knowledge sharing?

How do you handle stress?

Chapter 14
"Co-ing" and Evolving

SUBTOPICS: CO-EVOLVING ... JOURNEY INTO COOPERATION AND COLLABORATION ... THREE-WAY COOPERATION AND COLLABORATION ... CO-EVOLVING IN A CUCA WORLD ... SUSTAINABILITY ... ICAS AND SUSTAINABILITY ... SUSTAINABLE KNOWLEDGE ... A NEW GENERATION OF CO-CREATORS ... THE DISCOVERY OF COMMUNITY

TABLE: 14-1. THE ROLE OF CONTROL.

FIGURES: 14-1. THE JOURNEY TOWARD INTELLIGENT ACTIVITY IS A JOURNEY OF "CO-ING" ... **14-2.** THE FIELDS OF COLLABORATIVE COMPETITION AND COMPETITIVE COLLABORATION ... **14-3.** WHAT DO LIVING INFORMATION SYSTEMS LOOK LIKE? (CONVERSATIONS THAT MATTER) ... **14-4.** RELATIONSHIP OF ICAS CHARACTERISTICS AND SUSTAINABILITY AND HEALTH PARAMETERS.

TOOL: 14-1. BUILDING MENTAL SUSTAINABILITY

Living the "co" in our everyday activities is a critical pivot point in the Intelligent Social Change Journey. It denotes the recognition that we are not alone on this journey toward intelligent activity. Recall that intelligent activity represents a *state of interaction* where intent, purpose, direction, values and expected outcomes are clearly understood and communicated among all parties, reflecting wisdom and achieving a higher truth. Whether from a physical, mental or emotional focus, human experiential learning is about living in and with our environment. We now recognize that an individual cannot evolve or expand without interaction with others (Cozolino, 2006). We are social beings, and co-ing is the "co" of co-creating, cooperation, collaboration, community, co-evolving, and co-service, that is, expanding the entangled knowledge base of humanity and serving others so that they may serve others.

Figure 14-1. *The Journey toward intelligent activity is a journey of "co-ing".*

In this chapter, we take a closer look at the concept of co-evolving. We then explore the human journey into cooperation and collaboration, with a focus on the movement from competitive advantage to collaborative advantage in the current business environment. We briefly look at a current three-way cooperation and collaboration example. Co-evolving in a CUCA world leads us into a discussion of sustainability and, specifically, sustainable knowledge. Finally, we take a good look at the new generation as co-creators, and touch on the powerful role of community in this environment that, for those of us who are holdovers from different times, will never be the same.

Co-Evolving

At the highest level of evolution, co-evolving describes an interdependency of two or more species, with each affecting development of the other. The term originated from Ehrlich and Raven (1964) in their now-famous article, "Butterflies and Plants: A Study in Coevolution," which showed the relationship between families of butterflies and phylogenetic groups of plants. While the relationship of insects and the flowers they pollinate is often used as an example of co-evolving, co-evolving can insinuate a predator/prey or parasite/host relationship or competitiveness, as well as a mutually beneficial relationship.

As a species—and as individuals—we survive by successfully **co-evolving with our environment**. In changing times this is a continuous and difficult process because of the intensity and uncertainty of the environmental changes that occur. Co-evolving is a focus of Phase 2 of the Intelligent Social Change Journey. In this context, co-evolving means interacting with, influencing and, as necessary, adapting to the demands of the environment.

Let's look at the word more closely. Evolve is to develop gradually over time; in this sense, we differentiate "evolve" from "exist", thus emphasizing development (change) rather than existence, although clearly you cannot evolve unless you exist. Recognizing the various nuances that could be attached to the concept of evolving, we choose to consider the term in a positive context, that is, evolving *to* or *towards* something "better", with "better" in context to a perceived current state and the movement toward an improved, even transformative, state. Thus, the term co-evolve as used in this text represents *an interdependent developmental learning journey among two or more people*. This can be extrapolated to other levels such as two or more teams, organizations, or nations.

From the viewpoint of the individual, we now know that the self co-evolves with its environment through the process of associative patterning, the complexing of incoming information (extrinsic signals) with internally-stored patterns (intrinsic signals). The results are not necessarily based on the *number* of the extrinsic signals, but rather on neural interactions "selected and stabilized by memory through previous encounters with the environment." (Edelman & Tononi, 2000, p. 137) In other words, the more we know about a specific area that is in memory, the stronger the modulation with extrinsic signals that relate to that area. The more we know in an area, the easier it is to learn in that area. There is an amazing plasticity in the mind/brain, "endowing it with the flexibility to adapt to the environment it encounters, the experiences it has, the damage it suffers, the demands its owner makes of it" (Begley, 2007, p. 130). The bottom line is that the brain is continuously remodeled by the lives we lead.

<<<<<<<◇>>>>>>

INSIGHT: **The bottom line is that the brain is continuously remodeled by the lives we lead.**

<<<<<<<◇>>>>>>

Journey into Cooperation and Collaboration

Whether today or in days of old, cooperation and collaboration start at the family level in caring for and protecting our young. Expanding on information provided in Chapter 3/Part I, as Darwin realized in *The Descent of Man*—too late to recall the meme "survival of the fittest" that had taken on a life of its own—"Those communities which included the greatest number of the most sympathetic members would flourish best and rear the greatest number of offspring" (Darwin, 1998, p. 110). Thus, began the recognition that "cooperation and unity, rather than survival of the fittest, are the keys to the success of a species" (Kropotkin, 1902). In fact, cooperation was identified as *the key factor* in evolution and survival (Swomley, 2000).

Both cooperation and collaboration could be defined as the process where two or more people and/or organizations work together towards achieving mutually beneficial goals and objectives. Collaboration denotes closer alignment of the parties involved. This is the co-creation of value through open sharing, the leveraging of existing resources and creating new insights through the bisociation of ideas.

As our human mental faculties developed and expanded, recognition of the power of cooperation and collaboration did not immediately translate into our organizational models, which were largely based on control, whether this was via blood lines, religion or classes. Max Weber's bureaucratic model called for imperative control, which was management power over workers based on a hierarchy of relationships. See Table 14-1.

Focus on controlling physical activities

Control via Blood Lines	Control via Religion	Control via Class Separation

629-647 A.D.	1200 A.D.	Circa 1900 A.D.
Reign of Taizong (Golden Age of Chinese Imperial History)	Pontificate of Innocent III (Height of power of Roman Catholic Church)	Implementation of Max Weber's Bureaucratic Model
Value of learning and knowledge recognized and used to expand the imperial family's influence throughout bureaucracy. Instituted system of state schools and colleges reserved for children of the Imperial family and those of higher Imperial officials. Highest positions in government went to those who passed literacy exams.	Religious beliefs and rituals serving as the framework and justification for authority. Supervised religious, social and political life in the West. Centralized administration and tapped church's financial resources, taxing and putting under Papal protection bishops, monasteries, convents and churches. Codified Canon Law.	Imperative control (management power over workers through legal, ownership and charismatic legitimacy). Hierarchical structure, clear division of labor, rule and process orientation, impersonal administration, rewards based on merit, decisions and rules in writing. Knowledge linked to power; secrecy increased superiority and power.

Table 14-1. *The role of control.*

The rise of Knowledge Management, riding on the tail of the quality movement, brought management attention to the importance of knowledge as a strategic asset. Since knowledge is created by people, this led to a refocusing on people and new ways, such as communities of practice and social media, to ensure the flow of knowledge among people, improving decision-making at all levels of the organization and expanding the opportunity for creativity.

Learning and knowledge creation cannot be ordered to occur; they must be nurtured, providing the internal environment (meditation, safety, rewards and recognition) and external environment (stimulation, trusted others, exposure) such that it will emerge. The combination of creativity and collaboration create a collaborative entanglement that erases cause and effect relationships. The act of bisociating ideas is itself a representation of the creative leap of Phase 3, which can occur nearly every day of our lives.

Collaborative entanglement, a phenomenon occurring during the course of positive and creative interactions, is the dynamic process of mixing, analyzing, discussing, perceiving and interpreting knowledge from different perspectives. It produces emergent patterns. In a social setting, new thoughts and behaviors proposed through personal reflection emerge and build on other's thoughts and behaviors, becoming mixed with yet another set of thoughts and behaviors from the community, and so on. We call this mixing, entwining and creation of unpredictable associations the *process of entanglement*; the knowledge creation process in a group or community that works very much as does the human mind/brain.

Biological systems are remarkably smarter in their support of the body than we are in sustaining our work places and communities. Fortunately, we can learn and *are* learning from ourselves in this sense, and whether we reflect on this learning in the form of a reality or as an analogy is insignificant as long as we keep learning and creating knowledge (Bennet & Bennet, 2008c). Collaborative entanglement as a social phenomenon can be analogous to the natural activities of the brain, with the brain representing the researcher and the stakeholder community representing the knowledge beneficiary. All the living and learning of the host human is recorded in the brain, stored among some hundred billion neurons that are continuously moving between firing and idling, creating and re-creating patterns. Information is coming into the individual through the senses, which, assuming for the sake of our analogy, resonates with internal patterns that have strong synaptic connections. When resonance occurs, the incoming information is consistent with the individual's frame of reference and belief systems. As this incoming information is complexed (the associative patterning process) it may connect with, and to some degree may bring into conscious awareness, deep knowledge. The unconscious continues this process 24/7, with new knowledge stored in the unconscious and perhaps emerging at the conscious level.

<<<<<<<<>>>>>>>

INSIGHT: **Biological systems are remarkably smarter in their support of the body than we are in sustaining our work places and communities. Fortunately, we can learn and *are* learning from ourselves.**

<<<<<<<<>>>>>>>

The collaborative entanglement of humanity is reflective of the butterfly effect of complexity theory, and the real-time learning lesson of World War II, when we learned that an action taken on one side of the world impacts the other side of the world. As we now know, we are all energetically connected, part of a larger web of interactive energy. The idea of collaborative entanglement honors that knowing. Whether a family, an organization, a country, or the world, we are on this journey together, and the actions of the one affect others.

In Knowledge Mobilization theory, collaborative entanglement means to *purposefully and consistently* develop and support approaches and processes that combine the sources of knowledge and the beneficiaries of that knowledge in order to move toward a common direction such as meeting an identified community need

(Bennet & Bennet, 2007b). Thus, *collaborative entanglement engages social responsibility.*

In the business environment of today, organizations are recognizing the value of collaborative entanglement as collaborative advantage. *Collaborative advantage* can be described in terms of open communications, shared understanding, and decision-making that collectively and equitably moves collaborators in an agreed-upon direction. What is causing this shift? Underlying it is development of the mental faculties and the recognized value of innovation.

As we moved into Internet dominance, *concepts and terms began to emerge that tempered the hard edge of competition with elements of cooperation and collaboration.* An early concept was co-opetition. Applying game theory to business—with money representing points won or lost—co-opetition is described by Brandenburger and Nalebuff (1997) as part cooperation and part competition, creating a new dynamic to generate more profits and change the nature of the business environment. The underlying premise is that companies can achieve sustainable competitive advantage by changing the game to their own advantage, cooperating and/or competing where appropriate for maximum gains. Long-term gains come not only from competing successfully in the current environment, but from being an active participant in shaping the future environment and creating expanded opportunities. Clearly this cannot successfully occur without the ethical underpinning of collective values.

Amazon is an excellent example of co-opetition. Amazon works closely with other companies while also competing with them. For example, the Amazon Marketplace enables competitors of any size to use Amazon's online platform and technological capabilities to present millions of new, used, and rare books and other products to millions of customers. Competitor's products are displayed right next to similar products sold by Amazon. This is reflective of the lesson shared in the old movie, "The Miracle on 24th Street", where Macy's Department Store Santa Claus recommended Gimbal's products to parents when not available at Macy's.

Enter the new century. Different combinations of competition and collaboration comprise the interim currency of today as we move toward ever-increasing connection and collaboration in our global world. Figure 14-2 looks at the characteristics of competition and collaboration in terms of inside or outside organizational boundaries. Dependent on the primary focus—competition or collaboration—we can describe combinations of these characteristics and the behaviors they drive as collaborative competition or competitive collaboration, respectively. Note that while innovation can occur in all four sectors, we now recognize that innovation is a highly interactive, multidisciplinary process that increasingly involves cooperation and partnerships between a growing and diverse network of individuals and organizations (Kapeleris, 2012).

COMPETITION	COLLABORATION
INSIDE ORG BOUNDARIES	Individual focus driven by ego and need to achieve and/or win; Limits based on Individual's knowledge	Group/team focus driven by challenge and opportunity; Synergy can come into play; Limits based on collective knowledge and trust

Collaborative Competition   **INNOVATION**   *Competitive Collaboration*

| **OUTSIDE ORG BOUNDARIES** | Organization focus driven by perceived competitive advantage; Limits based on each organization's knowledge resources | Partnership focus* driven by challenge and opportunity; Synergy can come into play; Limits based on agreements, collective knowledge, and trust |

Figure 14-2. *The fields of collaborative competition and competitive collaboration. *Note: Teaming, partnering, and alliances are terms given to more formal relationships between organizations. They imply the intent of one or more organizations to work together to improve the effectiveness and efficiency of a common goal, and to reduce the costs of disagreements. (Bennet et al., 2015c. Used with permission.)*

Collaborative competition is a developed skill set that supports relationship building and leverages collaboration strengths. This approach cultivates a strategic mindset and a personalized, healthy approach to competition (Mayer, 2009). When friendly, it can inspire, spark creativity, and make work fun. For example, Dr. Kenneth Cohn (2008), a specialist in physician-administrator communication issues, shares two stories focused on enhanced healthcare collaboration. In the first story, a cardiologist kept track of starting times in the catheterization lab and used healthy competition to motivate other cardiologists to show up on time. He noted, "Cardiologists are a lot like alpha dogs who, when a bone is tossed their way, are eager to fetch" (Cohn, 2008).

Another example of collaborative competition is the Northwrite 2013 exercise. Sponsored by the New Zealand Society of Authors, Northland Branch, the focus of this competition was on writers working with writers, with the choice of collaboration approaches left up to the participants. The judges were pleased with the variety.

We discovered stories and poetry woven together; we witnessed cases of experimentation with language and form; we admired pieces that explored variety in voice and tone. From humor to suspense to the esoteric, these entries captivated and challenged us as readers, and as competition judges. (Northwrite, 2013)

Northwrite's bottom line is that the process of collaboration changes the outcome, takes the creative endeavor in new directions and creates something altogether original and surprising.

Many of the multi-player card games, board games and virtual games emerging over the past 100 years are based on the concept of collaborative competition. For example, several of the authors play the game of bridge. This is a game of co-evolving, with a diversity of objectives and different resources available every hand. The bidding part is all about acquiring enough information to strategically develop and bid a contract, making a plan for the direction you are going to head while playing the game out in the NOW. The plan cannot be an exact plan, because the available information about other players in the field is limited, including information about the opposing team and information conveyed by your partner—unless over time you have developed conventions within the rules of the game that enable you and your partner to have a higher level of intelligent interaction. Hopefully, the term "opposing team" carries with it the sense of a friendly game, urging you onward to see if your team can bid and successfully execute a contract and engage fully in this learning experience, but without the difficulties and negative feelings associated with hard competition. As we continue to play, we learn to recognize patterns of play. The similarities between many of our strategy games and life situations is amazing, but, then, that may be while games like bridge capture the attention of people year after year, and while virtual games fascinate the younger generations. This mind play is one way to develop our mental faculties, and, given the right games and attitudes, if we choose, we are able to extrapolate what we learn over into our daily lives. At the very least, the mind is actively engaged and learning, which carries healthy ramifications for the mind/body connection.

Competitive collaboration is when companies channel their competitive energy towards a common goal. It is a style of cooperation that demands real commitment and deep engagement from both parties. Competition can be a valuable human behavior. It is a great motivator. Rather than ignore this dynamic and expect purely altruistic motives, organizations are wise to work with it, channeling the competitive energies that abound in human nature toward collaborative behaviors that drive innovation (Carpenter, 2014).

A key principle is to recognize and reward people for contributions that *help advance ideas* as much as rewarding the people who *originate* the ideas. Carpenter (2014) says there are three design principles required for the effective application of this approach: (1) enable the provision and visibility of feedback; (2) recognize those who do it well; and (3) provide tangible incentives for collaborative behavior. For example, in the U.S. Department of Navy a community of practice provided awards to all participants who contributed to finding solutions to problems or issues addressed by the community (Porter, et al., 2002). Since the community interacted on a virtual platform, it was quite easy to observe member contributions. This could also be achieved through the process of peer ratings.

Singapore Airlines (SA) chose a competitive collaboration approach in the process of launching a full-service carrier in a 49:51 joint venture with Tata Group. Tata-SIA airline submitted its application for the grant of an Air Operator's Permit in April 2015. By collaborating with SIA, Tata found an opportunity in new areas of business and SIA recognized the synergy in this relationship. As Tan Pee Teck, SIA Senior VP for Product Services, recognized, "... there is some compatibility obviously in the relationship ... There is competitive collaboration and adversarial competition" (Teck, 2015).

In the interconnected world of today, hard competition can never again gain a long-term foothold. The journey from seeking competitive advantage to seeking collaborative advantage is well underway, a journey that produces win-wins instead of winners and losers, a journey where collaborative leadership at all levels of the organization, community, country and world emerges. See Bennet et al. (2015c) for an in-depth treatment of collaborative leadership.

Three-Way Cooperation and Collaboration

Before the turn of the century, organizations from the U.S. federal sector collaborated with academia and industry associations to figure out the things government knowledge workers wanted and needed to know in the field of Knowledge Management. This approach defined a conceptual framework for KM through developing criteria for accredited government certification programs. The result was a draft set of comprehensive learning objectives for government employees attending certification courses (Bennet & Bennet, 2004).

There were 14 learning objectives identified. The first, rightly so, connected the direct value KM added to the business proposition of the organization. The second included some unusual wording that shows unique insight. Learning Objective 2 was:

Have knowledge of the strategies and processes to transfer explicit and tacit knowledge across time, space, and organizational boundaries, including retrieval of critical archived information enabling ideas to build upon ideas.

This objective focuses on the flow of knowledge, both that which can be explicated (explicit) and that which is within us (tacit), across space and time. This understanding led to strategies such as "Retaining Valuable Knowledge: Proactive

Strategies to Deal with a Shifting Workforce", a Consortium Learning Forum Best-Practice Report sponsored by the American Productivity & Quality Center (APQC, 2002). Again, we see evidence that with knowledge comes responsibility, not just for the way that knowledge is used today, but ensuring future availability of what has been learned and how it may be adapted for future contexts. This is the element of collaborating with future implications in mind. For example, this is occurring when organizations take actions to mitigate pollution or other long-term effects on the environment. Solutions to such challenges may come by blending knowledge from a range of fields, from adapting current knowledge, or from a complete Creative Leap into new knowledge created by the unique circumstances (see Chapter 30/Part IV).

This three-way collaboration—horizontal, vertical and over time—has become a critical element of forward-thinking business models. For example, consider the KNOWledge SUCCESSion framework (Shelley, 2016), supporting sustained performance and capability growth through strategic knowledge projects. This framework is designed to stimulate conversations around strategies that engage both horizontal and vertical cooperation and collaboration *and* ensuring rich relationships *among the current project team and future project members*, that is, cooperation and collaboration over time. This three-way approach to knowledge sharing ensures the consistency and continuity of the project, and plows the way for the insertion of prior cycle learning and new ideas to sustain future project effectiveness. This is done by enabling the experience of success in iterative fragments, with these short cycles providing more flexibility for future decision-makers while decisions and actions remain aligned with the longer vision.

The biggest challenge facing many organizations is creating and maintaining a knowledge base that keeps the organization at its optimal performance. The way we interact with each other significantly impacts our success. To KNOW SUCCESS in a sustainable manner, individuals, teams and organizations need to actively manage their KNOWledge SUCCESSion (KS). Focusing on projects as vehicles of change and knowledge transfer, KS combines many interdependent aspects of knowledge to create synergies and align actions with overall organizational strategy. KS is about social interactions based in conversations, stories and shared insights that lead to inclusive interactions. These are connected through constant attention to asking questioning why actions are being taken and what value they create (both tangible and intangible) that is directly aligned with the goals of the person, team or organization. This approach leads to reflective constructive challenges that start with why and end with a carefully considered portfolio of projects that deliver immediate project outputs and create the foundations for future success. Thus, KS becomes the driver of innovation and capability development, and ultimately sustainable performance. Ongoing KNOWledge SUCCESSion builds our capability and confidence to successfully make the Creative Leap into a completely new future.

Co-Evolving in a CUCA World

In Chapter 13 we characterized the environment in which we live as CUCA, that is, accelerating change, rising uncertainty, increasing complexity, and the anxiety that accompanies change, uncertainty and complexity. Three of the drivers affecting this environment that represent forces for change are connectivity; data, information and knowledge; and speed. These forces can be viewed as either threats or opportunities. Let's explore the concept of co-evolving through the lens of these forces.

Enabled by the Internet, *connectivity* as a major force in our current environment refers to the connections among people, places and technologies, enabling totally new ways of moving and transferring data, information and knowledge among individuals, organizations and governments. Connectivity promotes collaborative entanglement. Anyone in the world can talk in real time at any time to almost anyone else in the world. Virtual conferences, video cameras and iPhones have become commonplace and ubiquitous. An ever-increasing number of conversations accelerates the flow of ideas and understanding. The building of relationships has moved from a focus on personal knowing to idea resonance (see Chapter 10/Part II).

A second major force in this environment is *data, information and knowledge*, with connectivity enabling these expanding resources. Organizations have new technologies and human systems that search and seek the data, information and knowledge needed to meet their objectives. These systems can validate the information, categorize it, identify the context and develop the best interpretation, thereby laying the groundwork for knowledge creation and application. In an environment where information is a bombardment, changing quickly, and is noisy and possibly random or with little meaning, the organization is forced to develop new systemic and human capabilities that can respond to this terrain.

Speed is a third major force; speed in the movement of goods and services, in the creation of new ideas through virtual collaboration, in the spread of information through increased bandwidth, in smart search engines and learning software, and in the sharing and diffusion of knowledge. Speed shortens time and creates a demand for faster decision-making. It increases uncertainty by limiting the time available to comprehend what is going on, exacerbating the problems of validation and assurance of information and knowledge. The continuing pace of acceleration demands that the human mind keep up.

An organic model of the organization co-evolving in this environment is the Intelligent Complex Adaptive System (ICAS) model (Bennet and Bennet, 2004). The ICAS is a knowledge organization, continuously reexamining itself and its external environment and, after doing so, adapting and redirecting its thrust. The ICAS represents an organization with an internal environment that combines the traits of teams, organizational intelligence, complexity and adaptability with external partners and connections. Taken together, these characteristics lead to an open, knowledge-creating, knowledge-sharing and knowledge-applying organization, which examples the porosity of a living organization ecologically connected to the outside environment.

As organizations change and take on new forms (co-evolve), they often do so through the creation and development of emergent characteristics, with the sources of these properties both structural and relational. Acting like a biological system, the ICAS has eight emergent characteristics that help provide the internal capability to deal with a CUCA environment. These are: organizational intelligence, shared purpose, selectivity, optimum complexity, permeable boundaries, knowledge centricity, flow and multidimensionality.

Intelligence is the capacity for reasoning and understanding or an aptitude for grasping truths (Webster's, 1996). When applied to organizations, Wiig (1993) broadens this view of intelligence and considers it the ability of a person to think, reason, understand, and act. In organizations this includes the capabilities to innovate, acquire knowledge and apply that knowledge to relevant situations. *Unity and shared purpose* represent the ability of the ICAS organization to integrate and mobilize resources to (1) provide a continuous line of focus and attention and (2) pull together the relevant parts of the organization when and where they are needed. *Optimum complexity* means having the right level of internal complexity to deal with the external environment while maintaining overall order and unity of purpose. *Selectivity* is the filtering of incoming information from the outside world.

Knowledge centricity is the aggregation of relevant information derived from the knowledge of the organization's components that enables self-synchronization and increases collaborative opportunities while promoting strategic alignment. Knowledge, the actual and potential ability to take effective action, is at the heart of the ICAS. *Flow* enables knowledge centricity and facilitates the connections and continuity that maintain unity and give coherence to organizational intelligence. *Permeable boundaries* allow a high degree of permeability in terms of information, people, and other energies needed to respond to opportunities as well as increasing and decreasing demands. *Multidimensionality* represents organizational flexibility, giving the organization the ability to continuously learn and apply new knowledge, to identify and deal with risk, and to think in terms of systems, that is, to perceive and analyze situations in terms of a wide scope of possibilities and long timeframes, all the while maintaining its organizational identity and unity. In other words, the organization must develop instincts and automatic competencies that are natural and become second nature at all times, what we call multidimensionality. Development of integrative competencies is an aspect of multidimensionality, calling for knowledge workers to expand their competency beyond their own discipline so they develop a broader perspective and understand the impact of their actions on other parts of the organization. Integrative competencies include system and complexity thinking, Relationship Network Management (see Chapter 10/Part II), and information literacy.

As part of the living organization, the information systems that support the ICAS are living systems (de Geus, 1997). What might these look like? To explore that concept, Figure 14-3 is a graphic representation to start "Conversations that Matter" (see Chapter 11/Part II).

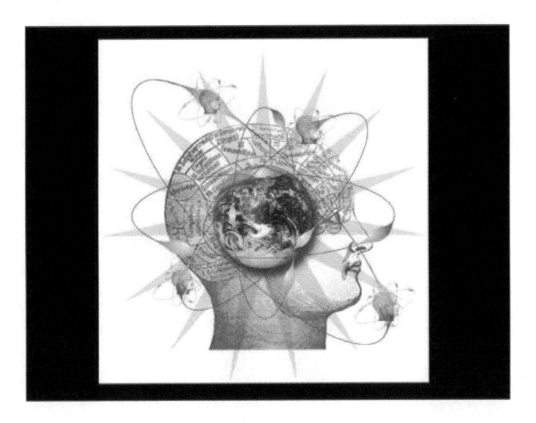

Figure 14-3. *What do living information systems look like?*
(Conversations that Matter)

Here are the descriptive results of several of those conversations.

The **Living Network** is an iterative and interactive communication and resource network comprised of changing information, people and processes. Flexible and adaptable to the changing needs of its members and the environment, it can change size, form and means of communication. Designed as an open and dynamic system, both definitive and ever-evolving, and user-driven, the living network brings knowledge sources and users together in an information exchange that can grow to a collaborative dialogue in virtual spaces, supporting global teams and communities. It is embedded with discovery tools and widgets, translation tools, and visualizations, and representation techniques for presenting multiple points of view and supporting individual's learning preferences. An example is *Facebook*.

The **Living Repository** is a collection and connection of databases filled with high quality information, the context of that information, and hyperlinks and connections to people who have expertise and experience in support of that information. It has personal interfaces, automated and automatically generated summaries at varying levels, messages and connections, and is ever evolving with both updates and deletions, becoming an integrated pool of knowledge from a variety of disciplines and people. An example is *Wikipedia*.

The **Living Document** is accessible, contextual, trustworthy, legitimate, accurate, current, and identifying—and providing access to—sources and the context of sources. A living document is interactive, flexible and adaptable, providing for the efficient inclusion of and connection to additional expertise. *It evolves; and is visibly related to people such that frames of reference can be assessed and questions vetted.* An example is the U.S. Constitution and the Constitutional Amendments.

These are not new models. For example, the ICAS concept was introduced at the turn of the century. While a dozen or so years ago businesses were befuddled by complexity, today complexity language has moved into everyday conversation. What is made quite clear by these models is that we as a global humanity have moved into the co-evolving phase of the Intelligent Social Change Journey.

Sustainability

Living in CUCA times, what are we trying to sustain? Physical life, responsibility, spiritual needs, value sets? In an organizational setting sustainability may mean social and economic survival. The same two things carry over to an individual. For example, survival would be maintaining the personal goals and perspectives of the individual (physical, mental, social, spiritual, etc.) However, for many people that is not be enough. We know that things can be better, and we want to improve ourselves, and help others improve themselves, perhaps making the world a better place for future generations.

In this context, recognize that "sustain" is not the same as "maintain". To maintain is to preserve something, retaining it or *supporting its existence*. To sustain, whether physical or mental, is to *strengthen and support*, to supply with *sustenance*. While these certainly sound similar, they are not. We maintain simple and complicated systems; we sustain complex adaptive systems, that is, living systems. For example, when you maintain a car, you keep it in working condition. To sustain a person or an organization in a CUCA environment requires growth. A good example is a sustainable forest. Sustaining a forest involves clearing out underbrush which poses a fire hazard, thinning trees when they are overcrowding and failing from lack of sunlight, seeding as needed, ensuring the ecosystem is balanced in terms of forest creatures and vegetation, etc. You get the idea. Sustain isn't keeping things the same, it's co-evolving with the environment.

In 2005 Mountain Quest Institute surveyed 200 senior executives in the U.S. Federal sector regarding the ability of their organizations to effectively function under the conditions of CUCA. The eight sustainability factors that emerged with a short description are as follows:

*Continuous learning = having a mindset and a self-directed program to continuously learn, create and apply knowledge.

*Adaptability = Can change habits, beliefs, and values as necessary to sustain performance in a changing environment.

*Flexibility = Keeping an open mind and attitude, willing to change positions and direction, adopt new perspectives and try new things.

*Quick response = Capable of reacting/responding quickly when needed.

*Resiliency = The ability to recover from setbacks and to resume high performance.

*Robustness = The ability to respond to a broad range of tasks or problems.

*Alignment = The capacity to maintain internal and personal consistency and cohesion while simultaneously staying flexible and adaptable to a changing environment.

*Stakeholder satisfaction = providing value that satisfies stakeholders.

We consider these eight factors as sustainability capacities and competencies which can be built into an organization. Capacity alludes to potential, the capability or power to do something or understand something; a competency is the ability to do something *well*. Thus, capacity can be planned into the organizational structure and processes, and competencies are developed through education, training and experience.

In the list above, stakeholder satisfaction is based on sustaining alignment while effectively co-evolving with a CUCA environment. Continuous learning—focused both on the domain of knowledge related to organizational direction AND on integrative competencies—provides the knowledge reservoir that supports adaptability, flexibility, quick response and resiliency. In the 1980's and into the 1990's, many organizations failed due to a foremost focus on efficiency. While some of these companies were able to simultaneously sustain effectiveness of their current products, there was no room for adaptability, flexibility and resiliency. In the name of efficiency, training and unused resources had been eliminated. As markets became global and customer demands shifted, these organizations were unable to keep up. They had reduced their capacity, which is necessary for adaptability, flexibility and resiliency in a changing, uncertain and complex environment!

The understanding of complexity is benefiting many organizations of today. For example, in today's CUCA world, many front-line organizations understand that continuous learning is critical to survival, as well as offering the potential for expansion into new markets. Recognizing learning as both a human and organizational capacity, this mindset incentivizes building capacity through encouraging continuous learning and intelligent choice of the focus of that learning. This is planned capacity to guide future decisions.

We contend that these factors also apply to individuals. Consider adaptability, which is required for humans in personal crises as well as when crises emerge in the environment in which they live. For example, if you have a crisis that is overwhelming, professed atheists may no longer be atheists. Ultimately, all humans have issues that challenge their beliefs and knowledge. These are growth opportunities where the self can choose whether to change or not, whether to expand or, preferring the safety of the known, contract.

This tool is built on our understanding from neuroscience findings that thought changes the structure of the brain, and the structure of the brain affects our thought. Thus, embedding positive thoughts regarding your personal capacity to handle future disruptions can have a mental, emotional and physical impact on your future behaviors. In the words of English philosopher James Allen (2016), "You are today where your thoughts have brought you; you will be tomorrow where your thoughts take you."

****

TOOL 14-1: Building Mental Sustainability

This tool engages the power of affirmations through semantic realignment, which is using verbs which indicate action followed by positive qualifiers (Bullard and Bennet, 2013). The exercise starts with personal mental programming.

STEP (1): During a few minutes of quiet time, start a list of positive traits and capabilities. Don't be shy; this is for your use only.

STEP (2): Take a deep breath in, hold it to the slow count of three, and then release slowly through your mouth, letting go of any negative thoughts or feelings, letting them float away on the out-breath. Now, imagine yourself as the hero of your life story—which you are, picturing yourself in your mind as you choose to look, and wearing whatever costume you choose to imagine. Have fun with this!

STEP (3): Remember, heroes have courage and noble qualities (see the discussion on Nobility in Chapter 22/Part IV). As this hero, recall situations in your life where the hero has come to the rescue of others. Pause in between recalling events to jot down a one-liner regarding the event in your notes. Then, close your eyes again, bring the avatar of you, the hero, to mind, and recall another event where the hero saved the day. NOTE: Small things count. When you have captured all that you can remember, review your notes and put them in a safe place where you can pull them out as needed.

STEP (4): The next day, begin a self-assessment of your thought and words in terms of negative and positive language. This will require heightened awareness of self, and may take a few hours to get used to! Whenever anything comes to mind or is spoken, assess the thoughts or language for negativity, and consciously rephrase that thought or language, eliminating all negative messages you are in the habit of using. Here are some ideas to get you started: (a) Eliminate negative expressions such as "I can't" or "I am not good at", which set intention (Remember, if you think you can or you think you can't, you're right!); (b) Eliminate command phrases like "I have to" or "I should" or "I've got to", which represent force rather than choice (Remember, learning increases through volition). Continue this process for as many days as it takes to eliminate negative language. When you can go through two days without any negative language, you are ready for the next step.

STEP (5): Pull out your list of positive traits and capabilities. Review the list, adding your new-found ability to engage the world from a positive frame of reference, and any other positive traits or capabilities that are not yet on the list. Bringing your hero avatar to mind, review the notes regarding his/her exploits, smiling or laughing at the antics these exploits represent. Fold the list and put it in your pocket, remembering to keep it in your pocket throughout the next 21 days.

STEP (6): Now you are ready to begin your affirmations. Once in the morning when you start your day, and once in the evening before going to bed, stand in front of a mirror. Looking in the mirror, picture yourself in the guise of your avatar. (It is okay to smile!) On Day 1, firmly repeat the first affirmation below, out loud. When you are done, nod a thank-you in the mirror and go about your day, remembering to carry your folded list of positive traits and capabilities and hero exploits in your pocket. Repeat this process for three days.

STEP (7): On Day 4 move through the same process focusing on the second affirmation below, and at the end repeating the first affirmation (one time is fine). Repeat for 3 days.

STEP (8): On Day 7 start with the third affirmation (three times), then say the first and second affirmations each one time. Repeat for 3 days.

STEP (9): On Day 10 repeat the process starting with the fourth affirmation. Repeat for 3 days.

STEP (10): On Day 13 repeat the process starting with the fifth affirmation. Repeat for 3 days.

STEP (11): On Day 16 repeat all five affirmations (each three time). Repeat for 6 days.

STEP (12): On Day 21 put away the list you have carried for 21 days (perhaps placing it at the bottom of the sock drawer where it can be pulled out any time it is needed as a reminder of who you are). Write out (by hand) the six affirmations below, fold them up, and carry them in your pocket for a minimum of 21 days. Know that this is WHO YOU ARE, and that you have the capacity to address any challenges and take advantage of any opportunities that come into your awareness. You are now in a position of choice.

THE SUSTAINABILITY AFFIRMATIONS:

(1) I know myself. I change my habits, beliefs and values as necessary to reflect my growth and sustain performance. I am adaptable.

(2) I adopt new perspectives and try new things. I have an open mind, positive attitude, and am willing to change position and direction when warranted. I am flexible.

(3) I react and respond quickly when needed. I am speedy and effective.

(4) I bounce back and move forward through any setbacks. I am healthy.

(5) I share my knowledge and wisdom with my trusted network, and I ask for help when it is needed. I am a high performer.

NOTE: It only takes 21 days to change a habit or embed a new habit. Use this tool, or any appropriate variation of it, as often as needed to program yourself the *direction of your choice.*

****

One word of caution. Long-term sustainability often requires trade-offs. Sometimes instant decisions have to be made in response to "wicked" problems that may conflict with long-term sustainability. For example, consider the cave man, who had to have more fat on the body than necessarily healthy in order to survive when food was not available. In today's environment, there may be a balance necessary between short-term desires and long-term survivability. For example, sustainability of the physical body would prohibit smoking, therefore calling for a potential sacrifice in behavior for some people.

ICAS and Sustainability

The eight characteristics of the ICAS organization and the eight sustainability characteristics, which are also health parameters in a CUCA environment, are all emergent qualities, and there is a direct relationship among them. See Figure 14-4. Again, note that continuous learning is significant and necessary for multiple characteristics of the ICAS to emerge.

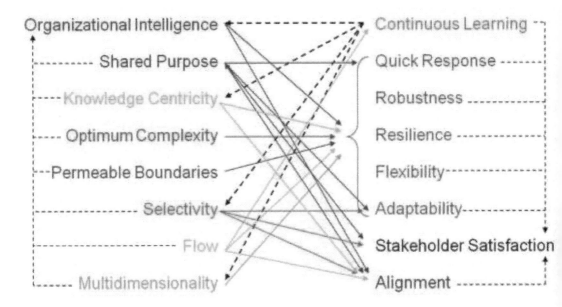

Figure 14-4. *Relationship of ICAS characteristics and Sustainability and Health parameters.*

Stakeholder satisfaction is emergent coming forth from the organizational capabilities. It is an external measure of an internal capability. Thus, the eight emergent characteristics of ICAS all participate in creating the ICAS organizational capability to satisfy stakeholders.

Sustainable Knowledge

While the issues and situations addressed in CUCA times are generally complex, the people and organizations involved in these issues and situations are complex adaptive, as is the self. Since the amount of knowledge needed to understand an issue or situation would correlate with the difficulty of understanding, and predicting the future effects of, any action on the situation, how do you gain that knowledge? How do you learn? In changing times, it is necessary to learn quickly and accurately, and be willing to take risks. If we cannot learn at least as fast as the environment changes, we are doomed to play catch-up and are tied to outmoded ideas and perhaps inadequate actions. But there are no easy answers. No one learning process is optimum for different individuals, and the learning process is highly dependent upon the nature of the knowledge needed, which is dependent upon the nature of the environment.

Is there specific knowledge that will help us take effective action in CUCA times? The knowledge needed will likely be quite different than the knowledge that worked for you in what you perceived as "normal times". Under relatively stable conditions, knowledge is developed through learning by studying, social interaction, and experience, all excellent ways to learn. Once learned, information can be reused or reapplied often, perhaps with some adjustment to account for different situations. As experience is gained, and larger patterns are identified, this information can often be pulled from memory and applied (knowledge) to take effective action based on those patterns.

However, during CUCA times it is likely to be difficult or impossible to use memory and experience as a guide because of the uncertainty of what will happen next. Another difficulty is that things may change so quickly that there is little time to figure out what to do. Because of the speed of change, uncertainty and complexity, past knowledge will probably be inadequate, and may even be dangerous.

A foundational approach to developing the capacity to react quickly and effectively, and respond to surprises, shocks and opportunities, is to develop the kind of knowledge that provides sustainability in its ideal form. Recalling our earlier discussion of sustainability, an individual would consider each factor from their own personal perspective and, if needed, develop their own information and knowledge base capable of responding to their situation. This knowledge base—or access to the information that supports it—would then be quickly available, that is, previously acquired, quickly validated and easily brought to mind. For example, if a focus area indicated a wide range of potential issues or problems, the individual would then develop a knowledge-based response system that was robust and capable of responding to this particular range of problems. That knowledge base would include information systems as well as trusted networks with appropriate knowledge resources. While this approach requires a level of forecasting that may sound forbidding, to some extent it is something every single individual does every single day. Most, however, have just not taken the time to develop this capability at the conscious level.

<<<<<<◇>>>>>>

INSIGHT: **To some extent, and for the most part unconsciously, every single day we are expanding our personal knowledge base focused on long-term sustainability.**

<<<<<<◇>>>>>>

Knowledge Capacities, introduced in Chapter 21, are sets of ideas and ways of acting that are more general in nature than competencies, more core to a way of thinking and being, that specifically support building capacity for sustainability. The intent is to embrace the power of the mind/brain/body (conscious and unconscious) to sustain us through CUCA times.

A New Generation of Co-Creators

In 1975, Csikszentmihalyi, the author of *Flow*, published a book entitled *Beyond Boredom and Anxiety*. This book focused on, in a culture ruled by *the pursuit of money prestige and pleasure*, how to make our lives more meaningful. As Csikszentmihalyi (1975, front cover) described, "We find ourselves on a never-ending search for ways to counteract the boredom, anxiety, and alienation that our work-oriented society has become." He, of course, is introducing the flow experience, that *exhilarating feeling of creative accomplishment and heightened functioning* (see Chapter 18).

Fast-forward four generations, with new minds and new hearts engaging the world quite differently. The good news is they *do* engage. "They organize themselves, publish themselves, inform themselves and share with their friends—without waiting for an authority to instruct them" (Tapscott, 2010), albeit an underlying pattern of this need for immediacy is an impatience with business models and processes of the preceding generation (Smith, 2013). Hadar (2009) describes this generation as optimistic and determined, and notes that they like public activism and Elmore (2010) points out that they are both high-performance and *high maintenance*, more likely to "rock the boat" than any prior generation (Johns, 2003).

Let's understand that this is a generation that is connected; from their viewpoint they always have been and always will be. Information is available at the tap of a finger. Their world has always been complex, and so to them it is simple; they hop from one thought to another, never needing to focus too heavily, because all they need is instantly available. They are superior integrators of information, use their feelings to select what is next on their action agenda, and thrive on interaction.

The implications of continuous social interactions (conversations, dialogues and multilogues) across an expanded global network (capacity) are staggering. When needed, these young decision-makers have the ability to develop context and generate ideas around a specific issue at hand (capability). Further, swimming around and diving up and down in the global shallows—which are filled with a diversity of views, perspectives, concepts and cultures—spurs uninhibited creativity and more significant innovation than surface swimming. Decision-makers in the connected, global world can be *mentally stimulated by interactions involving diverse views, perspectives, concepts and cultures* and are not bounded by local ideas.

Creativity and innovation thrive on different ideas and ways of looking at things, and flourish from connecting different streams of thought. From cross-domain stimulation of an open mind, new and often unsought patterns will emerge. A key phrase here is "open mind," that is, a mind not "limited" (whether purposefully or otherwise) to a specific direction, a bounded domain of knowledge, or immutable mental models. Open mind describes a decision-maker co-evolving with a CUCA environment and searching out relationships between the mission/vision/purpose/values of their organizational alliance and the potential offered within their environmental opportunity space (Bennet and Bennet, 2004). These are decision-makers seeking a window of opportunity in terms of space and time in a turbulent environment.

<<<<<<<◇>>>>>>

INSIGHT: **Creativity and innovation thrive on different ideas and ways of looking at things, and flourish from connecting different streams of thought.**

<<<<<<<◇>>>>>>

Because this new social way of being, thinking and acting taps into a huge diversity of experience, there is also an increased *appreciation of difference*, and with it comes a tolerance of diversity. "They are a true global generation; smarter and more tolerant to diversity than their predecessors" (Panetta, 2013). Immersion coupled with conversation and dialogue is quite the opposite of the Cold War isolation approach. *If they choose to do so*, the Net Generation may truly have the potential to create a global humanity.

Simultaneously, they can become quickly irritated when something they desire is not immediately forthcoming, and incredibly bored when unplugged, that is, when immediate access to the larger world is not available through their iPhones and tablets. They are a generation of immediate gratification, because this is the *fast* world we live in. We had an example of this in the Summer of 2016, when Ray-Ban, a global leader in the premium eyewear market, decided that Act Six of their #It Takes Courage campaign was "the courage to ditch the screen and truly connect in the real world" (Ray-Ban, 2016). Ray-Ban asked seven people from around the world who are online influencers and digital content creators, with millions of followers on various social media, to spend 48 unplugged hours in the vicinity of Greenbank, West Virginia, a cell phone tower-free location.

The influencers who participated in this event were: Gabbie Fadel, a YouTuber-Twitterer from Brazil; Giaro Giarratana, an Instagramer from Holland; Zhang Wei (Will), a Fashionista/Blogger from China; Jack Adams (Mumdance), an Electronic Musician from the UK; Matteo, a Digital Artist from Italy; Faith Silva, an Instagramer from the US; and Paul Ward, a Photographer from South Africa. They stayed at the Mountain Quest Inn and Retreat Center in Frost, West Virginia. During their "unplugged" experience, they visited the small newspaper office, talked to locals, brushed and played with the horses, interviewed an electromagnetic sensitive individual in her home, gathered around a campfire, ate together and shared stories.

The authors had the opportunity to do questionnaires before and after the influencers' experience, as well as observe them *during* the experience. Initial responses were as expected, some anxiety, some hesitation, discomfort at not being able to check email, but generally open to the new experience and very much living in the NOW. Several of the influencers admitted that they found joy with being globally connected, in chatting with people 24/7, of getting a message out to your audience instantaneously, with the immediate response from people. They truly enjoy influencing, and being an inspiration to, others.

Regarding their expectation for the event, it was one of change. One influencer exclaimed: "What am I gonna do? How will I spend my day without my Netflix account and my phone?" Another said, "I am expecting or hoping to gain some perspective, in what way I'm not entirely sure. But being this far out of your comfort zone can only be a positive thing." Post event responses showed shifts. On a scale of 1-10, with 1 being minimal and 10 being wonderful, they rated the experience at 9, 10, 11 and 10,000. They were all tired, but, as one shared, feeling stable and happy. *They all agreed that perhaps it was a good idea to get offline on a more regular basis, to interact face-to-face with people.* Individual responses about the experience showed inner reflection. For example, an insightful observation by one influencer was, **"There's no 'social' in social media."** And as far as what was learned, "I learned that with the right attitude new and strange experiences can yield interesting reflections on self and society." What is fascinating about this comment is that the "new and strange" experience refers to living a life that was considered "normal" some 20 years ago!

As can be seen, once the cycle was broken—a breather from virtual global connectivity which indeed took courage—these influences recognized the importance of having direct human "contactivity". Note that this was a situation involving changing their day-to-day activity, engaging what they described as a "new and strange" experience, a new environment in which to co-evolve. This is consistent with neuroscience findings in terms of the need for social engagement. Further, four of the influencers specifically spoke of "trusting" Ray-Ban in this experience. Thus, Ray-Ban was in the role of the trusted significant other necessary to move comfortably through change.

The Discovery of Community

By now, we are beginning to understand that co-evolving is all about living and working with others, whether that is a family, an organization, a local community or a world-wide community. Communities denote commonalities of some nature, whether those commonalities are physical (examples: sports enthusiasts, or living in the same locality), mental (common domain of knowledge such as science, or sharing common goals and objectives), or emotional (common attitudes, or common interests). Braden (2014) says that localized living—community—is the key to living in these times of extremes. He refers to localized in terms of food, services and energy, noting that (1) one size does not fit all, and (2) each geographical area has special needs and things that are both available and abundant.

This concept does *not* denote a movement away from globalization. Quite the contrary! From systems theory we have learned that a combination of small systems working together has more flexibility (and stability) than one large system, that is, as a hierarchy. The origin of hierarchies lies in the ability to withstand or survive shock. For example, if a given part of an organization is shocked, if it is hierarchical, the shock only damages the local level of the hierarchy and allows the organization to rebuild itself because of that hierarchy. (See the discussion of hierarchy in Chapter 10/Part II.)

<<<<<<<◇>>>>>>

INSIGHT: **Community provides a degree of stability while simultaneously enabling greater adaptability, flexibility and resilience**.

<<<<<<<◇>>>>>>

There appears to be a paradox, of course, that community provides a degree of stability while simultaneously enabling greater adaptability, flexibility and resilience. The answer underlying this paradox is that we reference a community based on cooperation and collaboration rather than control, which was the underlying foundation of bureaucracy. Similar to the earlier example of the intelligent complex adaptive system, this is a community that is co-evolving with its environment, utilizing its hierarchical relationship as a learning and operational platform, with the global world as a grounding structure, simultaneously independent and interdependent. (See Chapter 10/Part II on Grounding Change.) This is the same growth relationship attributed to individuation and Oneness (Chapter 4/Part I). From the perspective of energy Art, this same relationship is demonstrated by the diversity of orbs (represented as electromagnetic energy points of consciousness) that come together in the instant to form a tapestry of *Myst* representing a larger concept, then falling back to their individuated state. See Appendix C.

In our interconnected world community need not denote living in a single location or specific locality. A community support system can be sustained through virtual interactions as well. Take, for example, the Women of Wisdom group who held their annual retreat at Mountain Quest for several years. This eclectic group spent four days together sharing their individual learning and skill sets such as felt making and Reiki energy healing amidst planned moments punctuated with conversation, positive affirmations, story-telling, meditations, dancing, and drumming. A culminating talent show highlighted songs, poems and skits connecting with the participants and the perturbations of the day. How can a single event sustain community throughout the year? It can't. This event lays the groundwork for smaller sessions with rotating hosts and homes; for a continuous dialogue through a private web service, with counseling and other services openly offered according to the gifts and learning throughout the group; and for an overwhelming outpouring of love and active support as individuals move through life-changing events in their lives. *This is the definition of community*.

Questions for Reflection:

How do you achieve and advance collaborative advantage?

How do you sustain your knowledge base?

What differences do you see between the way you interact and the way the younger generation of decision-makers interact? Is there something you can learn from them?

Reflecting on the communities of which you are a part, how interdependent are your relationships?

Chapter 15
Managing Change
in a Knowledge Organization

An Example of a Phase 2 Change Approach

SUBTOPICS: THE ORGANIZATION AS A COMPLEX ADAPTIVE SYSTEM ... THE INTERNAL KNOWLEDGE ENVIRONMENT ... THE CHANGE APPROACH ... THE ADIIEA MODEL ... THE CHANGE PROCESS ... THE ELEMENTS OF CHANGE ... EMERGENT CHARACTERISTICS ... THE STRATEGIC INITIATIVE PULSE ... FINAL THOUGHTS.

FIGURES: **15-1**. CONTINUUM FROM BUREAUCRACY TO THE KNOWLEDGE ORGANIZATION ... **15-2**. ADIIEA LEARNING-BUSINESS MODEL ... **15-3**. FORCES AT PLAY AFFECTING RECEPTIVITY TO CHANGE ... **15-4**. THE STRATEGIC INITIATIVE PULSE (1) ... **15-5**. THE STRATEGIC INITIATIVE PULSE (2).

With the recognition of knowledge as an organizational asset came the awareness that knowledge could not be "managed" but rather had to be nurtured (Bennet & Bennet, 2004), and that an individual could not be ordered to learn but could learn best if they *wanted* to learn. In other words, the creation of new ideas and the expansion of knowledge (the capacity to take effective action, moving toward intelligent activity) cannot be controlled. People can control themselves in a way that is intelligent, conscious and creative in its own right, but control of others and our environment is an illusion. Being pressured or forced to learn minimizes the learning rate because it creates a level of stress and fear that may significantly detract and reduce learning capacity (Jensen, 1998). Further, an individual who tries to control others is vulnerable to their behavior. What *can* be done is to educate and nurture people, and provide a learning environment that facilitates knowledge sharing.

INSIGHT: **An individual who tries to control others is vulnerable to their behavior.**

The Organization as a Complex Adaptive System

Comprised of people who are complex adaptive systems (see Chapter 6), the organization itself can be considered a complex adaptive system. As a brief review, the complexity of a system is measured by its variety, the number of possible states that the system can have (Bennet & Bennet, 2004). A state is a specific configuration of the system. People and organizations are both complex adaptive systems containing many components that interact with each other. They are both partially ordered systems that unfold, evolve through time, and are mostly self-organizing, learning, and adaptive. To survive, they are always creating new ideas, scanning the environment, anticipating the future, trying new approaches, observing the results, and changing the way they operate. To continuously adapt they must operate in perpetual disequilibrium, which results in some unpredictable behavior. Having nonlinear relationships, complex adaptive systems create global properties that are called emergent because they emerge from the multitude of elements and their relationships (Bennet & Bennet, 2008b).

An organization has a large number of options and choices of actions it can take to adjust itself internally or when responding to, or influencing, its environment. The people in organizations are semi-autonomous and have varying levels of self-organization. They operate and direct their own behavior based on rules and (hopefully) a common vision of the organization's direction, working in small groups to take advantage of the local knowledge and experience of coworkers. It is the aggregate behavior (actions) of all these workers that can be observed as organizational performance. The interactions that create this performance are numerous, complex, and often nonlinear, making it impossible to derive global behavior from local interactions. The variety and diversity of individuals also contributes to the creation and characteristics of the aggregate behavior.

Given enough resources, if one person leaves an organization, the others immediately reorganize to fill the vacuum and the firm internally adapts to its new structure, often with some stress (and presumably some learning). As people move in and out of the organization, its global behavior may shift and change, adapting to its new internal structure as well as its external environment. This continuous flexing of complex adaptive systems keeps them alive and gives them the capacity to quickly change pace and redirect focus.

In the midst of all this change—and despite the need for the disequilibrium to adapt—most individuals and organizations have a tendency to seek stability. For example, emergent characteristics of an organization represent stable patterns that are qualitative and exert a strong influence back on the individuals and their relationships (Bennet & Bennet, 2004). Examples are culture, team spirit, attitudes toward customers, trust, consciousness, laughter, and emotions.

There are various mechanisms for influencing organizations as complex adaptive systems. These include structural adaptation (change the structure of the organization to change the problem); boundary management (managing the boundary conditions to shift the energy affecting the system); absorption (bringing the complex situation into a larger complex system, thereby resolving the original problem by dissolving the problem system); optimum complexity (ensuring you have as many options to deal with a problem than there are in the problem); simplification (reducing uncertainty to allow logical explanations for decisions); sense and respond (taking a testing approach by observing, then perturbing, and studying the response); amplification (shotgun effect; taking a variety of actions to determine which ones are successful); and seeding (the process of nurturing emergence). See Bennet and Bennet (2013) for an in-depth treatment of decision-making in a CUCA environment.

The idea of enabling state changes by identifying the critical nodes in a system and leveraging them is pragmatic and powerful. For example, Perturbation Theory, used to solve mathematical problems otherwise unsolvable, is based on the concept of simplification. A set of approximation schemes are mathematically developed starting with the exact solution of a simpler, related problem. In a middle step the *perturbation* occurs when the problem is broken into solvable parts. Thus, through simplification an approximate solution is discovered.

A typical organizational intervention that takes the sense-and-respond approach is to require a specified series of actions done in a specific fashion to ensure a desired outcome. These directives may or may not be cohesive with the culture, or the way work is done. If the new procedures are consistent, they may well be fully adopted. Even when the new procedures are not consistent with the culture, when oversight is strong, employees may follow the steps of the process to the letter, at least for a while. When management focus changes, or a management personnel change occurs, employees will slip back to earlier behaviors consistent with the culture. This phenomenon has been well-documented in the literature on management and culture (Forrester, 1994; Munck et al., 2002, Schein, 2004).

Most organizations today exist in a knowledge environment. As the globe shrinks and information traffic covers mother earth, data, information and knowledge significantly impact every individual and every organization. These forces, residing external to the millions of firms, government agencies and not-for-profits, play a significant role in both forcing internal changes to ensure survival and, at the same time, challenging change management as it works to effectuate those changes. This chapter looks at the difficulties in managing change in this new landscape, change that is needed to make organizations capable of operating collaboratively with a high quality output over the long haul.

We shall first look at those generic characteristics needed to survive in a knowledge-intensive world, that is, what an ideal knowledge organization would look like. We then consider the challenge of moving a bureaucracy or its variant to the ideal knowledge organization. In other words, we look at change management, offering some new and some not-so-new ideas that a change agent should consider. Several new models are presented to provide the reader different perspectives on the change problem. While each view taken by itself is useful, it is rarely enough. Change management is a systems problem and orchestrating change is a complex process requiring multidimensional understanding of both the system being changed and the change process itself.

The Internal Knowledge Environment

A good knowledge organization is one built on quality knowledge systems, systems that provide the right information to the right people at the right time, taking into account the way information is received, and perceived, to ensure that information flows freely and quickly. In other words, an internal environment where the technology is conducive to human use and where people want to share their own expertise and reap the benefit of others' experience. Individuals who are part of this environment will themselves become open systems by being both producers and learners of knowledge. They will have the ability to focus their attention on what makes the greatest difference and on what helps achieve the greatest good, defined in terms of the organization's mission and vision as well as the moral responsibility that comes with knowledge.

The above environment comes from what we have learned about ecologies that create and nurture innovation and the sharing of ideas. Environments conducive to innovation flourish best under decentralized organizational structures that, through their supporting infrastructure and inherent interpersonal relationships, create a natural expectation and acceptance of the responsibility all members have for initiating new activity. These organizations have simple processes for exploiting new ideas (including champions and resources, and encouraging and rewarding experimentation via loose deadlines; with minimal surveillance, evaluation, and administrative interference). Effective communication among all levels leads to the sharing of understanding, through both success stories and lessons learned, as a natural part of the culture.

The ideal knowledge environment builds on these learnings to include the need for effective continuous and interpersonal communications at all levels and the use of team-based structures. Continuous and interpersonal communications create an essential framework within which creative thinking, brainstorming, inquiry, dialogue, debate, scenario planning, discussion and rational analysis are encouraged. These are the ways in which synergy can create new thinking and paradigm shifts. For example, research has indicated a correlation between a pre-school age child's intelligence level and the amount of time the child spends with parents in interpersonal communication. A similar phenomenon may hold for organizational intelligence, that is, workers will be more creative, thoughtful and act smarter when they spend time interacting with each other, within the framework of a clear vision or goal.

The idea of creating an optimum knowledge-based organizational environment has at its foundation cohesive subgroups or teams, and networks of relationships where open and free exchange of ideas is the norm. The advantage of teams (as for any form of small collaborative group) is that individuals can get to know each other, developing trust and effective interpersonal relations which generate information and knowledge sharing through brainstorming, problem solving and decision making. Team learning can then occur naturally through the process of responding to changes in the external environment. As teams develop their own centers of learning, and as people move around within the organization, the seeds of team efficiency and effectiveness will expand throughout the organization and generate the desired knowledge environment. This is one factor in creating the desired change.

The Change Approach

Where an organization lays on the spectrum or continuum from bureaucracy to the concept of a knowledge organization such as the intelligent complex adaptive system (see Chapter 14) very much drives the approach required to manage change (see Figure 15-1). At the left end of the spectrum, you would work through the chain of command and mandate compliance, and, based on the Weberian bureaucratic model, share as little information as necessary to accomplish the desired change. As Weber believed and is still occurring in some organizations today, "Every bureaucracy seeks to increase the superiority of the professionally informed by keeping their knowledge and intentions secret" (Gerth & Mills, 1946).

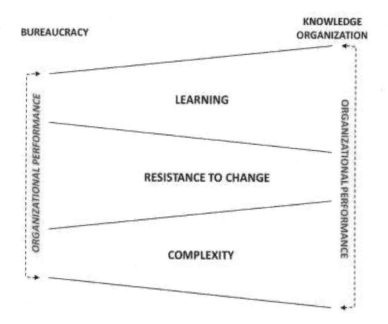

Figure 15-1. *Continuum from bureaucracy to the knowledge organization.*

At the other end of the spectrum the change manager's job is to demonstrate value and to educate, letting the organization itself build the response and implementation strategy appropriate for each organizational change element. In exploring the application of the science of complexity to organizations, Stacy suggests three basic needs for a complex adaptive organization. These are to provide workers with (1) a clear rationale for new direction; (2) a strong set of values they can share and operate within; and (3) the freedom to self-organize (Stacy, 1996). The precept is that the workers know what needs to be done and, given direction and values, they are able to organize themselves better than management can dictate. This approach is consistent with findings in complexity theory. However, it is effective only with organizations already in an advanced state of empowerment and knowledge sharing, that is, on the right side of the spectrum. Although some present-day world-class firms exhibit elements of this self-organizing approach, many of today's organizations have a distance to go.

This same concept of change management for a knowledge organization surfaced in a five-year study involving over 2500 individuals in 460 companies. The Jensen Group study on "Changing How We Work" found that, "'God's' reality is that if we designed Knowledge Management structures that created meaning, drove understanding, integrated content and facilitated conversations, change would change itself—at the appropriate speed" (Jensen Group, 1997). The study goes on to conclude that change management is, in reality, an "artificial solution imposed on an [sic] dysfunctional corporate knowledge system."

Success occurs over time, and comes with many faces. In fact, there is danger in premature convergence for this can limit potential. As much as we are inclined to desire change at Internet speed, there is a natural pace and rhythm of change that is specific to each organization. We will explore this concept further below.

Figure 13-1 shows that as we move from a bureaucratic structure to a knowledge organization, both individual and organizational learning increase and resistance to change decreases. However, we must be careful and not fall into the trap of believing that knowledge organization structures do not resist change. Knowledge organizations, being adaptive and learning, are much more comfortable with new ideas, products and organizational structures than a corresponding bureaucratic firm. However, if the anticipated change is affecting or perceived as affecting now or in the future a worker's job security, organizational status, physical location or career opportunity in any negative way, forces are created and resistance can be strong, subtle and possibly invisible in either organization. (See Chapter 3/Part I on forces.) Fear and psychological loss drive behavior far more than rational thought. How "loss" is defined by an individual is highly dependent on the degree of the individual's learning and flexibility, with the feelings of loss inversely related to learning and flexibility.

<<<<<<<◇>>>>>>>

INSIGHT: **As your environment becomes more complex, increased learning decreases resistance to change.**

<<<<<<<◇>>>>>>>

The ADIIEA Model

Becoming a knowledge organization requires an understanding of the relationships, not just existence, of learning, complexity, and resistance to change. For example, Figure 15-1 shows that as we move from the bureaucratic structure to the knowledge organization structure, individual and organizational learning increase and complexity increases. Thus, reducing resistance to change is directly related to our understanding of learning as a model of change. We hear that people fear and resist change, and we may even repeat this statement without giving thought to why people would buy a Lotto ticket, which would intentionally disrupt their life with change. Upon closer inspection, the resistance and fear are not directed towards *all* change, but to the "unknown" and "lack of control" found within *some* change (Lazarus, 1991).

Given that it is change itself that bureaucratic cultures resist, providing learning of the change process is necessary such that there are fewer unknowns and more understanding of the control each person in the knowledge organization has over the change process. Unfortunately, most organizations do not view "learning" as a model of organizational change. Instead, "learning" is viewed as "training" for individuals, which is held as a separate concept and model from the "work" process. As noted by Peter Senge, "Making learning an 'add-on' to people's regular work, has probably limited more organizational learning initiatives than any other factor" (Senge, 2006: 287).

To address this issue, a combined learning-business model was created, called ADIIEA (Lewis, 2013), which is named after the six phases of change: Automation, Disruption, Investigation, Ideation, Expectation, and Affirmation (see Figure 15-2). In his preface to the revised edition of *The Fifth Discipline*, Peter Senge (2006) quotes W. Edwards Deming: "We will never transform the prevailing system of management without transforming our prevailing system of education. They are the same system." The ADIIEA (pronounced uh-dee-uh) model describes learning from a storytelling pattern, and then describes the management and leadership activities required along the way, representing both learning and management.

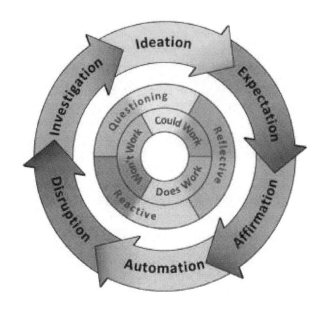

Figure 15-2. *ADIIEA Learning-Business Model.*

The *Automation* phase is where individual and organizational activities operate in routine (reactive / does work), on autopilot and status quo. A typical definition of "automation" includes "the technique, method, or system of operating or controlling a process by highly automatic means…" which includes training, codified processes, as well as robotics—yet we tend to only associate this term with robotics, forgetting that humans operate within the state of automation throughout most of the day. As robotics continue to replace trained labor, more humans will need to be able to navigate throughout the entire change cycle.

The management thinking models that came out of the Industrial Age are usually "prescriptive" in that they provide steps without first describing an underlying model. A key example is the DMAIC thinking model used in Six Sigma training. DMAIC stands for: Define, Measure, Analyze, Improve, Control. When we map these steps to the ADIIEA model, we find that: (1) Define occurs in *Disruption*, to identify a problem but not an opportunity; (2) Measure also occurs in *Disruption*, to measure production variation from expected; (3) Analyze occurs in *Investigation*, to inspect using statistical methods to find root causes but not to explore or discover; (4) Improve occurs in *Ideation, Expectation,* and *Affirmation,* to create improvement ideas and implement plans; and (5) Control occurs in *Automation* (the new routine), to maintain production variations to less than three defects per million units (six sigma measurement).

A knowledge organization cannot operate fundamentally from Industrial Age process models, but instead needs to operate from thinking models that describe change and learning. Starting from our normal routine (Automation), we encounter something out of the ordinary (Disruption) and begin to look deeper into the situation (Investigation). Then we think of some ideas (Ideation) and put a plan into action (Expectation). With a sound plan, we eventually see positive results (Affirmation), and over time, we settle into a new routine (Automation). From this descriptive model (ADIIEA), we can then infer the prescriptive management and leadership activities required, rather than starting from a point of memorized steps. This is how we can picture learning as THE business model, rather than learning as an "add-on" to business operations.

An interesting aspect of the ADIIEA Model is its focus on Expectation and Affirmation. It is not enough to have an idea. Rather, there is a need to set the expectation for that idea and through Affirmation ensure it is working the way it was expected to work. The creation process of intention and expectation is continuous, and critical. (See Chapter 25/Part IV.)

Because of the hierarchal structure and *base of command and control* in a bureaucratic organization, there are fewer directions to go, less variety in decisions and actions, and less potential to bring to bear than in the knowledge organization based on teams and knowledge sharing. Bureaucratic organizations were designed for stable, repetitive, error-free processes meeting their objectives. While the use of control in bureaucratic organizations is not new to history, in today's environment they are rarely sustainable. See Table 14-1 in Chapter 14.

In contrast, *knowledge organizations flourish on new ideas and change.* The amount of potential in a knowledge organization is limited only by the number and quality of ideas generated and implemented, and the array of possibilities within the resources available. Because of its multiple communication networks, feedback paths and constant variation of team structures, complex structures such as the knowledge organization discussed above have the ability to learn, adapt and take on far more variety of actions than a bureaucracy. Thus, although they are more complex than bureaucracies, they can use that complexity to respond more quickly and effectively to a non-linear, dynamic, knowledge-laden external environment.

The Change Process

We have learned through the years that when organizational change is mandated and certain actions occur in response to that mandate, individual behavioral change is highly dependent on the individual's receptivity to change and to the incentive to exchange old behaviors for new ones. Receptivity to change is affected by a combination of internal and external information and current beliefs, all of which are subject to continuous examination and update. This means that all incoming information is colored by the current beliefs and feelings, which we now understand from the perspective of the mind/brain as the process of associative patterning. This also means that all incoming information, whether originating from the unconscious mind of the individual or from the external environment, is under continuous examination and, as a result, the individual's beliefs themselves are also subject to continuous reexamination (see Figure 15-3). This powerful process goes on at various levels within all learning individuals and all organizations.

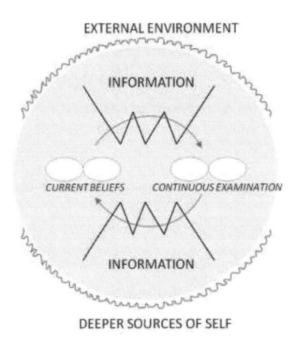

Figure 15-3. *Forces at play affecting receptivity to change.*

This process also operates continuously, and generally invisibly, in a learning organization. Incoming information is continuously examined in light of the organization's structural capital, i.e., that explicit information and knowledge which is within the organization. It is then considered in relationship to the belief set (in a healthy organization reflected in the mission, vision and strategy) and to the organizational culture (through values, behavior and expectations). Any new information needs to be made sense of through these lenses before it will be embraced by the organization. And the mission, vision and strategy should always be under continuous examination in light of incoming internal and external information. This under-the-looking-glass approach reduces what we call "resistance to change" since both "old" and "new" information and knowledge are subject to it.

From psychology (Freudian theory), we pull the concept of the ego, that aspect of personality that encompasses the sense of "self" in contact with the real world. The ego is largely a product of the personality. There is an in-depth discussion of personality in Chapter 4/Part I. To represent the *instinctive* aspects of personality, Freud used the concept of the *id* (Gerow, 1992). Viewing an organization as having a culture, an emergent characteristic similar to personality in an individual, we can extrapolate that culture is made up of both an *ego* and an *id*. The ego, whether reflecting positive or negative responses to the environment, provides that portion of the inner identity of the organization that faces the world with rational thinking, and the id represents past experience and beliefs converted to instincts and emotions through time.

The culture (ego and id) of the organization collectively represents a powerful energy force. While the organizational ego serves as the watchtower and processor for incoming information, the id provides the energy and spirit for action and resolve, with ego representing the rational, objective part of culture and id representing the emotional, subjective part. Whether viewed in the individual or organizational setting, the ego and id can be strong advocates or barriers to change, and both must be recognized and dealt with. An organization can be changed and turned in literally endless directions by recognizing and dealing effectively with both the organizational ego and id.

All too often, senior managers of today's organizations believe that since their workforce is empowered and flexible, they need deal only with the ego side of culture, providing a set of reasons why change must occur and a plan to accomplish that change. They may consider the id side as touchy-feely, and therefore unnecessary. Freudian theory reminds us that people act consistent with their personal knowledge, beliefs and feelings, especially in times of possible danger, and all significant organizational change will be perceived as threatening to some workers. This is consistent with the AUBFOE model of individual change presented in Chapter 6/Part I. Further, as we know, you cannot leave emotions at the door (see Chapter 12/Part II). Change must be addressed in terms of both the ego and the id.

A first step to receptivity is gaining attention. As the environment bombards the senses, attention itself rapidly becomes a scarce resource. Information doubles every 18, 9 or 3 months (depending on which study you read). There are currently over 800 million web pages, and Internet traffic is doubling every 100 days. By the time you read this book, these figures will have themselves doubled. See Chapter 25/Part IV on Attention and Intention.

Marketing experts have studied potential buyer response for decades. A lot of what they have learned carries over to the art of managing change in either government or the private sector. The importance of product name transfers to the perceived trustworthiness of information dependent on the sender. Market segmentation and customization map to the personalization of information as seen by its recipient. Product appeal and advertising campaigns relate to evoking emotion with the information sent.

And, finally, the importance of product value becomes the receiver's real or perceived need for use of the information. To get someone's attention, something of perceived value (to them) must be offered in return. When addressing effective Knowledge Management, Tom Peters says the crux of the issue is not information, information technology, or knowledge per se. "It's how … you get busy people … to want to contribute [or use information] … The answer turns out to lie more with psychology and marketing than with bits and bytes" (Peters, 1992).

Sensory inputs provide the stimuli for the organization culture's attention, or inattention. The external senses provide what Thomas Reid, a Scottish philosopher who lived, thought and wrote over 200 years ago, called a conception and an invincible belief of the existence of external objects. Reid credited a "double province" to the senses: to make us perceive and to make us feel, using the smelling of a rose as an example. When we smell a rose, two separate and parallel things happen: a sweet, subjective smell enters through our olfactory system and we perceive the external and objective presence of a rose. What Reid is getting at is that the sense of smell is something that directly affects us as individuals, a subjective experience, a feeling. But the perception of an external presence provides us with objective facts to make judgments about the external objective world.

The culture of the organization, then, carries the residue (memory) of feelings about the organization and the external world, while at the same time it is constantly under the influence of its own belief set, which is itself being continuously examined as new external and internal information flows within the organization. Thus, in the regular course of events, the organizational ego will modify itself and change or flow into a somewhat different ego. Such is the usual process with cultures. They change slowly, never losing all of their history nor accepting all of the new ways, with the id portion taking longer to adjust to the new changes than the ego. When an organization's culture undergoes traumatic shock such as massive layoffs, mergers, or impending dissolution, there is a frantic attempt to create alternate stories or self-images to handle the situation. But egos have their id partners, which carry the memory of the images and experiences of traumatic shock. If all humans behaved rationally, there would be very few overweight people, no smokers and wars would be history. If organizational cultures followed the rational part of their ego, most would be high-performance, knowledge-centric and adaptive, and potentially arrogant, with no balancing sensitivity.

The classic belief has been that organizations do not change without undergoing a traumatic emotional experience. While that may have been true in the bureaucratic structure, as organizations adapt to knowledge environments there may well be new learnings that will allow change without this historic need for trauma.

Once attention is gained, individual learning styles contribute significantly to each worker's ability to take in information along with its context and meaning. Nonaka and Takeuchi (1995) identify and discuss the four modes by which knowledge is transferred. These modes use some combination of tacit knowledge (which is internalized in each of us) and/or explicit knowledge (which can be codified in some form of media). The four quadrants are aligned to preferred learning styles. They are: tacit to tacit (individual learning through apprenticeship); tacit to explicit (group learning); explicit to explicit (organizational learning); and explicit to tacit (enterprise learning). While each individual has a preferred learning style, and each area of knowledge has its natural habitat, the challenge is to create a dynamic environment that permits all knowledge forms and all learning styles and perspectives to share understanding and create innovative solutions.

Even if individual attention is gained and the material presented in a variety of ways, taking into consideration learning styles and modes of receptivity, unless the receiver is operating in a processing mode consistent with the knowledge content, very little will be acted upon. Recent psychological studies show that an individual's attention focus changes, on the average, every 40 minutes. That means attention alone will not carry the day. Long speeches, videos or meetings will not of themselves produce the desired paradigm shift in either individuals or the organizational culture. So, what will?

Given the discussion above, it may be surprising that organizations can and do change. But, of course, they do. The following are offered as considerations when stimulating change:

* Organizations, like people, have an internal belief structure and an instinctual history that is constantly examining itself based on the flow of information from both internal and external sources.

* The organizational culture, that is, its ego and id, has the ability to turn the organization in literally endless directions.

* The level of learning within an organization can be inversely correlated to expected resistance to change.

* As the external environment becomes more complex, the bureaucratic organization is more difficult to control and its efficiency decreases.

* As organizations become more knowledge-based and true collaboration and empowerment occur, internal complexity increases, which can be used to support change.

The Elements of Change

We, and our organizations, are affected by changes in our environment, and to various degrees we can exert influence on that environment. We now consider planned change, where we strive to create the future reality of our organization.

A preparatory tenant for planned change is to determine if the need for change is real and the time needed is available. Is there a good business case for changing and has a viable strategy been developed? A second tenant is the willingness to let change beget change. Change can be initiated and orchestrated, but it cannot be rigorously controlled. The end-state is never precisely predictable. What frequently happens is that resistance is proportional to the level of control of the change process. Remove people's say in the change and you remove their motivation to cooperate, which increases forces.

A third tenant is the intention to see it through. False starts will generate confusion, produce discretions in both efficiency and effectiveness, and embed themselves in the cultural memory. Start change with the intent, energy, and resources to see it through, yet with a strategy flexible enough to meet the second tenant above.

The first element of planned change is a clear understanding of where the organization currently is (value and values, structure and processes, strengths and weaknesses) and an understanding of the desired future state (vision and mission, opportunities and strategies). What's different in a knowledge-based organization is that this crucial first step is the most important instrument of change. If the need for change can be communicated, understood, accepted and aligned across the organization, supported with implementation tools (which promulgate change in a non-threatening way) and incentives, change momentum will be well underway.

The value of change is made visible through the use of cross-organization and cross-product teams to define the new vision, the effective use of diverse modes of communicating that vision, and continuous commitment from senior and middle management to that vision and to the employees' welfare. The fluid exchange of ideas and understanding across the organization, resonating with the belief set of the organization, will determine what change will occur. That means (1) exchange at every level of the organization, horizontal and vertical, and (2) a focus on building a common understanding of the context (the need for change and the vision of the future) and defining pathways and connections to get there. Ultimately, this comes down to individuals, their relationships with each other, and the data, information and knowledge they have access to accept and apply.

Tools are critically important to change management, and can be used as learning vehicles, motivators and long-term facilitators. Tools may provide guidance on how to get from here to there (policies, guiding principles, instructional material); road maps that provide for process change (methodologies such as scenario planning); technology (from collaborative software to simulations); and communities and forums for the active exchange of successes and lessons learned. People and dollar resources such as change champions and seed funding can be instrumental in speeding up the journey.

Motivation is increased through tools that demonstrate the potential for greater efficiencies and effectiveness, with the associated rewards of personal productivity, better products and higher customer satisfaction. Since tools are objective, in that they do not carry the connotation of "past wrongs," they offer "new opportunities" to improve performance without the emotional baggage of "I must not have been doing it right before!" Tools do not challenge the internal belief systems or past behavior, rather they encourage change through taking advantage of an opportunity—especially when the user has the freedom of choice.

Facilitation occurs where tools encourage and foster better communication and collaboration. If people start talking and listening they will learn better and be more willing to change. Some tools act as an independent focal point for discussions, debate and inquiry. This "shared space" provides an effective way to bring people's perspectives together and communicate with a common focus and language.

Scenario planning is helpful because its process encourages creative, yet self-consistent, thinking and it gives the group an idea of what the future could look like, ergo a direction to move towards. This assures that change is directed and purposeful, providing a vision to spark the emotions and encourage dreams. (See the Tool: Scenario Building in Chapter 16.)

A simple and perhaps surprising tool is the use of space to foster communication and the sharing of understanding, which in turn facilitates change. The frequency and amount of conversation among workers is exponentially related to the closeness between their offices; the closer their offices, the more they talk to each other. By placing change agents throughout the organization, or having leaders, managers and supervisors spend more time managing by walking around, employees have greater opportunity for face-to-face dialogue to reduce their fears and better understand the need for change and its impact on their work and job security.

Cognitive tools such as lateral thinking, synectics, synthetic analysis and dialogue, and systems thinking have been found to be very useful in helping people comprehend the complex relationships that exist in their organization and to identify feedback and circular patterns of cause and effect which may either stifle or accelerate organizational change. See the articles by Bohlin and Brenner (1996) and Rooke and Torbert (1999) in *The Systems Thinker*. System dynamics (a form of advanced simulation) can change fundamental belief systems objectively as groups work together to build a common understanding of how their organization really works. System dynamics models provide the opportunity to experiment with cause and effect in simulated current or future organizations through sensitivity analyses and flight simulation runs. Groups of managers have used modeling to identify serious problems in their organization, recognize their own paradigm errors in how the organization really works, and develop and simulate correction strategies. Vennix (1996) and Morecroft and Sterman (1994) offer in-depth discussions of this process, and Bennet (1997) includes an Integrated Product Team flight simulator. The bottom line is that group and personal experimentation help create a willingness and a rationale for understanding and supporting change.

All collaborative technologies can provide value (Schrage, 1990; Coleman, 1997; and Skyrme, 1999). The more these mental implements are used, the more ideas are available for use, and the more opportunity for the organization to develop and fulfill its own unique collaborative advantage.

Incentives include high-visibility reward and award systems. They also include reinforcement from leadership. An essential positive incentive that came out of the Total Quality movement is leadership walking the talk. Leaders (including middle managers) must be a proactive part of the change process, consistently presenting the vision, clarifying the path and acting as role models for all employees.

It would be nice if we could paint that clear vision, snap our fingers, and achieve the desired end state—and perhaps we can in the future—but today the reality is that a transformed organization does not just happen. In many ways, organizations evolve like living organisms, growing much like a human child. A concerned parent has a great deal to do in a child's early years with relating information and incentivizing behavior, but as the child grows older self-incentives and incentives from the external environment take priority and the parent role becomes one of information sharing, guidance and dialogue. When the child enters adulthood, the parent serves more in the advisory capacity. During this cycle, growth visibly occurs in small chunks, with the parent first focusing on life threatening issues, then working with the basic qualities of the genes (ego, capability and value set) to create emergent characteristics that affirm and mold the belief set. Along this growth road, benefits accrue for both the child and parents as they learn about what it is to be human through each other's eyes. This metaphor offers insights for the growth of organizations from the first "Eve" (the first homo sapien sapiens) of 117,000 years ago through the bureaucratic organization to the beginnings of the knowledge organization. The growth cycle in individual organizations can also reflect this metaphor, as well as the change effort itself. While dependent on the environment, change behavior reflects its place in the growth cycle, whether in the individual or the organization. For every change there is a time.

Emergent Characteristics

As organizations change and take on new forms, they often do so through the creation and development of what systems theorists call emergent characteristics. These represent new properties that are totally different from the properties of the old structure, and they cannot be directly derived from the lower levels of the organization. For example, social organizations emerge from individual actions, and knowledge sharing arises from changes in behavior and new technology, yet social organizations and knowledge sharing are phenomena that are very different in kind from individuals or technology.

<<<<<<<◇>>>>>>>

INSIGHT: **Organizations change and take on new forms through the creation and development of emergent characteristics.**

<<<<<<<◇>>>>>>>

The connection between the early organization and its current emergent properties is extremely complex and difficult to follow via cause and effect chains. It is also difficult to predict the precise nature of the emergent characteristics. This is one reason why planned change is so difficult and the change process so hard to control. For instance, it is easy to create a vision of a team-based organization with high employee empowerment. But, the exact details of the best team structure or the specific way that employees should be empowered are very hard to predetermine. People are not machines and their variability and self-determination are essential for their efficacy. Thus, while a desirable emergent characteristic can be nurtured, it cannot be decreed.

Emergent characteristics can be best understood in relation to a clearly defined vision prior to the anticipated change. Emergent characteristics usually make up the key factors that will make the vision a reality, as well as providing local indicators or measures of success. Emergent characteristics grow from ideas, ideas that emerge from individuals in relationship with each other. These organizational ideas, much like the individual model at Figure 15-2, are constantly examined in light of new information (both internal and external). And these ideas, even while affected by their environment, are also constantly altering and creating their environment.

What do these emergent characteristics look like? Some examples that relate to the knowledge organization are: a sense of community, knowledge sharing, knowledge repositories, organizational flexibility and organizational learning. As discussed above, it may be impossible to identify the lower level causative elements that lead to the creation of these emerging characteristics.

Community. Community is formed through networks based on relationships. Teams, flexible work groups and communities of practice (COPs) and interest (COIs) are forms of building community. What is specific to COPs and COIs—concepts that emerged out of the Knowledge Management arena—is their particular way of looking at the world; they are organized around a shared domain of knowledge. COPs and COIs cross operational, functional and organizational boundaries and focus on value added, mutual exchange and continuous learning. While closely aligned with the strategic direction of the organization, they are maintained by making connections and providing value added for their participants. Critical factors to success include a sense of urgency, trust, respect, personal passion, open communications, and the participation of key thought leaders. The exact nature, form and participation level of COPs and COIs is dependent on the needs of the organization and the benefits to their members.

Knowledge Sharing. The sharing of knowledge is not natural to the organic growth of the bureaucratic organization. During the knowledge life cycle, data and information are used by an individual to create new knowledge built on context and understanding. As knowledge is shared across the collaborative base of an organization, this knowledge is (1) used to improve competing products and (2) used alone or in combination with other knowledge to create new ideas, new knowledge, that support the innovation process. New knowledge is a positive result of sharing knowledge. Another positive result is the efficient availability of the best knowledge to decision makers. The negative potential of sharing knowledge is its potential decay or loss of value as time elapses; needs change and new knowledge comes into demand.

It now becomes clear why, historically, managers have always considered their knowledge as a source of power. It is also clear why the knowledge organization of today—living in an environment with easy access to unlimited data and information—considers knowledge shared as their source of power. These knowledge organizations succeed based on the continuous influx of new ideas and innovation, and their superior ability to create, find and apply knowledge at the time and place where it is most powerful.

Knowledge Repositories. Knowledge repositories, automated libraries, computer services, databases, etc., offer a capability for not only storing huge amounts of data and information but also efficient and semi-intelligent retrieval and assemblage capability. As search algorithms, intelligent agents and semantic interpreters become more powerful, employees will be able to rapidly retrieve information needed for problem solving and decision-making. Although knowledge repositories may appear to be technology driven, they require a great deal of human effort to input the right information and motivate people to make effective use of them. Both of these may require culture changes that if successful will result in a new organizational strength. The value of the knowledge repository is not so much what resides in it, but what flows in and out of it to and from decision makers. (See the "Conversation that Matters" focused on the idea of the living repository presented in Chapter 14.)

Organizational Flexibility. Another desired emergent characteristic of the knowledge-based organization is the ability to quickly respond to changes in the external environment. Organizational flexibility requires workforce empowerment, clear vision and values, and willingness by management to encourage prudent risk-taking. A *freedom to take action* environment, coupled with open communications and fast, small, self-organized teams will result in *opportunity making and taking*.

Organizational Learning. Effective organizational flexibility also requires continuous learning, the fifth emergent property discussed here. Lifelong learning, changing and forgetting lay at the foundation of progress in the modern world and may well be the ultimate separators between success and failure for individuals, public organizations and private industry. (Forgetting is discussed in Chapter 20.) Without learning, change is likely to be wasteful or irrelevant; with learning, change carriers the opportunity for improvement.

The Strategic Initiative Pulse

Change can be managed through a set of strategic initiatives designed to bring about specific emergent characteristics. The introduction of change is a phased phenomenon. The timing of strategic initiative thrusts needs to be correlated with the system's ability to recognize value and begin implementation. Each organization has a receptivity rhythm that can be monitored based on feedback loops.

The model in Figure 15-4 demonstrates the Strategic Initiative Pulse (SIP) that was developed over three years of study of the Department of Navy (DON) Acquisition Reform Office implementation approach. Note that while this model deals with physical change and is based on engagement of forces, the mental development or pre-work has been done to ensure that the desired change is both possible and consistent with the desired end state. The SIP model is loosely analogous to Isaac Newton's fundamental laws of motion stating that *to maintain a change in motion you must have a continuous force*. If the pressure for change is a constant, change itself will accelerate. As a construct for understanding the SIP, we will artificially divide the organizational system into three forces or levels: the Proactive Forerunners, the Doubting Thomases, and the Resisters (including "rocks" who will rarely change).

Assuming cohesive thinking and compatibility between the organization's needs and the change initiative, introduction of a new initiative (I_1) requires consistent, persistent pressure at all levels of the organization. Examples of this pressure are provided in the AUBFOE individual change model in Chapter 6/Part I. Over time, intelligent and consistent pressure will result in recognition of the value of the change initiative by the organization. It is at the point of value recognition that the organization's Proactive Forerunners embrace the initiative and begin implementation.

If the Proactive Forerunners appear to be successful with I_1, implementation of the initiative quickly cascades down through the ranks of the Doubting Thomases. The greater the appearance of I_1 success by the Proactive Forerunners, the faster the

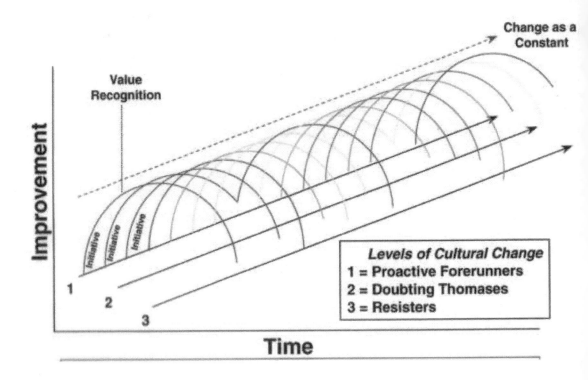

Figure 15-4. *The Strategic Initiative Pulse (1).*

cascade through the Doubting Thomases. Then, the hard work resumes. Consistent, constant pressure must continue as slowly, slowly, the top layer of resisters opens up. How long and how far down into the resister layer the system can continue this I_1 push is highly dependent on the resources of the change effort. For at some point behind I_1's introduction, and prior to system value recognition, I_2 has been introduced and is requiring the same consistent, persistent pressure for success. Then, near the value recognition point of I_1, and while I_2 is still in need of consistent, persistent pressure, I_3 has been introduced into the organization. As demonstrated in Figure 15-5, to achieve change as a constant (continuous change acceleration), value recognition points are built on overlapping change efforts.

Here is where the intelligent learning system comes into play, built on open feedback loops. It is best explained by example. Near the turn of the century when the U.S. Department of Defense (DoD) Secretary mandated the use of Integrated Product Teams (IPTs), within 48 hours DoD teams of every type began calling themselves "IPTs," while struggling to figure out exactly what IPTs were.

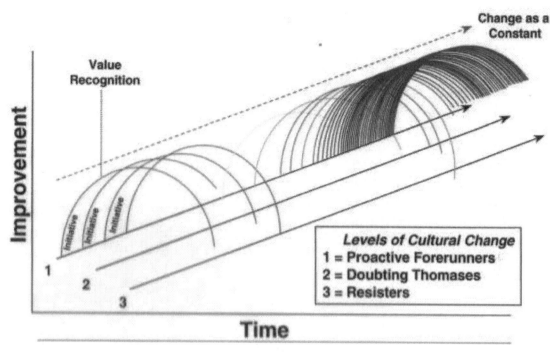

Figure 15-5. *The Strategic Initiative Pulse (2).*

Within a couple weeks of announcement of that policy, the U.S. Department of the Navy (DoN) Acquisition Reform Office virtually posted draft IPT guidelines. During the following two weeks more than 600 emails, phone calls and personal dialogues occurred across the staff, with employees asking: "When will the final guidelines be issued?" Approximately six weeks into the change process, a second "draft" version of the IPT guidelines was posted virtually. Over the following two weeks a flurry of questions ensued, but this time those questions numbered in the dozens instead of the hundreds. Three months into the change process you began to see programs differentiating between IPTs and other types of teams. When a third set of "draft" guidelines was virtually posted, the two dozen responses were focused more on providing *ideas of how to improve the guidelines* than on asking, "When do the final guides come out?" Similar response patterns to the introduction of new initiatives were observed over a three-year period, such that response times could eventually be granulated down to sub-elements of the organization, each of which had a different culture and a different receptivity rhythm.

The response patterns demonstrated that initiatives too closely introduced failed to move through the layers of the organization (see Figure 15-4). This, of course, is partially due to the reduction of consistent, persistent pressure, which is difficult to sustain when multiple initiatives are simultaneously introduced. Conversely, if too much time elapsed between change initiatives, the initial buildup to the point of value recognition became slower and more difficult (see Figure 15-4). As change behavior becomes embedded in the organization, the organization once again becomes comfortable, and slower to respond to change.

As demonstrated in the SIP, in this model change requires aggressiveness in terms of continuous, persistent pressure (engaging and directing force). This implies the power of energy directed into action. This infers to the intelligent use of force. When change is focused in the physical utilizing bounded knowledge, the transformation of any idea into realization is the result of this creative aggression. This model is what we bring from the past, what we have observed in others and how we have learned through experience, and, when repeated over and over again and successful, helps build our tenacity, persistence and self-confidence as actors in our individual world-scape. With the realization that thought precedes form, these attributes serve us well as (1) we move from a physical focus on moving energy to a mental focus on building concepts; (2) we begin to recognize that our thoughts have value beyond our individual world-scape and *we begin to share them in service to others that they may act*; (3) we open our learning to co-evolve with our environment, becoming part of a larger flow; (4) we continue expanding our awareness and consciousness, making increasing contributions to the larger whole and enabling others to make larger contributions; and (5) we move toward a state of balance, where the connections among the past, present and future clarify and come together to empower us as co-creators of our reality.

Final Thoughts

It is clear that there is no one simple solution to change and that every change effort is context sensitive. It is also clear that the change approach is dependent on where an organization lies on the continuum from a bureaucratic organization to a knowledge organization.

In this chapter, we looked at the internal knowledge environment of an organization in terms of a knowledge organization. We viewed organizational change and learning through the lens of an individual change and learning model, explored elements of change and the creation of emergent characteristics, and looked at the Strategic Initiative Pulse emerging from work with the DoN Acquisition Reform Office. The final paragraph of a chapter offers the author one final opportunity to share the knowledge and passion so important to sharing ideas. Our final thoughts are these: Vision your reality, then act accordingly, as if that reality is today, which moves us from the state of co-evolving with our environment toward becoming co-creators of our reality.

Questions for Reflection:

Have you increased your learning in order to deal with increasing levels of complexity?

Which elements of this change approach have you applied or will you apply in your change initiatives, and what is the impact of that inclusion or omission?

Chapter 16
Time and Space

SUBTOPICS: THE USEFULNESS OF TIME ... PAST, PRESENT AND FUTURE ... THE GIFT OF PLANNING .... EXPLORING TIME: BUILDING CONCEPTUAL RELATIONSHIPS ... THE RHYTHM OF CHANGE ... TAKING ADVANTAGE OF TIME AND SPACE

FIGURES: 16-1. CONCEPTUAL MODEL OF TIME AS LINEAR ... **16-2.** CONCEPTUAL MODEL OF TIME AS CIRCULAR ... **16-3.** CONCEPTUAL MODEL OF TIME AS A SPIRAL.

TOOLS: 16-1. INTEGRATING TIME INTO THE SELF EXPERIENCE ... 16-2. SCENARIO BUILDING

Time is the glue that holds space together. Time and space are interwoven. The higher the amount of intelligent activity, the closer together they become. The lower the amount of intelligent activity—the more unintelligent activity—the more forces are created and the more time and space are separated (MacFlouer, 2004-16). Thus, delays of time are inevitable in the presence of certain space conditions. As described in *Urantia* (1952):

> Time is a succession of instants that is perceived by analysis, while space is a system of associated points that is perceived by synthesis. These two dissimilar concepts are coordinated and associated by the integrating insight of each individual personality ... only man possesses this time-space perceptibility.

A difficulty we have in understanding space in the physical plane is due to the fact that while our material bodies exist in space, space also exists in these same bodies. It may help our understanding of space relationships, from a relative point of view, if we think of space as a property of all material bodies. As a body moves through space, it takes with it all of its properties, even the space which is within it. Thus, at the material level all patterns of reality occupy space. This, of course, begs the question of whether the pattern of an idea, a thought form, occupies space, that is, asking: *Is the immaterial non-spatial?* This is explored in Chapter 26/Part IV.

The advent of Quantum mechanics and relativity theory brought with it a new understanding of time, space and objects as in some way continuous. As Wilber (1993) describes, space is not blank but serves a surrounding function to objects. On the other hand, the boundaries of objects are defined by the space around them. Space cannot exist separate from objects, and objects must be enclosed by space, so in this sense space and objects are one. As Wilber (1993, p. 82) goes on to say,

> Furthermore, objects, in order to exist, must endure; that is, duration or time is necessary for the existence of objects ... Conversely, the existence of duration depends upon objects, for without objects to endure, there could be no duration;

and in this sense, time and objects are one. It follows that space and time are also one. Hence space, time, and objects are mutually dependent and inseparable.

Further, there is a direct correlation between space and intelligent activity. Space connects to time. Space allows activity to take place that is not intelligent and grows from this unintelligent activity, causing forces. Through thought we are able to reduce space. The more we join ourselves together in any thought, the less space between us, and the easier to use time in ways that are intelligent and "save time". For example, the faster we travel the more space curves and the less time it takes, and we don't use up as much time in the traveling.

If life becomes more forceful, we need to apply more intelligence, that is, be inclusive with others and work together. When we connect ourselves with more people and interact intelligently, improving dialogue, we connect ourselves with more of life and our perception of space decreases. For example, the Internet produced new forms of communication, allowing more interaction with others and reducing space.

<<<<<<<◇>>>>>>

INSIGHT: **When we connect ourselves inclusively with others and interact intelligently, we connect ourselves with more of life and our perception of space decreases.**

<<<<<<<◇>>>>>>

Light joins time and space together. If we were moving at the speed of light (from our physical perspective, that's 186,000 miles per second relative speed), there would be no space in between events; and everything would be occurring in one place. As science fiction writer Ray Cummings (1922, p. 46) succinctly expressed, "Time ... is what keeps everything from happening at once!" If we were moving with the light itself, at the speed of light, time would stop. Thus, light is a measure of the separation of time and space. Further, there would be no forces since energy would be integrated with space and time (MacFlouer, 1999). While these concepts can initially sound confusing, similar ideas have been promulgated for many years, initially through science fiction and, more recently, in research shared broadly through such vehicles as *Scientific American*, *National Geographic*, British Broadcasting Company nature productions, or *The Great Courses* presented by The Teaching Company.

****

TOOL 16-1: INTEGRATING TIME INTO THE SELF EXPERIENCE

Breathing is an important part of the Buddhist meditative experience to build awareness of bodily sensations and as the foundation of achieving mindfulness. Conversely, the strongest psychodynamic foundation for the self experience is hunger. By focusing on breath, we are able to release the anxieties of self and perceive the soft ebb and flow of time. As psychoanalyst Michael Eigen (1993, p. 46) explains, "the sense of self based on a normal experience of breathing is an unpressured sense of self which is not easily stampeded. For the sense of self structured by appetite, time is an irritant. The self structured by an awareness of breathing can take its time, going from moment to moment, just as breathing usually does. It does not run after or get ahead of time but, instead, seems simply to move with it."

STEP (1): Find a comfortable place to sit or lie down where you will not be disturbed.

STEP (2): Close your eyes. Take three or four long, deep breaths, filling your lungs completely on the in-breath and emptying them completely on the out-breath.

STEP (3): Feel your body relax; do a slow scan of your body, feeling it gently relax into the chair or bed on which you sit or lie.

STEP (4): Refocus on your breath, now a gentle, slow in and out. Feel your body welcoming the breath; imagine it moving through your system, reaching all of your body from within.

STEP (5): While continuing relaxed breathing, imagine the air surrounding your body entering through every cell on the surface of your body, softly greeting and intermingling with the breath within. Feel a soft inner breeze lift and lighten your body.

STEP (6): Staying in this place of floating, refocus on your breath, gently moving in and out. Enjoy the experience in sequences of NOW. When you are ready to return to your physical reality, slowly shift your awareness away from your breath and open your eyes, thanking your body for the experience.

****

The Usefulness of Time

Time is a perspective, the result of something taking place. In the journey of life, we use time to grow ourselves, creating and harnessing energy through thought, feelings and activities. It serves as a way of measuring what we are doing, and serves as a record-keeper of those activities.

Fluid and changing, time also serve as a measure of consciousness for those who are creating events in space. It is used to give order to sequences of events that occur in our lives, defining both the duration of events and the space (amount of time) in between them. In the course of this process, time provides the opportunity for our senses to join together, process information and make decisions. For example, take an action and feedback loop which provides the opportunity to reflect and identify mistakes in a logical sequence, all of which feeds into developing and understanding larger concepts and patterns, the process of meaning-making on which our judgment and decisions in the present are based. As is described in *Urantia* (1954, p. 1295):

> Experience, wisdom, and judgment are the concomitants of the lengthening of the time unit ... As the human mind reckons backward into the past, it is evaluating past experience for the purpose of bringing it to bear on a present situation. As mind reaches out into the future, it is attempting to evaluate the future significance of possible action. And having thus reckoned with both experience and wisdom, the human will exercise judgment-decision in the present, and the plan of action thus born of the past and the future becomes existent.

From a Quantum physics viewpoint, time appears to be both a wave function and a particle. Particles are confined to atomic structures, and the four forces (nuclear strong, nuclear weak, gravity and electromagnetic energy) have been identified as coming from these. Particles of time actually go backwards instead of forwards (MacFlouer, 2004-16), so time can only be measured as a particle when you look at it from the future to the past. If you are looking at time from its relationship to space, it appears that space is static, with things moving through that static space and time moving as a wave coming in the opposite direction through space. Using MacFlouer's example, think of space as a container that is spongy, with movement through space causing space to expand. As a wave, time is expanding with space.

Note that time occurs with and without accompanying forces. As a pragmatic example, an individual can literally float in thought, losing all track of time, or, conversely, be caught up in thoughts such as "I don't have enough time" or "We're late", which are accompanied by bursts of energy (physical and emotional in terms of stress) to resolve the perceived issue. Almost everything we think of as a time issue deals with knowledge, information and our interaction with others. The more forces are engaged over time, the faster we age. Thus, stress has a direct correlation to the amount of overall time available during a lifetime, with a low level of stress serving as a measure of the effective use of time. See the discussion of optimum arousal in Chapter 13.

At the same time (pardon the pun in the usage of this phrase), the larger the space between events in time the more forgetting that takes place and the more difficult it is to connect events that occur. Memory improves when there is less space between events. In Phase 1 of the Intelligent Social Change Journey (see Part II), we recognize a linear cause-and-effect relationship between actions taken and results. As change and the environment in which that change occurs becomes more complex, we move into Phase 2 of the ISCJ, where individuals and organizations learn to co-evolve in a CUCA environment (see Chapter 12/Part I). In this second Phase, it is not necessary, nor desirable, to recall the exact events that have occurred. These events, along with their context, have become part of larger patterns that are stored as invariant forms, that is, what is stored is what is necessary for the individual to re-create and connect knowledge to that which is of importance to the individual. That which is important is determined by the level and amount of focus (awareness and attention) and the strength of emotional tags. Memory was introduced in Chapter 5/Part I and is discussed in more depth in Chapter 18.

Throughout history, different cultures have perceived time in different ways. In modern Western culture, there is a linear progression. The future lies ahead and the past trails behind. For example, consider the flow of a river, or the path of an arrow or bullet on a target range, or a hiker on a trail. This is consistent with thinking about time as a wave. Conversely, in the modern-day African tribe from Mal (Dogon) or the Na-Khi of Tibet and China, there is the instinctive conception that the past is ahead (ancestors stand before you) and the future lies behind (descendants will follow you). This is consistent with thinking about time as a particle.

<<<<<<<<>>>>>>>

INSIGHT: **As discovered through Quantum physics, particles of time actually go backwards instead of forwards, so time can only be measured as a particle when you look at it from the future to the past. This is the instinctive conception believed by the modern-day African tribe from Mal (Dogon) and the Na-Khi of Tibet and China.**

<<<<<<<<>>>>>>>

In the Neolithic era in China (around 6000 B.C.), time was perceived as a circle and visioned as a serpent or dragon eating its own tail. Similar concepts are found in Egyptian, Hebrew and Greek history, and also appear in ancient hieroglyphic languages in Tibet and as part of the Vedic tradition of India. Time perceived as a spiral appears in ancient European societies such as the Celtic culture, as well as in Africa. For example, the African Tabwa tribe associates time with the shape of a shell, moving clockwise on the outside and counter-clockwise on the inside. This same pattern of alternating energy flows is reflected in Cooper's (2005) drawing of the rings of the Master Universe.

Time has also been considered an illusion, albeit a useful illusion. For example, the Vedic, Buddhist and Dogon literature perceive time as a reflection or image of a more fundamental reality on another plane of existence. Similar to our use of forces, we can also think of time and space in terms of opportunity—the opportunity to try different approaches to accomplishing something in life, and different solutions to problems, until we find the one that we feel is the best, offering us the opportunity to do it over and over again until we get it "right" in terms of achieving a desired future state.

Past, Present and Future

An interesting finding in Quantum mechanics is the discovery that electrons and protons can move backwards and forwards in time. As chaotic and strange as this sounds, there is argument that when time is separated from space, you end up with tachyon particles that move backwards in time. Carroll (2016) explains that all directions in space, including time, are created equal. He provides the example of videoing a pendulum rocking back and forth, which appears the same whether you run the video forward or in reverse. This simple example of a general principle says,

> For every way that a system can evolve forward in time in accordance with the laws of physics, there is another allowed evolution that is just 'running the system backward in time.' There is nothing in the underlying laws that says things can evolve in one direction in time but not the other. Physical motions, to the best of our understanding, are reversible. Both directions of time are on an equal footing. (Carroll, 2016, p. 55)

There is no before or after in nature. We live in the *present*, the NOW. Everything occurs simultaneously, everywhere at once, and the evidence is right at hand. As Wilber (1993, p. 84) describes,

> … simply stop reading and look up, where you will discover an infinite number of processes all happening at once: sun shining, heart beating, birds singing, kids playing, lungs breathing, dogs barking, wind blowing, crickets chirping, eyes seeing, ears hearing … These phenomena do not proceed one another nor follow one another in time—they are all happening everywhere at once, no before no after … [Nature] has the whole of its existence simultaneously, and that is the nature of Eternity.

Wilber (1993) contends that memory *creates* an illusion of time; that when we remember a past event it is only a dim picture that exists as a *present* experience. Similarly, Watts (1968, p. 82) calls memory a present trace of the past, only existing in the *present*. For example,

> … remember something. Remember the incident of seeing a friend walking down the street. What are you aware of? You are not actually watching the veritable event of your friend walking the street. You can't go up and shake hands with him, or get an answer to a question you forgot to ask him at the past time you are remembering. In other words, you are not looking at the real past at all. You are looking at a present trace of the past … From memories you infer that there have been past events. But you are not aware of any past events. You know the past only in the present and as part of the present.

Thus, it is that these memory traces provide us the connective tissue (a line, a succession) to link the past and the future, cause and effect, before and after, and yesterday and tomorrow.

The same concept applies to the future, since thinking about the future occurs as a *present* thought. As Schrödinger (1983, p. 145) states, "Mind is always *now*. There is really no before and after for Mind. There is only a *now* that includes memories and expectations." Thus, the present NOW includes all time, and as Wilber (1993, p. 86) concludes: "… it is only in confusing present memory with past knowledge that we conjure up, out of this present moment, the vast illusion called 'time'."

Similarly, Carroll reminds us that memories are features of the current state of the Universe, whether those memories appear in history books or photographs or are part of the neuronal patterns in our brains.

> The current state, by itself, constrains the past and future equally. But the current state plus the hypothesis of a low-entropy past gives us enormous leverage over the actual history of the Universe. It's that leverage that lets us believe (often correctly) that our memories are reliable guides to what actually happened. (Carroll, 2016, p. 62)

In this current state of NOW, we can perceive patterns and frequencies from the past and flip them to project patterns into the future.

The Gift of Planning

Planning is forethought—a mental activity focused on achieving a specific goal—and is associated with all three phases of our change model. As described above, when we expand consciousness, we expand our ability to see patterns and develop good predictive success, and help others do the same. Thus. planning, related to forecasting and predicting the future (see Chapter 22/Part IV), is an interactive part of consciousness. As an executive function of the frontal lobe, planning encompasses neurological processes that formulate, evaluate, select and sequence thoughts to move toward a desired goal. From the instant those thoughts emerge we are on the path of creation. As Mulford (2007, p.72) describes:

> When we form a plan for any business, any invention, any undertaking, we are making something of that unseen element, our thought, as real, though unseen, as any machine of iron or wood. That plan or thought begins, as soon as made, to draw to itself, in more unseen elements, power to carry itself out, power to materialize itself in physical or visible substance.

In the Industrial Age, plans became the mechanism to create the conditions (resources and events in time and space) to maximize the likelihood of future success. As Alerts and Hayes (2005) assert, there was the general faith that a systematic approach consisting of decomposition, specialization and optimization of components would handle even the really challenging problems. Military plans included five elements: missions, assets, boundaries, schedules and contingencies. In a steady environment this approach worked most of the time. However, it became problematic in more dynamic environments.

While planning was centralized, there was also the acknowledgement that in a changing, uncertain and complex environment, execution must be decentralized, where "the flexibility and innovation necessary for accomplishing the mission typically resided with those implementing the plans much more than with those developing them" (Alberts & Hayes, 2005, p. 48). Deliberate planning was the process to achieve force synchronization.

Through cultivating deliberate acts and movement. you increasingly lay a solid foundation of courage, both moral and physical. Note that deliberate acts do not always imply slowness. Just as thought moves rapidly, so too may it move the body when it is required. This can occur when the thought is clearly planned, seen and outlined in mind before it is allowed to act on the body. As Mulford (2007, p.44) describes:

> It is so seen or planned, and so acts to use the muscles in the rapid thrust and parry of the skilled fencer, and similarly with the professional danseuse, in fact in all superior accomplishments, be they of painter, musician or other artist. These, however, in many cases, are but partial controls of mind. Outside of his art, the artist may have little mental control or deliberation, and as a result be 'nervous' vacillating, easily disturbed, whimsical and timid. The mind is our garrison to be armed at all points and disciplined to meet any emergency.

Planning is a property of intelligent activity and always has a purpose. It is different than forecasting (predicting what the future will look like) in that the planning process maps potential futures, and generally includes multiple scenarios for potential future events. Scenarios are the articulation of possible future states, constructed within the imaginative limits of the author. While scenarios provide an awareness of alternatives—of value in and of itself—they serve as planning tools for possible future situations. The plan becomes a vehicle to respond to recognized objectives in each scenario.

<<<<<<<◇>>>>>>

INSIGHT: **Planning is a property of intelligent activity and always has a purpose.**

<<<<<<<◇>>>>>>

Planning is a learning process which includes two parts: the creation of myths about social realities and the process of emergence (Michael, 1977). For an expansion of our planning capability we look to the expanded experiential learning model developed by Bennet et al. (2015b). This model adds a fifth mode of social engagement to the experiential learning model, that is, in our focus, recognizing the global connectivity of people and the need for interoperability in the strategic planning approach, which brings an emergent quality into the process. Built on decentralized execution, an example of this is the *power to the edge* approach adopted by the U.S. Department of Defense in response to accelerated change and increased volatility (Meyer & Davis, 2003). This approach moves toward the metaphor of evolution in support of continuing innovation, concluding that organizations need to experiment rather than plan. As Alberts and Hayes (2005, p. 227) describe, "various kinds of experimentation activities ... need to be orchestrated as part of a concept-based experimentation campaign to conceive, refine, and fully mature innovation." They contend that the planning process needs to move away from a centralized, top-down, engineered process to,

> ... a process that works bottom-up; one that creates fertility, seeds ideas, nurtures them, selects the most promising, weeds out the losers, and fertilizes the winners. Only an empirically-based experimentation process that employs an appropriate set of measures can accomplish this. (Alberts & Hayes, 2005, p. 228).

A first step is the redesign of traditional exercises into incubators of innovation as a complement to experimentation, which they see as the fundamental mechanism to cope with change and fuel adaptation. They also recognize the necessity of interoperability and the power of sharing and collaborating. This is the co-evolving model of the Intelligent Complex Adaptive System provided as an example in Chapter 14 (Bennet & Bennet, 2004).

While mental thinking can potentially prepare people for future events, it is recognized that there is no linear extrapolation into the future in a changing, uncertain and complex environment (CUCA); that is, the environment of the Phase 2 (co-evolving) change model of the Intelligent Social Change Journey. This is why Alberts & Hayes (2005) feel that specific scenarios of interest, largely scripted, cannot provide sufficient freedom to produce the disruptive innovation that is needed. However, the experimentation and *power to the edge* approach advocated does *not* take into account the power of thought.

There is always an element of the unseen when we create a plan, or any business, invention or undertaking. This element is our thought, which, while it may be unseen is as real as any visible material object. As soon as it is made, that plan or thought draws to itself other unseen elements which provide the power to execute the plan or the thought, the "power to materialize itself in physical or visible substance" (Mulford, 2007, p. 72). Unfortunately, when we have fear or expect negative consequences we are also creating a construction of unseen elements which draw forces similar to that thought. This is the law of attraction described by Hicks and Hicks (2006) and described by Mulford (2007, p. 72) as building in unseen substance, the things we think about, "a construction which will draw to us forces or elements to aid us or hurt us, according to the character of thought we think or put out."

Marrying the mental faculties and the creative imagination, the planning process includes identifying goals and objectives, creating strategies to achieve these goals and objectives, organizing the resources and means to accomplish the strategies, and implementing those strategies. The secret of success is ensuring that the planning process represents intelligent activity, that is, *a state of interaction where intent, purpose, direction, values and expected outcomes are clearly understood and communicated among all parties, reflecting wisdom and achieving a higher truth.*

<<<<<<<<>>>>>>>

INSIGHT: **The secret of success is to ensure that the planning process represents intelligent activity.**

<<<<<<<<>>>>>>>

A tool for future thinking is scenario planning, or scenario building. In our earlier discussion of meaning in Chapter 5/Part I, we said that higher-order consciousness, as seen in humans, includes the ability to build past and future scenarios. Further, we discovered that planning, related to forecasting and predicting the future, is an interactive part of consciousness. Now you might be surprised that we will say that management is all about the future. Decisions are made based on expected outcomes, that is, things that will happen in the future. Management decisions are based on improving future organizational performance (Wade, 2012).

Scenarios are a form of story that serve as planning tools, providing a structured process for consciously thinking about—and planning for—the longer-term future. Introduced in the 1950's by Herman Kahn, scenario planning was first used in military war games in the 1960's, with a focus on the "predict and control" approach. Later, the emphasis shifted to analyze "cause and effect" relationships in order to better prepare for the future. As a foresight methodology, it is used to consider possible, plausible, probable and preferable outcomes. Possible outcomes (what might happen) are based on future knowledge; plausible outcomes (what could happen) are based on current knowledge; probable outcomes (what will most likely happen) are based on current trends; and preferable outcomes (what you want to happen) are based on value judgments (Bennet et al., 2015c).

****

TOOL 16-2: Scenario Building

Scenario Building is a creative and shared process that involves groups or teams while allowing time for reflection and creative dialogue about the current and future environment and what the organization may become. This specific process was developed for the U.S. Department of the Navy.

STEP (1): Identify a central issue or question. This step involves clarifying the strategic decisions the organization faces that are critical to the future, establishing the inter-relationship among them, and establishing a horizon time.

STEP (2): Identify the key decision factors within the immediate (micro) environment. This is generally done through brainstorming and answering a series of relevant structured questions.

STEP (3): Identify the larger drivers of the key decision factors in the macro environment (social, technological, economic, environmental and political).

STEP (4): Develop the structure for the scenario by grouping high impact/high uncertainty forces and drivers and potential responses. Wild cards, that is, low-probability, high-impact events such as a terrorist attack or disrupted water supply may be considered. Pre-thinking these events offers the opportunity to examine their implications and make better decisions should they occur. This process develops a ranking of possibilities.

STEP (5): Explore the implications of each scenario in relation to current and future strategy, and identify early indicators. This step should result in core strategies and contingency strategies. The aim is to identify strategies that are robust across all scenarios, given what is known and what might occur in the future.

STEP (6): Flesh out the details of the scenarios, creating a logical cause-and-effect flow with a timeline.

STEP (7): Refine and rewrite the scenarios to take them into a narrative form that is easily understood.

HINT: Consider the tenets of Appreciative Inquiry as you develop and refine these scenarios. (See the discussion of Appreciative Inquiry in Chapter 9/Part II.)

While these scenarios may prove useful, a significant advantage of this process is the perceptions, awareness and attitudes of the participating strategists relative to their organization, its environment and its evolution into the future. In other words, they will become much more sensitive to changes and potential risks and opportunities that may arise, and potentially more open, and responsive, to unknown and unperceived events.

****

Creative imagination has a role to play in scenario planning. In Chapter 9/Part II we said that there are two parts to creative imagination. When creative imagination is disconnected from the mental faculties such that pictures in our mind are unstructured and conflict with one another, it is not actionable and considered fantasy, although still may offer ideas for future actions. The second part is factual creative imagination and represents actual or potentially actual occurrences based upon the situation and context of an event or series of events; this is actionable in the situation and context at hand (MacFlouer, 2004-16). See Tool 92: Practicing Mental Imagining.

The focus on critical uncertainties necessary to move through scenario planning is often quite difficult. Wade (2012) argues that scenario planning is all about thinking the unthinkable. Yet, we are moving closer to understanding that we are co-creators of our reality (developed in Chapter 23/Part IV) and the powerful impact of attention and intention (discussed in depth in Chapter 25/Part IV) and thought (expanded in Chapter 26/Part IV) in this process of co-creation. Thus, an intelligent approach is necessary for effective scenario planning, that is, building scenarios that are based on factual creative imagination while simultaneously ensuring the opportunities offered by every situation are creatively planned into the scenario, always ending with multiple options, multiple choices.

Ultimately, planning is about the future and, as we have learned along the way, living is a continuous journey of change. There is a moral challenge associated with planning. Planning is intended as a fundamental guideline, with the objective of planning to *maximize the options of future decision-makers* (Churchman, 1977; von Foerster, 1977). While we cannot control the future, we can nurture its unfolding, and prepare for the potential of creative leaps. Thus, planning itself becomes a tool for change, and helping others learn how to use this tool fully—a *pass it on* strategy— becomes a powerful way to help the best future emerge.

Exploring Time: Building Conceptual Relationships

Without committing to a prescriptive way of thinking about time and space, let's consider conceptually how these different beliefs affect our understanding of time. We begin with laying out our assumptions for the conceptual models we intend to visualize. Here is our starting point:

* In our physical reality, all things exist as patterns of energy.

* As energy, everything is interconnected.

* Time and space have some relationship.

* Time does not exist at the speed of light.

* We are all vibrational beings (made up of ever-moving atoms, electrons/neutrons/protons, quarks, etc.)

* Since energy conserves itself, the life force is infinite, whether perceived as "me" or "we".

* Consciousness is the ability to focus, a level of awareness, the relationships among that of which we are aware, and the relationships among our self and that of which we are aware.

Our first conceptual model at Figure 16-1 considers time as linear. At the speed of light there is no time or space, thus the individuated "Me's" in the model, perceived as separate in linear time, work as a collective whole. Linear time is perceived as a continuous series of "now's" with memory of past NOW's available.

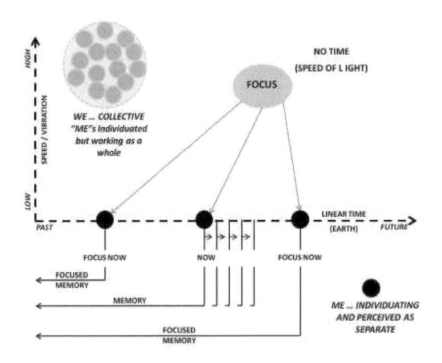

Figure 16-1: *Conceptual model of time as linear.*

If we consider time as circular, this conceptual model presents quite differently (Figure 16-2). Again, at the speed of light (in the center of the circle) there is no time. In this circular model, the past, present and future are all happening simultaneously, with the focused NOW of the individual "me" a choice anywhere along the parameter of the circle. Note that time is only fractured into the past, present and future because we perceive it that way. The more complete the experience of NOW, the more focus on the NOW, the more it is happening in the NOW.

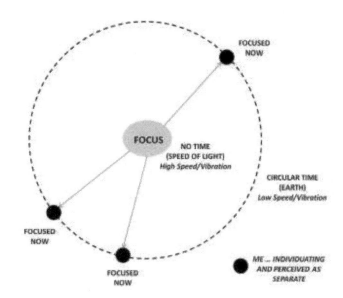

Figure 16-2: *Conceptual model of time as circular.*

The idea of a spiral provides the opportunity to focus at any point located in the spiral. The point of no time could be perceived as at the small tip of the spiral or as coming from a place apart from the spiral. See Figure 16-3. From a conceptual viewpoint, recall that our galaxy takes the shape of a spiral. As a mental exercise and using the conceptual model of time as a spiral, what might this say about our galaxy and our focal point within that galaxy?

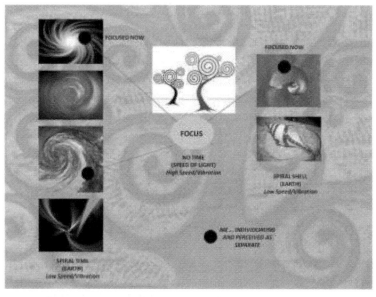

Figure 16-3: *Conceptual model of time as a spiral.*

These conceptual models are meant to trigger YOUR thinking about the relationship of time and space, and YOUR relationship to these concepts as a conscious being. You are encouraged to create your own model utilizing the unique learning and frames of reference reflecting your individuated experiences in life.

The Rhythm of Change

Reflect for a moment. Without time and space would there be rhythm? Would there be change? Within our perception, time measures motion, and motion itself is a kind of change. A change in the motion of an object implies that time has passed, that is, the time when the object was at one place and then another (a runner or train), or the time when the object was one thing then became another (changing water to ice or steam). Without time and space would there be learning?

As introduced in Chapter 15, change can be managed through a set of strategic initiatives designed to bring about specific emergent characteristics. The timing of these strategic initiative thrusts is correlated with the system's ability to recognize value and begin implementation. Highly dependent on the consciousness level of the organization, there is a receptivity rhythm that can be monitored based on feedback loops (Barquin et al., 2001). It is loosely analogous to Isaac Newton's fundamental laws of motion, stating that to maintain a change in motion you must have a continuous force. If the pressure for change is a constant, change itself will accelerate. See Chapter 17 for a short treatment of the rhythms of life. In Chapter 24/Part IV there is an example of the use of rhythm in promoting propaganda.

Taking Advantage of Time and Space

Because it is so entangled with consciousness and intelligent activity, all of this conversation about time and space can become confusing. However, it does lay the groundwork for figuring out how to take advantage of time and space in our everyday lives. As McMoneagle (2017) says from his personal experience in remote viewing,[16-1] while time and space are an illusion, the experience is real.

Recognizing the importance of time has brought us, individually and as organizations, to a focus on time management, that is, planning and exercising efficient and effective use of time spent on specific activities. This would include setting priorities, carrying out any activity around those priorities, and reducing time spent on non-priorities. The popular "80-20 rule" called Pareto analysis was based on the idea that 80 percent of tasks can be completed in 20 percent of available time, thus providing a way to sort out priorities. This simple tool, which helped bring priorities into mind, provided a way of balancing thought, moving those priorities in the same direction, reducing forces, and allowing more creativity.

Let's briefly look at a few ideas of how to use time.

First, the mind has the ability to hold time in place. While we almost always live in memories of the past and anticipation of the future, if we choose, we can stop the thinking of the mind and access the quiet mind of the present. While this may take some practice, one approach to getting this started is to focus your attention on the small soft spot at the top of the head. When all your attention is on this spot, there is not much room left for a stream of thought or monkey chatter.

Second, the measure of what we create is determined by time. In the physical plane, we push (over time) through forces to create, with the creation a result, and measure, of our effort. Thus, from the physical plane viewpoint, time is primarily about the past.

Third, time and space enable development of patterns. As advocated earlier in this chapter, patterns from the past can be used to extrapolate the future. For example, consider changepoint detection used by statisticians. Changepoint detection is the identification of a definite change in patterns beyond normal fluctuations, that is, looking across a large population base for small changes happening at the same time or in close proximity. A result might be recognition of a large number of people in a specific area calling in sick with similar symptoms, which could lead to early detection of a flu epidemic. The recognition of existing and creation of new patterns is essential to the development of conceptual thinking necessary for co-evolving (Phase 2 of the ISCJ).

Fourth, when we focus our energy for the benefit and health of others, we discover that time and space become closer, with the perception of more time available and an ease of moving through space.

Fifth, time provides a vehicle to correct mistakes, to experiment, to learn. When we move along an uncomfortable path, once our awareness is raised, we have the opportunity to choose differently. Time and space provide opportunities for the future. As the popular adage goes, *it's not over until the fat lady sings*. This strikes home for one of the authors who in her early years was an opera singer.

Sixth, in the present we have the opportunity to retrospectively review thoughts and actions, reflect on those thoughts and actions, mentally restructure them and perceive different outcomes. Much like scenario planning, this retrospection sets the groundwork for taking different actions in the present and future.

Seventh, time and space enable the discovery of higher levels of truth. As we identify events that are similar, we are able to construct conceptual models that help explain these events. The continuous discovery of new examples provides the opportunity for new truth to emerge.

And so forth through time …

Questions for Reflection:

How can you leverage this deeper understanding of the time/space continuum to enhance your Intelligent Social Change Journey?

Do you effectively manage time in implementing your complex changes?

If you had to build a social-conscious time management model, what would it look like?

Given that its theoretically possible to turn time backwards, what from your past would you change?

Chapter 17
Connections as Patterns

SUBTOPICS: INFORMATION INCOMING ... PATTERNS OF THE PAST ... EXPLORING ENERGY PATTERNS IN THE MYST ... PATTERNS AS STORY ... THE STORY OF SELF ... THE RHYTHMS OF LIFE ... FINAL THOUGHT

FIGURES: 17-1. REPRESENTATIVE TEXTURES OF THE *MYST* PHENOMENON ... **17.2.** THIS *MYST* PHOTOGRAPH ENTITLED "ENTANGLEMENT" ENGAGES THE META-PATTERN OF TUBES ... **17.3.** THE FORMING OF THE *MYST* ... **17-4.** IN THIS PHOTOGRAPH ENTITLED "THE GIFT OF LIGHT", GIVEN NO EXTERNAL INFLUENCE AND AN APPROXIMATE 100×100 PIXEL SQUARE, THE PROBABILITY OF THE PINK SHAPE APPEARING IN THE PHOTOGRAPH IS 10^{-94}.

TOOLS: 17-1. THINKING PATTERNS

To clearly see the direction we are heading, it's a good idea to first understand where we have come from, where we are, and how we got from there to here. This has proven incredibly difficult in an increasingly complex environment where invisible forces combine to form emergent characteristics that at best are difficult to directly connect to those forces. However, when we are able to identify the iteration (repetition) of patterns, we are better able to connect potential indirect cause and effect relationships in the future. In short, in the NOW we learn from patterning the past in order to better predict the future.

Underlying the physical Universe there is energy and patterns of energy. The term "pattern" comes from the French word *patron* which refers to a specific theme that reoccurs in events, objects, or movement. Patterns can be based on repetition (the same thing appearing again and again), periodicity (recurrence at regular intervals), similarity (likeness, qualities or features in common), or symmetry (balanced proportions, exact correspondence in position) and translation (a change in form or state, transference to a different place).

As introduced in Chapter 2/Part I, if a specific pattern or set of patterns is not random, then it contains information. However, whether a specific non-random pattern is *recognized as information* depends on the individual looking at the pattern. For example, if the pattern is a Chinese symbol and the observer does not understand Chinese and is not capable of interpreting the pattern of the symbol, then the observer acquires no information from the symbol. However, to a Chinese observer the same symbol may contain huge significance and meaning.

Building on this idea, any given pattern may contain different information for different observers. Many people have different interpretations, that is, they get different information from the same pattern. These differences happen for a number of reasons. First, we tend to see what we are looking for, what we are interested in, or what strikes an emotional chord in us. Since no two people are alike (different DNA, beliefs, passions, etc.), the things we are looking for, interested in, or emotionally charged about can be quite different. Second, as has been previously discussed, the interpretation and meaning of incoming patterns are very much a function of preexisting patterns in the brain. Each individual has had different experiences in life (culture, family, activities, work, etc.), all of which are reflected in the patterns in the individual's brain.

Humans are ALWAYS looking for relationships among things—events, happenings, people, thoughts. We are part of the grand search for patterns, for creative association (Gell-Mann, 1994). The human mind has evolved to discover patterns. In fact, "the human mind yearns for the beauty of order and pattern" (Whitfield & Ayensu, 1982, p. 9). With each individual's pattern detection and formulation system fueled by all that it is to be human, an entangled matrix of thoughts, feelings and experiences emerge within and without throughout life. *Around us weave the energies of probability, randomness and chaos married to characteristics of change, uncertainty and unpredictability.* Just as we take the events of our lives and create a story of us, whether real or imaginary, we discover and invent the patterns which we seek, driven by the need for structure, connections and meaning.

<<<<<<<<>>>>>>>

INSIGHT: **Just as we take the events of our lives and create a story of us, whether real or imaginary, we discover and invent the patterns which we seek, driven by the need for structure, connections and meaning.**

<<<<<<<<>>>>>>>

Nature herself repeats patterns at various levels, building multidimensional patterns of iterated cells. It wasn't until 1975 that Benoit Mandelbroth, a mathematician working for IBM at the time, who later became Sterling Professor of Mathematical Science at Yale University, observed the presence of repeating patterns, much like Russian nesting dolls, within the complexity of fractal images. He explored "seemingly separate entities, from the shapes of coastlines to plants, blood vessels, human pursuits, music, architecture, even stock markets and clustering of galaxies" (Courteney, 2010, p. 219). Through mathematical analysis, he demonstrated that, no matter how chaotic it appears, there is an underlying order to *everything* in our Universe. He called the underlying patterns *fractals* and concluded that the appearance of disorder is merely a *function of limits of perception* (Mandelbrot, 1983). This was the beginning of fractal geometry, which revealed the design principle of Nature. This also demonstrates a human paradox, that man is simultaneously subservient to nature at the material level while possessing a unique liberty, freedom of choice and action. As succinctly stated in *Urantia* (1954, p. 1221), "Man is a part of nature—he exists in nature—and yet is able to transcend nature."

More recently, Sheldrake (1989) forwarded the hypothesis of formative creation, which proposes that *memory is inherent in nature*. This suggests that all-natural things inherit a collective memory from previous populations of similar natural things. Further, through repetition, these collective memories become habits. Thus, habits are inherent in all living things. And as that extends to humanity, "All humans too draw upon a collective memory, to which all in turn contribute" (Sheldrake, 1989, p. xvii). This process in which the past becomes present, involving formative causal influences transmitted through both space and time, Sheldrake calls morphic resonance.

Similarly, Usatynski (2008) has cultivated the field of instinctual intelligence, which refers to basic instinctual programs within the human that have innate intelligence aimed at survival in an unpredictable environment. These would relate to the programs described in Chapter 4/Part I as part of the personality. This intelligence requires learning, the continual modification of our nervous system as it adapts to continuous change, and then the passing on of that learning to future generations, who in turn change and pass on to future generations. We participate in this transformation through our expression of life. As Usatynski (2008, Preface) says,

> The most primal impulses are brought into alignment with the **most precious of human qualities like compassion, generosity, patience, and intelligence** [emphasis added]. Modern scientists are finally acknowledging what the ancient mystics have always known: our basic instinctual programming can not only learn and adapt—it can actually evolve.

A romantic treatment of this concept is that of the character of *torchbearers* forwarded in *Urantia* (1954, p. 909): "Social inheritance enables man to stand on the shoulders of all who have preceded him, and who have contributed aught to the sum of culture and knowledge." The marked increase in world travel and unparalleled improvement in methods of connection and communication have made this social inheritance highly visible, as well as having a great impact on the furtherance of civilization and the advancement of culture. For those who have traveled the Ph.D. learning trail, it is similarly described as a journey of "becoming" built on the thought of those who have come before.

Because at every level of complexity individual organisms (systems, holons) are indeterminate, morphic fields are probabilistic in nature when interacting with material forms. Sheldrake (1989, p. 120) provides the following description.

Random fluctuations in the electrical potential across the membranes of nerve cells affect their tendency to 'fire,' and this has important consequences in the functioning of the nervous system. For these reasons alone, it seems natural to assume that morphic fields are probabilistic in nature.

Thus, Sheldrake's morphic field appears to share properties of both Pierre Teilhard de Chardin's Noosphere (a consciousness field) and a Quantum field (a probabilistic field), perhaps different frames of reference for describing the same energy field.

Numbers lend themselves well to the creation of patterns. We use numbers to create grand designs for exploring our Universe. As Broadway drama critic Brendan Gill says,

> When it comes to dealing with time—a mystery whose nature remains largely inaccessible to us—we try to accommodate to the mystery by forcing patterns of numbers upon it. We divide it into units of measurement, such as seconds, minutes, hours, days, weeks, months, years, and decades, that give it the appearance of partaking of some Grand Design, useful to us for the planting of crops, the keeping of records, and the prediction of things to come. But we have no proof that any such Grand Design exists outside our senses …. (Gill, 1984, p. xx)

An interesting neuroscience finding is that patterns stay in the mind longer than facts. Goldberg (2005) points out that the aging brain can accomplish mental feats that are different than younger brains. Although older people forget names, acts, and words, they have the capability of remembering high-level patterns and meaningful insights that we often consider as wisdom.

Information Incoming

We started this book with the assumption that everything—at least in our physical reality—is energy and patterns of energy, and that information is a form of energy. Looking from an organizational framework, how do we find meaning in the plethora of information that is assailing our senses every moment of every day?

In our world of technology, data mining, including the use of artificial intelligence such as automated reasoning programs, emerged to support identification of patterns. For example, the use of supermarket loyalty cards in exchange for discounts enables the tracking of detailed purchasing patterns. Prominent methods in data mining include link analysis, software agents, machine learning, neural networks and, more recently, cognitive systems from the creation of artificial intelligence to development of systems that can supplement and expand the capability of the human mind.

Link analysis does just that; it uses mathematics and technology to connect people and organizations to events. Identification of these connections enables human experts to investigate each link and record detail, and to discover new nodes that connect to existing ones or new links between existing nodes (Devlin & Lorden, 2007). A subprocess of link analysis is geometric clustering, looking at the relationships among clustered events. For example, geometric clustering is the process used in social network analysis, which is a process for mapping the relationships among people, teams or across organizations. It is particularly effective in assessing the flow of information through communication and collaboration, and geometric clustering enables identification of people who are central (overly central?) and peripheral (underutilized?) to an organization. The extent to which a group is connected, or the extent to which it is split into subgroups, can be an indicator of a problem, difficulty, or strength in moving information from one area of the network to another (Bennet & Bennet, 2004).

Software agents come out of artificial intelligence research. These are self-contained computer programs that act autonomously to accomplish specific programmed tasks. For example, drug stores use software agents to mitigate the potential danger among prescription drugs, and banks use software agents to monitor the pattern of credit card activities. Machine learning is also a product of artificial intelligence research. Development of learning algorithms—which connect differentiating features of the information being searched—are essential for exploring the patterns of big data to identify key features and higher order patterns.

Neural networks, which are excellent for recognition of patterns, are another kind of computer program, which refers to the attempt to create a program that could simulate the way the human brain works. This attempt was a formidable task. It is not simply the large number of connections (synapses) in the human brain that make this difficult, and it is not *what* the human brain does, but understanding *how* it does it— that step portrayed in a myriad of cartoons that says "then a miracle occurs"—that challenges the designer's intellect. For example, building on the early connection machines made by Thinking Machines, Inc. (Hillis, 1987), at the turn of the 21st century Brown University set out to build a brain-like computer, what was called the Ersatz Brain Project. While only focusing on a microcosm of the brain, when the project was over the team had recognized that by requiring software to use brain-like constraints new ways to tackle old problems emerged (Anderson & Allopenna, 2008). Further, they realized that an important application of such a machine would be the realization of a large network where individual nodes having complex internal structures would provide flexibility and associative capabilities beyond semantic networks. The understanding was beginning to be voiced that as we design machines to mimic our minds, we need to make sure that those machines are equipped with sufficient diversity. They need a similar diversity to that which distinguishes humans from most other animals and from machines built in the past, "stemming from what we each have made of ourselves: a colossal collection of different ways to deal with different situations and predicaments" (Minsky, 2006, p. 6).

Cognitive systems move beyond Artificial Intelligence approaches to exploration of this technology to aid learning and decision-making. In 2005 cognitive science and technology became a core research focus for Sandia National Laboratories. For Sandia, cognitive systems include technologies that utilize computational models of human cognitive processes or knowledge of specific experts or other individuals (Sandia, 2007). These systems accurately infer user intent, remember experiences and provide simulated experts to help users analyze situations and make decisions. Through modeling a virtual "you" and simulating thinking patterns, individual strengths can be reinforced and weaknesses mitigated. Imagine this as the basis for a learning system, a human-technology partnering that is already happening today. This is clearly not the AI of the past. As described by Chris Forsythe, intent is modeled to a specific individual; knowledge is associative, with emphasis on pattern recognition not just rule-based representations and logic; and this is a dynamic complex system that may easily adapt to changing circumstances (Forsythe, 2003).

While not the subject of this book, there is so much more underway that even as we attempt to capture a few of those ideas, something new is emerging and those ideas become antiquated. What we have tried to convey in a very limited way is that, just as with the human mind/brain, possibilities abound, and the only limits are those imposed by ourselves.

Patterns of the Past

An approach to studying the changing times and the content and context of a situation is to identify patterns of change and the underlying principles or environmental drivers that are generating that change, unpredictability and apparent complexity. Much of this kind of knowledge resides in your unconscious, particularly if you have previously and deliberately looked for these characteristics. Thus, you may not be consciously aware of them but your unconscious can, and often will, be aware of them as you observe and study a situation. While perhaps outside of your awareness, you are creating knowledge in the form of understanding, meaning, insight, patterns and heuristics in your mind, albeit mostly in the unconscious part.

As we are exposed to more diverse and varying conditions, the brain creates new patterns and strengths of connections and thereby changes its physiological structure (Kandel, 2006). It is also true that the structure of the brain—containing a huge number of networks of neurons—significantly influences how incoming signals representing new thoughts (patterns composed of networks of neurons) are formed. Through the process of associative patterning, these new patterns entering the brain associate or connect with patterns already in the brain.

Pattern thinking is not primarily thinking through patterns, although over time this will occur. Rather, it is using your inside world to look for patterns in the outside world, and bringing them into your conscious awareness. The intent of pattern thinking is to let the pattern emerge as a mode of understanding a situation, purposefully thinking about external patterns in order to better anticipate and respond to change, that is, to expand your understanding, solve problems, create new ideas and improve your capacity to forecast the outcomes of decisions.

Thinking *about* patterns is different than thinking *with* patterns. If you start with a specific pattern in mind, no doubt you will find it. This is the same phenomenon that occurs when you purchase a new car and you begin seeing similar cars every time you are on the freeway, although you'd never noticed them before. However, pattern emergence can be stimulated by other patterns. For example, the systems thinking approach developed by Peter Senge is based on matching a recurring set of relationships (archetypes) to a situation at hand (Senge, 1990). While this force-fitting can certainly help facilitate an understanding of causal relationships in simple and complicated situations, recall that complexity infers difficulty in understanding something due to the large number of unpredictable and nonlinear relationships. Yet once you have used the models of complexity over and over again, you begin to *think systems* and discover systems patterns beyond the archetypes. Both systems thinking and complexity thinking are forms of pattern thinking, enabling the individual to build the ability to recognize, comprehend and learn how to influence complex systems (Bennet & Bennet, 2008b; 2013).

From the neuroscience perspective, pattern thinking involves mental exercise that stimulates the brain. The best mental exercise is new learning in multiple areas of the brain, acquiring new knowledge and doing things you've never done before (Amen, 2005). Making new connections, seeing new relationships, and bringing patterns into your conscious stream of thought does just that. For example, there are patterns over time: trends, cycles, spikes, curves, sinks, sources, and so on. Forecasters use scenario planning: setting up patterns, creating self-consistent patterns over time and looking at what happens. Scenario development can be used to create applicable knowledge by starting with the recent past and developing several possible scenarios for the future. Here you may have to identify trends by averaging over time, considering the most desirable, acceptable and least desirable possible outcomes. Knowledge can be developed from creating, studying and playing with the possible results of these scenarios. Other ways to think about forecasting is in terms of laying out a trail (a pattern) with milestones (symbols), and, of course, through dynamic modeling.

There is an important role that symmetry and parsimony play in patterns and in the physical world. Symmetry is the exact correspondence of form on opposite sides of a centerline or point (*American Heritage Dictionary*, 2006). Parsimony is the principle of least action or energy and conservation. Nature is fond of doing things in the most economical and efficient way. Since symbols are short forms of larger patterns, they help facilitate thinking about symmetry, and can help us recognize simpler solutions to issues and situations. (Symbolic Representation as a Knowledge Capacity is introduced in Chapter 21.)

When addressing a difficult situation, while there is generally not a visible cause-and-effect relationship, the amount and depth of study offer potential for discovering a solution or solution set. Individuals who are continuous learners, regardless of their focus of learning or areas of passion, will often see patterns that suggest action directions. While once in the middle of a situation, even the most rigorous focus and attention to detail may not present solutions, this focus and learning is supplying the unconscious with additional information to complex with all your experiences of life and identify patterns of response. In other words, while you may not have immediate answers, you are accelerating your unconscious learning (the unconscious can detect patterns that the conscious stream cannot) and increasing the potential for intuitive insights.

The above discussion brings home the fact that the mind/brain develops robustness and deep understanding derived from its capacity to use past learning and memories to complete incoming information. Instead of storing all the details, it stores only meaningful information in invariant form. This provides the ability to create and store higher level patterns while simultaneously semantically complexing incoming information with internal memories, adapting those memories to the situation at hand. Through these processes—and many more that are not yet understood—the brain supports survival and sustainability in a complex and unpredictable world. For example, our very survival is dependent on recognizing patterns such as weather cycles that drive our planting, harvesting and storing of food (Lipton, 2005).

****

TOOL 17-1: THINKING PATTERNS

In the latter part of the 20th century, the authors included the phrase *every decision is a guess about the future* in all of our briefings on decision-making. However, in working with the implementation of Knowledge Management in the U.S. Department of the Navy at the turn of the century, it became clear that the practices considered as *best* in one part of the organization failed in another part of the organization. This was early in the implementation process, when the understanding was just emerging that knowledge is context sensitive and situation dependent. *Yet there were similarities*; the *types* of things that were similar.

As more implementation examples of similar practices became available, recognizable patterns began to emerge. At this point, we began to purposefully look for patterns. If we found similar patterns occurring, we could more accurately predict the outcome of our implementation process. In other words, it was no longer a random guess about the future. Similarly, Lipton and Bhaerman (2009, p. 217) found, "If a pattern can be recognized, then the accuracy of predicting a future event is relatively high ... if events are found to be random, then all predictions are essentially guesses with an accuracy based on chance." This tool is focused on tapping into the innate human ability to recognize patterns.

STEP (1): Find a place where you will not be disturbed and briefly close your eyes and take several deep breaths. Open your eyes. Then sit comfortably, ready to take notes.

STEP (2): Consider the group of things or series of incidents in which you are searching for connections. If this is a group of things, briefly write down each item's characteristics such as how it looks and what it is made of, how it is created/developed, its purpose, how it is used, etc. If this is a series of incidents, briefly write down for each incident the subject (who or what) and the verb (action occurring) and any descriptive adjectives that come to mind describing the incident, the people involved, the place and timing, the outcome, and the why (if known).

STEP (3): Look across the group and consider the *differences* among the things or incidents. Note these as characteristics.

STEP (4): Look across the group and consider the *similarities* among the things or incidents. Note these as characteristics.

STEP (5): Considering both differences and similarities, identify categories into which these differences and/or similarities could fall. Keep searching until you can bring two or more characteristics of *different things or incidents* together into a category. Repeat until you have discovered all the categories that connect the things or incidents.

STEP (6): Now look at how the categories fit together. *ASK:* How do these things relate? Are these different things the same *types* of things? Are there patterns emerging?

STEP (7): Repeat Steps 3-6 until you are satisfied you have discovered all there is to discover.

HINT: This process works better in a facilitated collaborative group looking from multiple frames of reference!

****

Note that there is a difference between pattern identification and trend extrapolation. Patterns deal with repeatable associations and connections; trends deal with movements in the same direction over time. Throughout the history of futures research, trend extrapolation has been the most popular forecasting tool, and it is still a habit of many organizational planners today. Trend extrapolation is recent-past oriented and carries with it the assumption that people are objective. It does not delve into the more distant past, nor consider the future potential non-rational behaviors of human beings.

For example, behavior pattern analysis includes human actors such as the leaders of companies who carry a picture or perception of the character and purpose of the company. Their personal gestalt or worldview is going to be imposed on the technical, economic or financial aspects of any situation. As Simmonds (1977, p. 26) describes, "The resulting decisions may be wise or less wise, but they include the ambitions of the people involved, the friendships and the personality clashes, the power struggles and the ups and downs of real life." Using this broad, adaptive framework allows detection of directions of change, thus providing the opportunity to anticipate their implications. "The more complex, the more fluid, the situation—the greater the power, the greater the insight, of this kind of approach." (Simmonds, 1977, p. 26)

Exploring Energy Patterns in the *Myst*

We will use the *Myst* phenomenon that occurs on the 450-acre farm of the Mountain Quest Institute (MQI)—and other natural settings around the world—to briefly look at the process of pattern identification and recognition. While the phenomenon is quite unusual, the approach to exploring the phenomenon has been quite rigorous and heavily supported by development of the mental faculties.

The *Myst* phenomenon as a form is built on small dots of electromagnetic energy in the air, which are called orbs. As discovered through research and repetition, the orbs attract water molecules in the air which, in the instant present in various shapes such that they can be captured by a camera, and then disappear. While this pattern exploration will only represent a small piece of what has been a seven-year research project for the Bennets, it will hopefully serve as an example of how to explore patterns in nature, or perhaps your own patterns from the past.

Much like other patterns in nature, the *Myst* is somewhat chaotic, never exactly repeating a pattern, though consistent in many similar elements. Since ultimately we are looking for meaning in patterns, in addition to looking for those things which repeat themselves (characteristics, appearance, response, etc.), we search for *common principles* behind similar patterns that occur. For example, MQI's Quarter Horse Paint mare named Vision Quest is brown and white. While her mother (Calamity Jane) had different markings or patterns, nonetheless they are both Quarter Horse Paint mares that are brown and white. These are high-level similarities, although digging deeper into personality characteristics would also provide similarities as well as differences. The question then becomes whether the set of similar characteristics applies to all/most Quarter Horse Paint mares that are brown and white? Pattern formation in developmental biology is the mechanism by which equivalent cells assume complex forms and functions. In science pattern formation is the visible and ordered outcomes of self-organization built on a set of common principles. Are there underlying common principles behind the *Myst* phenomena? How deep can we delve to help identify differences, discover similarities and uncover meaning? Meaning, of course, is our most desirable goal.

Patterns can provide information, and by studying them carefully we may gain insights and understanding of what they mean. One approach to pattern recognition is the assignment of labels to a given input. An example is developing a classification or clustering system. For the *Myst* phenomenon we chose descriptive words based on visual representations of the phenomenon in terms of texture. These included: Circles (Standard, Crystalized); Clouds (Formed, Swoops, Splashed); Pocked; Fluff; Dots; Soft Light; and Bright Light. While one presentation can include multiple textures, forms or figures appear to be more exclusive in terms of texture. See Figure 17-1. Over time observation of these attributes gently leads us to think of specific characteristics in terms of energy output, which in turn leads us to explore potential sources of those energy outputs, or at least ones of which we are aware. For example, specific textures appear when there is a higher level of water vapor in the air, or during a clear night versus a cloudy night, or when there is a full moon. Thus, we begin to develop an understanding of the relationships among various aspects of energy in the night setting of the farm.

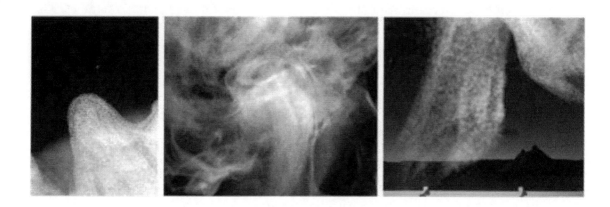

Figure 17-1. *Representative textures of the Myst phenomenon. (L-R) Dots (Rounded and Bounded); Fluff (with Light Striations) (note the arrows); and Circles.*

Shapes themselves, as form, are patterns, or metapatterns, that bound space. In Chapter 16 we introduced the relationship of space and form. Form exists in space and space exists in form; thus, at the material level, all patterns of reality occupy space. Space and form are mutually dependent and inseparable (Wilber, 1993). Let's briefly explore the significance of form.

Metapatterns are patterns of patterns (Bateson, 1979), grand-scale, inclusive patterns that help us understand ourselves and the functioning of the Universe. As Volk describes,

> ... a metapattern is a pattern so wide-flung that it appears throughout the spectrum of reality: in clouds, rivers, and planets; in cells, organisms, and ecosystems; in art, architecture, and politics ... representing all of human creativity.

The sphere is a metapattern. Perhaps it could be expected that orbs take the shape of a sphere. The omnipresent sphere is a universally abundant shape, the shape from which all living things emerge and the beginning point of complex individuals (Volk, 1995). Examples range from human ovaries to eggs; the fertilized eggs of frogs, sea urchins and worms to the green balls in freshwater algae colonies in various kinds of marine plankton; pulsars to black holes; and moons to planets and suns. Even atoms were originally thought of in terms of space-filling balls. As Volk (1995, p. 6) describes:

> When alone in space, like a miniature star, a hydrogen atom's cloud of charge density created by its single electron extends and fades into spherical infinity (the so-called 1s electron: s for spherical) ... The sphere thus appears to reign as dominant shape in the astronomically immense, the atomic infinitesimal, and the ancient or nascent living. No other shape is so universally abundant, so insistent as the omnipresent sphere.

<<<<<<<◇>>>>>>

INSIGHT: **The sphere, a universally abundant shape, is the shape from which all living things emerge, and is the beginning point of complex individuals such as the human.**

<<<<<<<◇>>>>>>

There are many reasons why the sphere emerges as the prominent shape throughout nature. Energy is always conserved; you cannot create it or destroy it; you can only change its form and/or move it around. A compacted surface area has significant biological advantages, providing the smallest surface and strongest structure for the greatest volume. Because it is a low maintenance shape, many cells are spherical. For example, the majority of cells in the human immune system (T-cells, B-cells, and the natural killer cells) are spherical.

In space, a liquid ball develops a "skin" that is self-created from surface tension. A leaky faucet demonstrates this same behavior as the water forms into a drop, naturally forming a skin as the fluids drive to achieve "states of lowest energy, which translates into the lowest total area of free surface" (Volk, 1995, p. 12).

<<<<<<<◇>>>>>>>

INSIGHT: **Energy is always conserved; you cannot create it or destroy it; you can only change its form and/or move it around.**

<<<<<<<◇>>>>>>>

When moving, spheres are omnidirectional, and, because roundness minimizes drag, when propelled they can spin in any direction with minimal air resistance. Further, throughout history the sphere has represented power. For example, the sphere (an orb of power) appears in the portraitures of European royalty and is often depicted in the hand of Jesus. Thus, physical attributes of spheres such as omnidirectionality, surface area and strength are part of the sphere's archetypal attributes equating power, equanimity, idealization, and perfection (Volk, 1995). These connections are observed in *Timaeus*, when Plato describes the origins of the Universe.

> Creator compounded the world … as far as possible a perfect whole and of perfect parts … leaving no remnants out of which another such world might be created … that figure … which comprehends within itself all other figures … the form of a globe, round as from a lathe, having its extremes in every direction equidistant from the center, the most perfect and the most like itself of all figures … the surface smooth all around … because the living being had no need of eyes when there was nothing remaining outside to be seen. (Hutchins, 1952)

Counterparts to the sphere, and also considered metapatterns, are sheets (flat planes, similar to a pancake) and tubes (rounded lines, similar to a spaghetti noodle). In the biological world an example of sheets are the green leaves on plants used to absorb light, with a surface area enhancement that is 20-40 times greater than volume (Volk, 1995, p. 31). Another function of sheets related to energy transfer occurrences is the ability to capture motion. Examples are the ear drum (capturing sound waves) and the sail of a sailboat (capturing wind currents). Sheets also transfer matter, as occurs in the leaf as it gathers carbon dioxide, disposes of oxygen, and transpires water to cool the leaf (similar to human sweating). Energy and matter also carry messages through light, the universal bearer of differences that make a difference (Bateson, 1979). Sheets are different than spheres in their surface-to-volume ratios as well as in their directionality. For example, tossing a Frisbee is very different than throwing a baseball. Given the general viewpoint of two-dimensions in pictures, it is difficult to identify sheets in the *Myst* phenomenon, although it is assumed that they are present.

Like sheets, tubes have a greater surface area than spheres with equivalent volumes. In nature they too are used as transfer surfaces. For example, a pine needle captures photons and exchanges gases much more efficiently than if its biomass were shaped as a ball. Also, like sheets, tubes change momentum with their environment. However, they are not interchangeable in places that need surface because of their unique shapes. Examples include a kite (sheet) attached to a string (tube), and a canoe (sheet) guided by an oar (tube attached to a sheet). As Volk states, "Where the press of maximizing area overwhelmingly drives the design, sheets will dominate" (Volk, 1995, p. 34). A third major attribute of tubes is the ability to transfer forces along lines. Biological structural tubes are about reach. "The most efficient use of materials in support systems that reach out occurs in cylindrical bodies" (Wainwright, 1988, p. 17). As connectors, tubes are directional. They can also be thought of in terms of relationships between objects in space. There are multiple examples of tubes in the *Myst*. One excellent example is a photograph titled "Entanglement" in the *Myst*-Art Gallery. These tube-like structures appear to be in relationship at their base with the larger *Myst* energy and to host faces at their extremes. See Figure 17-2.

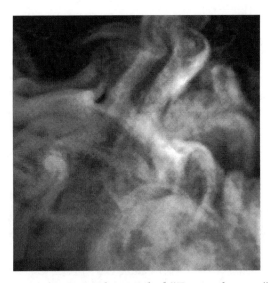

Figure 17-2. *This Myst photograph, entitled "Entanglement" engages the meta-pattern of tubes.*

Defining form within space, the surfaces of spheres, tubes and sheets can all be considered as borders which function as barriers to disruption. Distinct bounding surfaces can be found in all scales of life. For example, the generic design in biology's border is first to repel the drive toward disorder and second, via repetition to facilitate growth. These surfaces provide a system of walls and bridges that serve both to separate and connect. The closest example would be the patterns in clouds. While clouds lack a defining skin (such as the boundaries of the human body), they sometimes terminate against the dark sky thus showing edges, and sometimes are fuzzy and indistinct, even wispy in nature (similar to the *Myst*). While these borders are casual, clouds are still recognized as things that are distinct, worthy of notice, and therefore named.

The complex, often shifting nature of the borders of clouds described above (moving in scale from large to small) is an example of fractal geometry. In the classical Euclidean geometry objects exist in integer dimensions, that is, single dimensional points, one dimensional lines and curves, two-dimensional plane figures (like circles and squares), and three-dimensional solid objects (like spheres and cubes). Depending on the amount of space it takes up as it twists and curves, a fractal curve in nature will have a dimension between one and two; a fractal landscape will have a dimension between two and three.

Similar to clouds, the shifting nature of the borders of the *Myst* may provide an example of fractal geometry. Some of the *Myst* photographs demonstrate two properties: (1) When part of the image is magnified it is essentially indistinguishable from the unmagnified version (self-similarity, or invariance under a change of scale) and, (2) some parts are irregular fragments. In nature the patterns that are the most highly symmetrical are often the most random. While they are not always visible, there are always differences at some level. If these are not clear examples, the forming of the *Myst* provides some examples of underlying fractal patterns. See Figure 17-3.

Figure 17-3. *The forming of the Myst. Note the underlying patterns (right) when enlarged.*

As a final example of pattern exploration, another approach is to investigate the *probability* of a specific characteristics occurring. Probability is one way of helping to validate whether an event is based on an independent source. For purposes of this work, probability is considered the quality or condition of being probable or the likelihood that a given event will occur. This is often expressed as the ratio of the number of actual occurrences to the number of possible occurrences. Randomness is having no specific pattern, purpose or objective; relating to an event in which all outcomes are equally likely to occur. Non-randomness, then, means that the pattern, action or event can be anticipated from past and present patterns, actions or events, if (and only if) one has understood patterns over time (sequences) well enough to predict the next pattern action or event.

There is a difference between non-randomness, predictability and uncertainty. Predictability means that one can successfully anticipate the next event, action or occurrence. Uncertainty means that one cannot successfully anticipate (predict) the next event, action or occurrence.

If the patterns in the *Myst* are random, then most likely it would be the result of the weather or other environmental conditions. If the patterns in the *Myst* are non-random, then there is some force—perceived or felt, internal or external, understood and/or beyond understanding—that is forming and shaping the *Myst*. So, a first step in understanding the *Myst* and exploring the patterns in the *Myst* is understanding the probability that the *Myst* is non-random.

One element to consider is color. While there may be more shades of colors involved in some of the photographs, for simplicity here we assume three primary color tones: white, black and pink. By definition, if a color is random then the probability of selecting any one of these colors is equal. This is the same as throwing dice. If there is a different number on each side of a die (1-6) and if the die is balanced, the result should be random. The concept is similar with a perfectly balanced coin. In a random coin toss, the odds of tails versus heads should be the same, that is, both heads and tails have the same chance (50/50) of being on top.

With our three tones of colors, excluding external stimuli, it should be equally probable for any one color to appear in each pixel, that is, the probability of getting a black pixel is 1/3 or 33%, the probability of getting a pink pixel is 1/3 or 33%, and the probability of getting a white pixel is 1/3 or 33%. So, in an unweighted environment with no external influences the probability of each pixel being a specific color is 1/3 or 33%. In short, if each pixel of the camera's image were random, then the pictures would be nothing more than a messy, complex mixture of black, white and pink dots.

If we look at a specific order of a string of the same color, the probability changes. For example, the probability of getting three black pixels in a row is 1/3 X 1/3 X 1/3 which is 1/27 or 3.7%. The probability is becoming very low. Suppose I get from this phenomenon a hundred dots in a row? The probability is then $1/3^{100}$ which is equal to 1.94 X 10^{-48} (that's .194 with 47 zeros in front of it). This is a very, very low number, yet it is the probability of getting 100 black dots or 100 pink dots or 100 white dots in a row. Referring back to the picture frame and assuming an area of 100 pixels square (based on the width and height of the camera frame), there are 10,007 dots in the square. When we do the calculations, the probability of getting a random picture in that area with a specific pattern is 10^{-47}. To help understand this probability factor, let's consider it in comparison with the number of estimated particles in the Universe, which is 10^{70}. If a given picture without environmental influence is truly random, the probability of getting it is smaller than the number of particles in the Universe! Putting aside the interpretations of the shapes themselves, in the photograph shown in Figure 17-4, the probability of this block of pink randomly appearing in the *Myst* picture without environmental influence is approximately 10^{-94}.

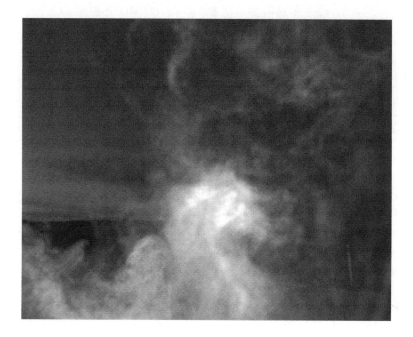

Figure 17-4. *In this photograph entitled "The Gift of Light", given no external influence and an approximate 100 x 100-pixel square, the probability of the pink shape appearing in the photograph is 10^{-94}.*

We have briefly explored three elements of pattern thinking: categorizing characteristics of the phenomenon; the relationship of meta-patterns; and the role of probability, with a single example of each provided in terms of exploring the *Myst* through pattern thinking. All this, of course, is based on directly experiencing the phenomenon of the *Myst*. Remembering that the mental faculties are in service to the intuitional, we would continue the search for patterns through every framework that makes sense. Then, we would look for higher order patterns across the patterns we have identified and described. Only then, with all that has been learned well in hand, would we turn inward and ask *how we feel* about the phenomenon, reviewing each aspect of our learning and repeating that question for each as well as addressing it as an overarching question. In concert, this would be a good time to take a close look at your mental models, and reflect on your openness to new ideas, simultaneously bringing to mind limits to your understanding and your openness to learning. Now you are in a position to explore meaning in terms of personal ramifications—what this phenomenon may mean to you in terms of beliefs, thoughts and actions—and what potential this learning holds for humanity at large. In terms of the *Myst* phenomenon, if you are looking for us to advise you in this regard, you will be disappointed. It is a personal experience for each of us to discover.

While this exercise took several pages, it provided a number of examples of the application of pattern thinking. We now briefly look at patterns as story before delving into the emotions as a personal guidance system.

Patterns as Story

The stories we tell and hear are instruments of change. Knowledge is experiences and stories, and "intelligence is the apt use of experience and the creation and telling of stories." (Schank, 1998, p. 16) Schank says that our knowledge of the world is more or less equivalent to our experiences. We understand experiences in terms of those experiences already in our memory that we understand, so that new ideas are dependent on old ideas. This is, of course, the process of associative patterning that is connected throughout this book as appropriate. Context helps us relate incoming information to the experiences already in our memory, and stories provide that context.

Oakshott (1933, p. 9) offers that experience, "of all the words in the philosophic vocabulary, is the most difficult to manage." We can place ourselves in situations to learn, but since learning is an emergent quality, *we cannot predetermine what we will learn* or, indeed, the significance of what we will learn to our future thinking and acting. Experiential learning is discussed at length in Chapter 9/Part II. There are many ways that information can come to the attention of the mind and thereby interact and influence your thoughts and perceptions of the world, and individuals may, and can, make sense of their experience in many ways, utilizing both inward reflection and social engagement. For example, social engagement might include discussions with friends, collaboration with colleagues, or engagement in communities of practice (Merriam et al., 2007). In today's connected world, virtual exchanges and idea resonances occur on a day-to-day basis, moving through the former barriers of geographic location, culture, age, education, professions, and values and belief sets.

Idea resonance, introduced in Chapter 10/Part II, bears a quick review. With the rise of bureaucracy in the 1900's, idea resonance was primarily built on relationships, that is, the valuing of ideas based on attunement with trusted and respected others who were personally known to the decision-maker. This makes sense. Trust was built up over time as we had a series of continuous cause-and-effect relationships with others, complete with feedback loops. Since travel was difficult and communications were limited, both personal and professional interactions were focused on specific groups of people whom we came to know well, thus enabling choice of whether or whether not to open ourselves to these individuals.

Building on the idea of resonance, let us briefly consider the concept of reverberation. An idea does not simply exist, and then cease to exist, that is, unless it is held and focused within and not allowed to reach its potential (see Chapter 20 on stuck energy). All change carries with it the quality of reverberation. We recognize that change does not happen in isolation. People—and organizations—are complex adaptive systems with many interrelated elements.

The quality of reverberation is a repeating echo that may have far-reaching or lasting impact and/or different impacts, highly dependent on the situation and context at hand. When multiple people are involved in or affected by change, there is the potential for a range of responses. If the change is a result of intelligent activity, then there is not only the potential of a resonance of ideas but progression or expansion of that idea based on an openness and willingness to learn from each other, without limits based on our perceived knowledge. Recall from the assumptions set out at the beginning of this book, that all knowledge is imperfect and/or incomplete intelligence. Because the effectiveness of all knowledge is context sensitive and situation dependent, knowledge emerges, shifts and changes in concert with our environment and the demands placed upon us. Thus, for continued expansion to occur there is the need for a sense of humility in the acceptance and consideration of new ideas, whether or not they fit into our previous learning, beliefs or understanding. When a "position" is taken in terms of past knowledge (regardless of the form this knowledge takes, i.e., beliefs, values, etc.) forces are created that prevent intelligent activity, thus limiting effectiveness of action.

There is a synergy that can emerge through the echoes of reverberation. This occurs when two or more individuals or groups between or among whom no forces exist reflect and consider the thoughts and feelings of the other, with an emergent quality representing the best of multiple streams of thought and feelings. This process is described as a *harmonic reverberation*.

Human memories themselves are story based. Memory recall is improved through temporal sequences of associative patterns such as stories and songs. Written, oral and visual storytelling are sequential narratives in a serial fashion. Hawkins (2004) explains that just as it is difficult to remember an entire story at once, the memory of a song is an excellent example of temporal sequences in memory. "You cannot imagine an entire song at once, only in sequence." (Hawkins, 2004, pp. 71-72) Neither are the stories ever remembered the same. Remember, we are verbs, not nouns, changing every instant of life. Stories are invariably the result of authorial aspect, changing every time they are remembered and retold.

While all experiences are not stories, stories are remembered because they are patterns and come with many indices, multiple ways that the story is connected to memory. "The more indices, the greater the number of comparisons with prior experiences and hence the greater the learning." (Schank, 1998, p. 11) In order for memory to be effective, it must have not only the memories themselves (events, feelings, etc.), but memory traces (or labels) that attach to previously stored memories. These indices can be decisions, conclusions, places, attitudes, feelings, questions, etc.

For example, a simple story can convey deep emotion and compassion. In 1997 when there was a mid-air explosion of Silk Air Ml 185 in Palembang, a Singapore Armed Forces helicopter was second to arrive at the site. Reflecting Singapore's commitment to humanitarian efforts, one participant in the rescue effort shared the following story:

> What we saw was unexpected and is difficult to describe. Pieces of twisted metal and mangled passenger seats half submerged in the murky waters of the Musi river. Luggage and body parts floating with the current. A lifejacket and teddy bear entangled in tall grasses at the river's edge. Our teams dove into the grisly work of search and salvage, hoping beyond hope that the river-soaked teddy bear had a live owner. It didn't. (Bennet et al., 2009, p. 326)

The Story of Self

One of the main jobs of consciousness is to tie our life together into a coherent story, a concept of self (LeDoux, 1996). As introduced above, moving through various life experiences, the individual singles out and accentuates what is significant and connects these events to historic events to create a narrative unity, what Long describes as a fictionalized history.

> [J]ust as the novelist is selective with respect to character development, plot, etc., so the person who seeks the connective threads in the history of his life … has singled out and accentuated the moments which he experiences as significant; others he has allowed to sink into forgetfulness. The result of this process is narrative unity as something akin to fictionalized history …[The] narrative unity which results from this process is not discovered; it is the result of selective attention, emphasis, dim remembrance, and possibly even forgetting. The person makes choices about the importance of persons and events, decides on their meanings, though there may only be a minimal awareness of the resulting order as a partially created one. These choices and decisions – like those of a novelist – are not arbitrary; they are guided by the desire for the "good story." The finished product is the "fictionalized" history of a life, neither a lie nor "the truth," but instead a work of imagination, evaluation and memory. (Long, 1986, pp. 75-92)

The autobiographical self—the idea of who we are, the image we build up of ourselves and where we fit socially—is built up over years of experience and constantly being remodeled, a product of continuous learning. Recall that Damasio (1999) believes that much of this model is created by the unconscious. While this is undoubtedly true, *it is the conscious mind that perceives the idea of self* and through active experimentation with objects and the external world is typically very aware of the perceived boundaries between the individual and the external world.

The story of you lives in the mind—the what, why and how of your life, a summary of the conclusions you have about yourself and life, which often include the harshest judgments you have about yourself. Walsch notes that this is not the "looking within" place where we search for answers to life. As he reminds, "Burrowing deep within that mess rarely produced clarity. In fact, I will say that it never does, because your story is not real. It exists only within your mind. It may seem very real to you, but it is not reality." (Walsch, 2009 p. 36)

<<<<<<<◇>>>>>>>

INSIGHT: **The story of you—which exists only in your mind—is not real.**

<<<<<<<◇>>>>>>>

It seems that evolution created the mind/brain to ensure survival through its meaning-making capacity, not just its memory. For example, in addition to Hawkin's (2004) invariant forms, Sousa (2006) points that we tend to remember things that have meaning, and the close ties between emotion, meaning, and remembering bring out aspects of the mind/brain/body that emphasize meaning. (See the discussion of meaning in Chapter 5/Part I.) The narrative language and connective tissue of stories communicates the nature and shape and behavior of complex adaptive phenomena. This is because stories capture the "essence of living things, which are quintessentially complex phenomena, with multiple variables, unpredictable phase changes, and all of the characteristics that the mathematics of complexity has only recently begun to describe" (Denning, 2000, p. 113).

Schank (1995) goes so far as to measure intelligence in terms of the number of stories an individual has to tell, and in terms of the size of an individual's indexing and retrieval schema that provide a mechanism for determining *what* is relevant to current experiences, and the ability to *search and find* that which is relevant. This is consistent with the power of the mind as an associative patterner.

<<<<<<<◇>>>>>>>

INSIGHT: **Because simple stories have the capacity to convey or highlight intricate patterns, they can be used to open minds and create new futures.**

<<<<<<<◇>>>>>>>

As we integrate the experiences, reflections, comprehensions, social engagements and actions of our story, we move to the position of observing the observer, floating above the drama of life and soaking in the richness of a lifetime of experiential learning. Is age the determinate of this aggregate and, accordingly, a dimension of intelligence? We think not. Short periods of time can be experientially rich, and the diversity of mind reflects the diversity of humanity. We can be sure, however, that every living creature is at some level experiencing, creating a story of their lives and, hopefully, learning and expanding.

In a newspaper article entitled "The Story of You" that appeared in the April 26, 2000, edition of *The Washington Post*, reporter Weeks cites Bernstein as saying "The future of literature lies on the screen" and Greco as saying "Books will become objects of nostalgia." (Weeks, 2000, p. C1) In our current reality we see the truth of this and even greater shifts coming down the way. While print media is seeing a resurgence, nonetheless, today, more and more authors write for electronic reading screens, and as the medium has changed from the oral tradition to paper to screen, the concept of story has changed. This chapter began with a simple definition of story as that which has a beginning, middle and end. With the increased use of hypertext on the Internet, even this simple definition is called into question. Modern day Internet storytellers are experimenting with short moving images and music, and only the occasional sentence here or there. For example, one Internet story website asks visitors to post their own stories or family photos, and invites readers/viewers to express their own innermost feelings, building those feelings right into the story being presented so others will respond to those and become part of the story, "changing and shaping and expanding and making more rich the story." (Weeks, 2000, p. C8-9) In short, the reader is becoming the storyteller, and the storyteller is becoming the reader.

The Rhythms of Life

In the previous chapter we introduced the rhythm of change. Rhythm is all around and within us as we journey through life. This is beautifully demonstrated in the movie August Rush, as a young protégée flows with the swishing of breezes back and forth across a grain field; picks up the beats of car horns, street cleaners, foot traffic on the streets of New York; and turns this rhythmic cacophony of sound into an exquisite sonata.

We are immersed in the rhythmical fabric of our reality: the striking of the ocean waves against the shore, the incessant mumble of cicadas as they execute their nightly circadian rituals of sound, the chorus of birds welcoming the dawn, the soft and continuous beating of our hearts, and the rise and fall of our breath. We are rhythmical creatures, made that way through evolution. There is a correlation between external rhythms of the environment and the internal rhythms of life on the

Earth. For example, the 24-hour day and our cycle of sleeping and waking. Rhythms are frequencies, the timing of events, a regular pattern. Cycles refer to the ordering of those events. Thus the 24-hour marks a rhythm of time, and the cycle of sleeping and waking occurs during that rhythm.

In his study of the work of Lao Tzu, Wing (1986) believes that we are creating a dialogue with the Universe when we translate our personal experiences in the language of nature. For example, when launching a new project, we might see a resemblance to the initial need to overcome gravity. This reflection of physical laws in our lives,

> … forms a direct and interdependent relationship with an elegant, impartial, and evolving Universe. When we align our lives to the rhythms of this Universe, we begin to understand its purpose and we begin to reflect its significance in our own lives." (Wing, 1986, p. 23)

We now are in a position of greater discernment and discretion, with the ability to recognize truth, facilitating intelligent activity and achieving "the fulfillment that comes from leaving what we touch with our minds a little more evolved than we found it." (Wing, 1986, p. 23)

From the cosmos we have the energy of the sun, the spinning and orbiting earth, winds and weather, cycles of cold and the pull and phases of the moon. As Whitfield and Ayensu (1982, p.15) describe: "Each of us on Earth, each of the 10 million species that has evolved on and now swarms over its surface, carries the time signature of the planetary motion of our world indelibly stamped within it." There is a physical vibrational basis of these signatures which are "the mechanisms that generate our rhythmical environment, an environment that has made us rhythmical creatures."

What is rhythm? It comes from the Greek word *rhythmos* which is derived from *rhein*, to flow. In a general sense, rhythm is the ordered alternation of contrasting elements. In music, it is the placement of sounds in time. The notion of rhythm also occurs in other arts, for example, poetry, painting, sculpture and architecture, as well as in nature (biological rhythms). (*Encyclopaedia Britannica*, 2016) The musical unit of time is called a beat; and the Italian word *tempo* is used to describe the fundamental beat of a music offering. However, the tempo of a musical work is not mathematical or metronomic, that is, it is not perfectly regular for any length of time. Along with sound fluctuations, modifications—or tightening and slackening—of the rhythm provide character and emotional emphasis, much like the human voice when communicating thoughts and feelings. These modifications are called *tempo rubato*, which means "robbed time." Note that even the human heart beat has a tempo rubato. As previously noted, if it was mathematically regular, it would wear out by our mid-30's!

Rhythm could not exist outside of time. Rhythm is established by a pattern that *exists over time*, a series of repeated activities, events or occurrences happening regularly and evenly over time. Activity is directly linked with energy coming from the environment, and these are often cyclic and rhythmical. As Whitfield and Ayensu (1992, p. 15) describe,

> The fact that patterns of activity are so often cyclical or rhythmic in organization is the result of a series of constraints which operate on living things and the ecosystems in which they live, and which favour some processes rather than others. It is difficult to conceive of efficient locomotory systems, for instance, which do not have the cyclical features demonstrated by all running, swimming and flying.

A key characteristic of rhythm is frequency, which is the number of complete, even cycles over a period of time (per second, minute, day, year, etc.). Frequency, a measure of time and space, was introduced in Chapter 3/Part I as one consideration of force. It is frequency that offers us patterns from the past that can be flipped to project patterns of the future, as addressed in the previous chapter.

To shape that future, Houston (2000) urges each of us to get in touch with our rhythm, our essential self. As is her gift, she expresses this quite elegantly and from the heart:

> In this Universe of ours, from the tiniest particles to the Galaxies of galaxies, everything is rhythm, pulse, beat, music. The music of the spheres is no mere metaphor, and its cadences are the stuff that supports life and all its becomings. Get in touch with the rhythm, which is your essence, your essential self, and the rest unfolds in the music that is meant to be. We are each of us melodies in the Divine symphony, and we can join the orchestration of the whole with the music of our minds. (p. 290)

Final Thought

As can be seen, patterns and rhythms are interwoven into our experiences of life. While often occurring outside of our awareness or so common that we take them for granted, these patterns and their rhythms provide clues to our physical, mental, emotional and spiritual expansion. In preparation for the creative leap of Phase 3 of the Intelligent Social Change Journey, we invite you to join us in expanding the music of our minds and co-creating your new reality.

Questions for Reflection:

How aware am I of the way my mental models have been formed by my past experiences and am I open to changing them?

How are my current mental models limiting my intelligent social change journey?

Do I see myself in my story as the subject rather than the object?

Chapter 18
Easing into the Flow

SUBTOPICS: LIFE FORCE ... THE ENERGY CENTERS ... INFORMATION AS ENERGY ... ENERGY ENTANGLEMENT ... THE FLOW OF LIFE ... THE OPTIMAL HUMAN EXPERIENCE ... FINAL THOUGHTS

TOOLS: **18-1**. CONNECTING THROUGH THE HEART ... **18-2**. DISCOVERING FLOW

From the most basic perspective, the physical Universe is made up of energy and patterns of energy—nothing more, nothing less. Albert Einstein proved that everything in our material world—both animate and inanimate, organic and inorganic— *radiates* energy. The Earth and her people are an enormous energy field full of continuously flowing entangled subfields. As Houston (2000, p. 147) so aptly describes, "The Universe, we are coming to understand, is a flow that arises moment by moment from the abyss of energetic nourishment in a process of continuous regeneration."

The idea of flow is a familiar one. We watch the flow of water as it moves down a riverbed or fills our drinking glass. We feel the flow of air as a breeze plays with our hair and our lungs move rhythmically in and out, in and out. We sense feelings of joy and sadness, calm and anger flowing through us. And, sometimes, since energy follows thought, we can perceive the thought of another without the hearing of words. Close your eyes for a moment and try to recall a time when you knew what someone was thinking without hearing the words.

The flow of energy is consistent with the flow of nature. For example, consider the difficulty of swimming upstream or cutting across the grain of wood. All matter and energy, whether based on physical, emotional or mental structures, is being continuously impacted and changed by outside forces. We now understand that information—and knowledge, our capacity to effectively act on that information—is partial and incomplete because all knowledge is context sensitive and situation dependent, all of which is in continuous flux among entangled complex adaptive systems such as people and organizations and the environment within which they function. When we become part of that flow, that is, *cooperate with* the flow, we co-evolve with our reality. In this process we begin to recognize patterns, extend the reach of our minds through contemplation, and develop an expanded future vision. Conversely, when we bound our beliefs and cease learning, we create blockages. This will be discussed in Chapter 20. Note that a complex adaptive system cannot stay in stasis for very long without either expanding (organization, growth) or dissipating (chaos or collapse).

Lao Tzu felt that powerful people radiate knowledge, but that this knowledge is more of an intuitive knowing emerging from the experience and direct understanding of nature (Wing, 1986). Powerful people influence and change the world, exhibiting compassion and generosity, because they "**instinctively realize that power continues to flow through them only when they pass it on** [emphasis added]. Like electricity, the more energy, inspiration, and information they conduct, the more they receive" (Wing, 1986, p. 13). Note his words that power continues to flow through them *only* when it is passed on. This is an important trait of all energy, including information and knowledge, and is an underlying intent of this book.

Our bodies—matter, or energy that has taken on form—are transformers of energy. The old worldview of the body as a sophisticated machine, based on Newtonian physics, is gradually giving way to a new scientific worldview of the body as a *complex energetic system*. This worldview is based on a new perspective of Quantum physics that "the biochemical molecules that make up the physical body are actually a form of vibrating energy." (Gerber, 2000, p. 5) From this new worldview, 80 percent of the etheric/dense physical plane is made up of energy; 66 percent of the astral/emotional plane is made up of energy; and 50 percent of the mental plane is made up of energy (MacFlouer, 2004-16). In other words, regardless of whether we look from a Newtonian or Quantum viewpoint, our everyday lives are engaged in manipulating and using energy. We are energy beings. As Collinge describes:

> When we think of our anatomy, we ordinarily think of our bones, muscles, organs, and other physical tissues. However, we also have an *energetic* anatomy. It is composed of multiple, interacting energy fields that envelop and penetrate our physical body, govern its functioning, and extend out into the world around us. This anatomy serves as a vehicle for the circulation of vital energies that enliven and animate our lives. (Collinge, 1998, p. 20)

Taking a consilience approach, let's explore these vital energies from a variety of perspectives.

Life Force

The Japanese word *Ki* describes the *essential life force*, the subtle infrastructure of our physical body, and the energy and warmth radiated by the living body, human or animal. Subtle energy is defined as low intensity vibrations/frequencies sourced from both physical (electromagnetic, Quantum, galactic) and metaphysical (consciousness, thoughts, spirit) causes. Everything that is alive contains and radiates *Ki*. Without this energetic backbone, we would have no life force and cease to exist as living, breathing, animated beings. When we open to the flow of life force, we don't have to "do" it; rather, there is an unfoldment, perhaps captured by the notion of surrendering to the flow and letting it "do" to us, fully embodying the concept of co-evolving in the NOW experience (Phase 2 of the Intelligent Social Change Journey).

This energy has been recognized and explored throughout the history of mankind, and called by many different names. As Eden (2008, p. 18) describes,

> Numerous cultures describe a matrix of subtle energies that support, shape and animate the physical body, often displaying intelligence that transcends human knowing ... It is hardly a new idea to suggest that subtle energies operate in tandem with the denser, "congealed" energies of the material body.

Mary Coddington (1978) fills an entire book describing this energy in terms of different cultures: *Ankh* in ancient Egypt; *Pneuma* in ancient Greece; *Prana* in the yoga tradition of India and Tibet; *Megbe* by the Ituri Pygmies, *Mana* by the Polynesian Hunas; *Orenda* by the Native American Iroquois; *Ruach* in Hebrew; *Barraka* in Islamic countries; *Holy Spirit* in the Christian tradition; and described as vital energy, bioenergy or biomagnetism in the West.

In Chinese medicine and philosophy this energy or life force of the Universe, which flows around the body and is *present in all living things,* is called *chi, ch'i, qi, Chi, Ch'i,* or *Qi* (Encarta, 1999). The manipulation of this energy is the basis of acupuncture and Chinese martial arts. A popular portrayal of this energy in Western popular culture was in the use of the "Force" in the *Star Wars* films. Note that *Ki*, by whatever name it is called, is not affiliated with any religion. It is older in concept and fact than any religious philosophy, and is considered the source of life itself.

Reflective of one of the author's lengthy association with the Japanese culture, for purposes of this discussion we have chosen to use the familiar term *Ki*, which literally translates as *breath* or *air* and we define as *the vitalizing energy of life*. This term is quite appropriate when contemplating the fact that our breath is continuously bringing energy into physical matter from the larger ocean of consciousness. There is a natural expanding and contracting, and when *Ki* departs the living organism, life has departed. If we briefly pause after an out-breath, we can perceive ourselves in an instant of death. This same state occurs in the instant after a sneeze. This is a place *in between* that is pregnant with possibilities and, metaphorically speaking, reflecting the changing of the seasons.

Ki is considered "an electrical type of energy that creates the body and determines the state of health" (Stein, 1995, p. 16), what is described as electromagnetic energy, which comes largely from the Sun but can also come from the Earth. For example, *Ki* is developed in deep oceans. The four forces identified by conventional physics—electromagnetic, gravity, nuclear and weak nuclear—were introduced in Chapter 3/Part I.

As conveyed in that chapter, *all* people are affected by these forces, and many consciously "feel" or respond to them. For example, when *Ki* moves in the body, the blood moves, so a warmth may be felt. When *Ki* is deficient the blood flow slows, and there may be a feeling of cold (Tsang, 2016). It is not surprising that the human is able to sense energies, even those not yet identifiable through our sophisticated technologies. As biofeedback researcher Dr. Elmer Green of the Menninger Foundation explains,

> ... [some energies] have not been detected with scientific instruments because these instruments have no parts above the [physical] level. Humans have all the parts and can therefore detect a greater spectrum of energies. Instruments are made of minerals, and lack the transducer components needed for detection .... In other words, living beings are coupled to the cosmos better than scientific devices, which are, after all, quite limited tools. (Green & Green, 1989, p. 304)

The term *transducer* refers to a device such as a microphone that translates signals from one form of energy to another. William Collinge, a researcher of subtle energy and integrative medicine, says that "the ability to detect and work with subtle energies is based on a transducer system that involves our endocrine glands, our nervous system, and our own biofield—to which these systems are coupled." (Collinge, 1998, p. 17) The biofield referenced here, a subtle phenomenon which cannot be measured by technological instruments, is the field through which *Ki* flows, acting as a transducer, an energy bridge to the physical body.

The human body not only receives and processes energy but also generates energy. While most people with electromagnetic hypersensitivity describe "feeling" the energy rather than "seeing" it, there are some individuals who do have the ability to visually see the electromagnetic energy surrounding living forms. This energy is often referred to as an aura, with the field around the living form called the auric field. Different types of energy produce different auras. For example, human auras would include energy focused at the physical/etheric, emotional, mental and spiritual levels, all interpenetrating each other and changing in form and color dependent on our thoughts and feelings (Mulford, 2007). The easiest aura to see is the one that directly surrounds the physical body. It can be seen by shifting focus, much like is done with aura photography. These energy fields have been captured through Kirlian photography, the use of a high-frequency oscillator to photograph energy fields around living entities.

The Energy Centers

To fully explore the energy centers that process the vital energy of *Ki* in the human body involves the marrying of science and spiritual traditions and the East and the West. Focusing on the physical body and the accompanying electromagnetic (etheric) field connected to the physical body, *Ki* flows through pathways that are called chakras, meridians and nadis.

There are seven primary chakras, or energy centers, located in the electromagnetic field that is connected to the physical body, and many, many smaller chakras that facilitate the flow of *Ki*. Each primary energy center is unique, having connections to one or more of the seven senses used to process incoming energies, and connecting to various organs of the body in terms of their functionality and health. It is this flow of *Ki* that gives life cohesiveness, allowing different centers to communicate with each other and integrate into a single life. If there is not enough *Ki* flowing through the centers, the senses cannot communicate with each other and the body begins to fail. While it is not our intent to provide an in-depth treatment of the chakra system here, we briefly introduce the primary centers.

The root energy center, located at the base of the spine, is associated with sexual energy and procreation, as well as our basic sense of hearing. The auditory nerve is the most complicated and connected nerve in the body. It links up with all parts of the brain, with as many as 30,000 nerve fibers at work in the inner ear alone, making the ear the greatest supplier of sensory energy, and the greatest changer of brain energy and direction (Bullard & Bennet, 2013). Having 90 times greater range than our eyesight, our hearing serves as a connection to others, hearing best the sounds of other human beings around us. The ability of humans to discern the experience of others is critical to the creation of civilization and to develop a meaningful life. Of the ears, Murray Shafer, a Canadian composer, said quite succinctly, "With our eyes we are always at the edge of the world looking in, but with our ears, the world comes to us and we are always at the center of it." (Campbell, 2014, p. 74)

The sacral energy center, located at the base of the spine or spleen, is associated with our sense of smell, which provides a way to pick up information that is at a distance from the physical body. This energy center helps to unify and balance the energy centers, and supports inner reflection and meditation. The solar plexus energy center, located at the naval, is associated with the sense of touch and how we pick up information close to the physical body, allowing us to sense small degrees of change. It is also very involved in how we *emote*, that is, expressing emotion in a dramatic way. This energy center is connected to the digestive system and liver, the chemical warehouse of the body which converts energy to what is needed, allowing us to live in the physical world.

The heart energy center, long associated with love and the recognition of Oneness and connections, and indeed home to our internal sense of connection, allows us to love life itself, developing an understanding of life and leading to expansion of our consciousness. There is a resilience here, supporting the continuous change in which our body thrives. When we are young, there is Heart Rate Variability (HRV), that is, the distance from the peak of one heartbeat to the next varies. As we get older and become more rigid in our behaviors and thinking, the distance from the peak of one heartbeat to the next becomes more even. This regularity limits our life span; for when the heart beats in an even fashion it wears out much faster. Heartmath (2016) says this resilience can be regained by establishing coherence between the heart and brain. The quick methodology starts with breathing a bit slower and deeper than usual while focusing on your heart. You can tap your fingers gently in the heart area to help that focus occur. Then, think and feel positive, perhaps focusing on someone special in your life, or perhaps focusing on something for which you are extremely appreciative. It is that simple—and can be that difficult, for life is filled with past memories and current perturbations, all of which have a tendency to creep in and out of our focus.

When fully functioning, the human has the power to comprehend and empathize with others (with empathy moving into compassion), and to sense and understand the connection to a larger force, giving us an awareness beyond our own life. The energy field of the heart and the Earth's energy field are coherent, that is, *they are part of a unified field.* More and more we are recognizing the impact of electronics on the Earth's energy field, and it begs the question: How are these electronics impacting the human heart?

****

TOOL 18-1: Connecting through the Heart

Neurons are not only located in the human brain, but in the heart, with the capability to think, feel and remember. Because these neurons are quite often not as actively engaged in everyday life as those firing within our heads, there are fewer mental models to limit the movement of our thoughts and feelings. This exercise is focused on connecting to the larger energy field through your heart.

STEP (1): Find a quiet place where you will not be bothered for a half hour. Make your body comfortable (sitting or lying down) and close your eyes.

STEP (2): Think about where your thoughts originate, and place your hand where you think that occurs. This will generally be on one side of the upper head, or on the forehead between the eyes. This "thinking spot" will serve as the starting point of your journey. Put your arm down and let your body relax.

STEP (3): Take several slow, deep breaths, breathing in through your nose and out through your mouth, consciously releasing any tensions or random thoughts with the out-breath.

STEP (4): Imagine an elevator inside the middle of your head next to the thinking spot where your thoughts originate. The door opens, and you enter the elevator.

STEP (5): The doors close, and you begin moving downwards. It is a beautiful elevator, see-through so you can observe yourself from within. Slowly, imagine the downward journey of the elevator, moving through the throat, down the neck, into the upper chest, and ever so slowly down right behind your heart space. Take your time;

there is no hurry. Keep all of your thoughts focused from the location of your elevator. If you have difficulty imagining this slow journey, take your hand and gently trace the journey down from your thinking spot. Down, down, down, until you reach your heart space.

STEP (6): The elevator doors open and you enter your heart. It is warm, softly beating, and quite welcoming. Keeping your focus in this place, imagine yourself growing larger and larger You are energy, with no barriers. From your heart space, you expand outward, encompassing your entire body, then move beyond the body, expanding wider and wider beyond the confines of your body. You feel free, and continue expanding, wider and wider, until you fill the room or area immediately surrounding your body. Keep your focus outward, and continue expanding, expanding, wider and wider. You, as your heart, now fill the house or field within which your body resides. Do not stop, continue expanding, periodically stopping to enjoy your growth, your freedom. Move beyond the local area to the larger geographical area of which you are a part. Keep expanding, more and more, wider and wider. You pass, and expand beyond, trees and houses, roads and the cars moving along them, up through the clouds, down into the Earth, ever-growing, expanding, expanding. The slow rhythm of your heart gently pulses through the field. You have no limits. You become as large as the Earth, and expand beyond, reaching the limits of the solar system, and expanding beyond. Continue expanding as far as you are comfortable. Then, pause and enjoy the feeling of this expansion. The lightness, yet the power of the energy of which you are a part. Observe what is beyond and, if you dare, continue expanding.

STEP (7): When you are ready to return, think about your body and where it resides, and slowly bring your awareness back to your body. You may repeat this process any time you choose.

NOTE: If you reflect on any issues or problems going on in your life after experiencing this journey, they may have lost their level of importance. Experiencing this journey, understanding that we are so much more, provides us with a larger systems perspective from which to view local situations.

****

The throat energy center, long associated with communication and providing a sense of others and how to speak to others, is also associated with our sense of taste, which is both a comparative sense and a discriminating and discerning sense. It is also connected to the lungs and breathing, and critical in controlling respiratory illnesses. The brow energy center, located between the two eyebrows, is associated with ways of seeing as well as structured energy. This is often associated with the concept of the "third eye", an inner sense of seeing. When there is too much energy flowing through this center it becomes difficult to retain our vision and use it in discriminating and discerning ways. The crown energy center, located at the top of the head, centers our senses themselves, connecting us to the larger Universal whole, providing a sense of morality, and opening us to discover our purpose and role in this larger whole, that is, our role as co-creators. For an in-depth treatment of these energy centers, see Leadbeater (1997), MacFlouer (1999) or just Google the Internet.

The free and balanced flow of *Ki* is the cause of good health (Rand, 1991, p. 1-9). Since *Ki* nourishes the organs and cells of the body, supporting them in their vital functions, the disruption of *Ki* brings about illness. In this regard, there is a direct connection between the thoughts and feelings of an individual and the flow of *Ki*. For example, *positive thoughts increase the flow of Ki and provide good feelings as well as health*. Negative thoughts disrupt the flow of *Ki* and bring about "feeling poorly". Negative thoughts and feelings in terms of blockages will be discussed in more detail in Chapter 20.

Discoveries in neuroscience since the turn of the century have confirmed the role of thoughts and feelings in the physical health of our body. As forwarded by Bennet et al. (2015b, p. 134), **"Thoughts change the structure of the brain, and brain structure influences the creation of new thoughts."** This feedback loop highlights recognition of the interdependence and self-organization of the mind and the brain in the sense that each influences the other. This also reminds us of the importance of both physical and mental health. It is now understood that "Positive and negative beliefs affect every aspect of life" (Bennet et al., 2015b, p. 136). This neuroscience finding has widespread application for learning and change, and is consistent with what we are learning through vibrational medicine. See the discussion of positive thinking in Chapter 9/Part II.

While the energy centers introduced above are focused at the physical/etheric (electromagnetic field), the emotional, and the mental levels—all three of which are addressed throughout this book as planes, and heavily involved in change—while we are living in the physical, a primary function of all of these energy centers is supporting the free flow of energy throughout the physical/etheric system.

All of our senses are involved in this process, alerting the body to external and internal events. For example, from the viewpoint of anatomists, there are two nervous systems in the human body, the cerebro-spinal and the sympathetic. However, there is also a third grouping known as the vagus nerves. The cerebro-spinal system starts at the brain, moves down through the spinal cord, and reaches throughout the body through the ganglia, with nerves issuing between every successive two vertebrae. The sympathetic system has two cords running the length of the spine, from which sympathetic nerves form a network of systems called the plexuses, which in turn serve as relay stations to smaller ganglia and nerves. The vagus nerves arise from the medulla oblongata, then descend independently deep into the body, entangled with the other two systems. Thus, signals are continuously being generated and communicated throughout the body.

Information as Energy

While we've talked about information as energy previously, let's explore this a bit deeper in terms of the mind/brain. Both memory and learning are expressed physiologically in the formation of new synapses, the connections between neurons, and the strengthening of existing synapses (Begley, 2007). "Brains have complex rules of guessing that allow them to extract information from incoming signals and create meaning and understanding without storing the full incoming signal" (Hawkins, 2004, p. 75).

For years, memory was thought to be stored somewhere in the brain. It is now widely agreed that there is no "grandmother" cell that "represents" a grandmother, no separate center in the brain where memories about grandmother are permanently stored. Instead,

> ...a long line of evidence shows that information storage follows a principle that is conserved across both vertebrates and invertebrates. Memory appears to be stored in the same distributed assembly of brain structures that are engaged in initially perceiving and processing what is to be remembered. (Squire & Kandel, 1999, p. 72)

Edelman's third theory postulates that memory is nonrepresentational; that is, a memory is not stored in the sense that a computer stores data. Rather, memory is the ability to repeat, recreate, or suppress a mental or physical act or past experience. These acts, being sequences of flows of interconnecting neuronal patterns, are internally experienced as thoughts, feelings, etc. These patterns may also cause muscles to change shape and therefore influence physical actions. Memory is seen as the capability of the brain to change its internal patterns and sequences of patterns to create the repetition of performance. This is facilitated by the associative patterning process. As Edelman and Tononi (2000, p. 95) detail:

> In a complex brain, memory results from the selective matching that occurs between ongoing, distributed neural activity and various signals coming from the world, the body, and the brain itself. The synaptic alterations that ensue affect the future responses of the individual brain to similar or different signals. These changes are reflected in the ability to repeat a mental or physical act after some time ... for example in 'recalling' an image. It is important to indicate that by the word *act* we mean any ordered sequence of brain activities in a domain of perception, movement, or speech that, in time, leads to a particular neural output. We stress repetition after some time in this definition because it is the ability to re-create an act separated by a certain duration from the original signal set that is characteristic of memory. And in mentioning a changing context, we pay heed to a key property of memory in the brain: that it is, in some sense, a form of constructive *recategorization* during ongoing experience, rather than a precise replication of a previous sequence of events.

Thus, memory is not a fixed rule that pulls up a past representation. It is *recreated* each time by the dynamic links and patterns between neuronal groups (Bennet & Bennet, 2008c). This explains why memory is often unreliable and rarely recreated exactly.

<<<<<<<<>>>>>>>

INSIGHT: **Because memory is recreated each time it is pulled up, it is rarely exactly recreated and often unreliable.**

<<<<<<<<>>>>>>>

Humans have three distinct forms of memory storage capabilities: sensory memory, short term memory (including working memory) and long-term memory. Sensory memory is quite short, generally a few seconds in endurance, and refers to information received through the senses. Short term memory takes over when information is transferred from sensory memory to our consciousness (Engle et al.,1993; Laming, 1992). While short term memory lasts longer than sensory memory, it is still initially very limited, engaging approximately 5 to 9 bits of information for approximately 30 seconds or so (Miller, 1956). However, a second phase of short-term memory is working memory, which occurs when material is kept in conscious focus for a longer period of time (Baddeley, 1997), and can happen when we are studying, repeating or rehearsing, focusing (for a period of time) on a core issue, etc. Because short term memory can only handle 5 to 9 bits of information, displacement occurs when it is full and a new bit of information enters. An example is trying to remember a phone number and the last couple of digits dropping out of memory.

Heffner (2014) says there are typically six reasons information is stored in short term memory: through the primacy effect (first information received), the recency effect (last information received), distinctiveness (stands out, different), frequency (rehearsed, repeated, "memorized"), associations (linked to something important, acronyms) and reconstruction (filling in a memory blank in the instant). One way to sharpen short term memory is through rehearsal, which can bring in multiple senses through visualizing, hearing, speaking, singing, and keyboarding information repeatedly.

Another way is through chunking, that is, bringing ideas and concepts together to create understanding through the development of significant patterns useful for solving problems and anticipating future behavior within a domain of focus. A study of chess players concluded that "effortful practice" was the difference between people who played chess for many years while maintaining an average skill and those who became master players in shorter periods of time. The master players, or experts, examined the chessboard patterns over and over again, studying them, looking at nuances, trying small changes to perturb the outcome (sense and response), generally "playing with" and studying these *patterns* (Ross, 2006b). In other words, they use working memory, pattern recognition and chunking rather than logic as a means of understanding, memory recall and decision-making.

Long-term memory is relatively permanent and can be thought of in terms of declarative memory and nondeclarative memory. Declarative memory includes the areas of semantic memory, factual knowledge such as meanings, concepts and math (Lesch & Pollatsek, 1993; Rohrer et al., 1995) and episodic memory such as events and situations (Goldringer, 1996; Kliegel & Lindberger, 1993). Note that declarative memory may take the form of explicit or tacit knowledge. Nondeclarative memory includes those acts and habits which are done by rote due to extensive practice and conditioning. An example would be riding a bicycle, which involves embedded tacit knowledge that has become part of the structure of cellular memory, what we refer to as embodied tacit knowledge.

Memory encoding, storage, and recall/recognition/retrieval all occur at the level of invariant forms, what Hawkins (2004) describes as "a form that captures the essence of relationships, not the details of the moment" (p. 82). The entire cortex is a memory system, storing sequences of patterns, recalling patterns auto-associatively, and storing patterns in a hierarchy (Hawkins, 2004). As a working definition, *memory systems* refer to the full set of memory patterns stored throughout the mind/brain/body.

There is no equivalent concept in computers for invariant forms. While a computer would encode data using 1's and 0's, the invariant forms that are encoded in the human mind would be associated with a previous memory, image, sound or emotion. As Hawkins (2004, p. 66) describes regarding a simple thought experiment,

> This task is difficult or impossible for a computer to perform today, yet a human can do it reliably in half a second or less. But neurons are slow, so in that half a second, the information entering your brain can only traverse a chain one hundred neurons long. That is, the brain "computes" solutions to problems like this in one hundred steps or fewer, regardless of how many total neurons might be involved.

Of course, the brain is not computing the answers to problems at all. It is rather *associating* new incoming information with stored patterns, the process of associative patterning (Bennet & Bennet, 2004), with a continuous stream of information from the environment moving through the seven human senses.

This brings us to a discussion of what is generally known as the binding problem. To form a complete memory, fragments of associated patterns need to be combined in some way, thus the term "binding". As Christos (2003, p. 51) describes,

> Fragments of attractors need to be combined in some way (called the "binding problem") to form a complete memory. The hippocampus may be involved in this function. Another particularly interesting candidate is the thalamus, which is the gateway to all sensory information entering the neocortex and for some reason also receives reciprocal information from each of the areas in the neocortex that it

sends information to. It is also known that neurotransmitters like norepinephrine are implicated with learning and are thought to be released from the locus coeruleus when something is to be learned. This needs to be coordinated with the task of observation.

Note the usage of the term "attractors". This concept of attraction becomes more prominent as consciousness expands (see Chapter 37/Part V).

A second issue has to do with memory traces, which do not necessarily involve pathways identical to incoming information. The greater the differences from the original incoming thought, the fuzzier the memory (Stonier, 1997). This is where Edelman's neural Darwinism comes in, the fact that pathways are continuously being corrupted or weakened. The less the pathways are used, the faster they become corrupted (Rosenfield, 1988). There is a competition of thoughts (neural Darwinism) coming into consciousness. There are, however, exceptions. As Stonier (1997, p. 154) describes,

> The evolution of the brain has created special categories of nerve traces which become relatively incorruptible. For example, those created during the developing embryo relating to vital functions are probably stable during our entire lifetime. Those involving imprinting phenomena in juveniles, likewise, are less prone to decay. The same thing may be said for those which become habits and those learned during emotional stress.

We will address memory in terms of "forgetting" in Chapter 20.

Energy Entanglement

(permeable and porous boundaries)

What we have learned through science is that the human body is *not* a separate part of the environment. Indeed, both organic and non-organic energies are exchanged in every instance of life. As brought in at the beginning of this chapter, through the very act of breathing we are in a continuous energetic interaction with *Ki*, and then there are the continuous interactions of life such as intake and output through our digestive system.

We also now know that we are in continuous two-way communication with those around us, and that the brain is continuously changing in response. As Cozolino and Sprokay (2006, p. 13) explain,

> It is becoming more evident that through emotional facial expressions, physical contact, and eye gaze—even through pupil dilation and blushing—people are in constant, if often unconscious, two-way communication with those around them. It is in the matrix of this contact that brains are sculpted, balanced and made healthy.

The interactions of our energies with others shape our relationships with those others, and profoundly influential dynamics are introduced through the *interaction of energetic states* (Collinge, 1998). For example, it is not necessary for the exchange of words or body language to convey deep emotions such as anger or love, which can be "felt" from a distance. If it was visible to our eyes, and as detailed in Chapter 26/Part IV, we could see the currents of our very thought flowing back and forth among people. As Mulford, 2007, p. 35) expresses, "There is no limit to the power of the thought current you can attract to you nor limit to the things that can be done through the individual by it." As this book progresses, we hope that the reality of this expression will become clear.

As introduced in Chapter 5/Part I, a more recent discovery through the study of cell biology provides additional insights regarding the energy field within which we live. Lipton discovered that human thought and behavior is part of what appears to be a large simulation. Information from the environment is transferred through *receptor and effector proteins*, much like a set of antennas attached to the outer membrane of every cell. Thinking of ourselves as part of a larger virtual reality helps us understand the importance of the energy—and signals—coming in from the environment. It has been long recognized that the Earth is surrounded by a geomagnetic field, an energetic anatomy similar to our own. For example, Collinge (1998) sees the energy centers, channels and fields emanating from the earth as analogous to those of the human body. As he says, "The entire earth and biosphere in which we live is one gigantic living organism, with its own metabolic and energetic qualities" (Collinge, 1998, p. 20)

This invisible field can be characterized as a nervous system running throughout the Universe, connecting all things. As we are reminded in the international, award-winning documentary film *Inner Worlds, Outer Worlds* (2012), *we are part of one vibratory field that connects all things*. This field "has been called Akasha, Logos, the primordial OM, the music of the spheres, the Higgs field, dark energy and a thousand other names throughout history" (back cover). This is the Noosphere described by the French geologist/paleontologist, Pierre Teilhard de Chardin as "a human sphere, a sphere of reflection, of conscious invention, of conscious souls" (de Chardin, 1966, p. 63) The word "noosphere" is a neologism that employs *noos*, the Greek word for "mind".

Scientists with electromagnetic theories that are congruent include: Harold Saxton Burr (Electric Fields of Life); Hameroff and Penrose (Orchestrated Reduction or Orch-OR); E. Roy John (Electromagnetic Information field); Ervin László (Akashic or A-Field); Benjamin Libet (Conscious Mental Field); Jibu and Yasue (Quantum Braijn Dynamics); Johnjoe McFadden (CEMI Field Theory—CEMI is Conscious Electromagnetic Information); Michael Persinger (Electromagnetic Consciousness); Susan Pockett (EMF Field Theory—EMF is Electromagnetic Field); Hermes Romjin (EMF Photon Theory—EMF is Electromagnetic Field); Rupert Sheldrake (Morphic

Fields/Morphic resonance); and William Tiller (K*Space). Several of these theories are called out as appropriate throughout this book.

When the Bennets published a new theory of the firm in 2004, *flow* was one of the eight emergent characteristics required for an organization to co-evolve with a CUCA (increasing change, uncertainty, complexity and anxiety) environment (Bennet & Bennet, 2004). In this work, *flow* is characterized as enabling knowledge centricity and facilitating the connections and continuity that maintain *unity and shared purpose*, and give coherence to *organizational intelligence. Flow*, moving across networks of systems and people, is the catalyst for creativity and innovation, with social capital the medium of exchange in this human framework.

Flow was introduced in terms of the flow of data, information and knowledge; the movement of people in and out of organizational settings; and the optimal human experience. While all three of these are certainly related to the idea of *flow* introduced here—with an emphasis on flow as the optimal human experience—we further expand the term to include the *flow of life events over time* and those events in relation to *the development of the self* and *the growth of humanity*.

The Flow of Life

Mahatma Ghandi said that we should *be the change we want to see in the world.* In the KMTL study[18-1] conducted by one of the authors, a thought leader in the field of Knowledge Management offered that through the creation of knowledge that we were creating both little drops of rain and, in some cases, monsoons. As he describes,

> If you think of knowledge broadly as all of the understanding that we as human beings have gained through experience, observation or study as the dictionary says, what we are doing either in the production of individual knowledge or in the development of this discipline that helps us to find and apply knowledge ... then it is as little drops of rain that start to flow down the hill that come together in little streams that eventually become big rivers flowing into the ocean. From that point of view, I think that we, whether as thought leaders or participants, are making that contribution. In some cases, it is little drops of rain, and in other cases it may be monsoons. (Bennet, 2005)

And so it is with life. There is a flow, a current, punctuated by our concept of time, within which thoughts and actions (events) occur. Much like falling in love, when an individual finds their flow, life is forever changed. The analogy made above by the KMTL study participant points to the beginning of the flow, to the thoughts and actions that come together to start the flow, some little and some large. Then, when other thoughts and actions are consistent with the flow, they expand and create a larger flow. Thoughts and actions that are inconsistent with the flow, that is, heading upstream against the larger flow, must be quite strong to make any headway, and can easily be overcome by the larger flow or swept to the side, out of the current. This description is beginning to sound very consistent with the flow of energy in a probability field.

In describing authentic happiness, Seligman warns that there are no shortcuts to flow. All the cognitive and emotional resources that make up our thoughts and feelings are engaged in the concentrated attention that flow requires. As Seligman (2011, p. 11-12) blatantly states,

> There are no shortcuts to flow. On the contrary, you need to deploy your highest strengths and talents to meet the world in flow. There are effortless shortcuts to feeling positive emotion … you can masturbate, go shopping, take drugs, or watch television. Hence, the importance of identifying your highest strengths and learning to use them more often in order to go into flow.

Seligman's model of positive psychology, which engages the flow state, includes the elements of positive emotion, engagement, meaning, positive relationships and accomplishment.

The process of flow is much like the workings of the prefrontal cortex of the human mind/brain. There are six layers of hierarchical patterns in the architecture of the cortex, with each layer storing an invariant form of the "most important" information coming through the lower level. "Most important" refers to value as well as the content that will provide the best accessibility (in your personal mental framework) to thought when it is needed. A parallel practice in information systems storage is to provide various levels of summaries and key words, easily searchable, all with connections to related information for depth and context as needed for the situation at hand. See Bennet and Bennet (2013) for a more in-depth treatment of this process. In terms of value, the more important a thought is to you and what you think and do, tagged with strong emotions, the more connections a thought has and the higher it is referenced (in invariant form) in the frontal cortex. Thoughts and feelings that are repeated over and over again through a variety of experiences affect your core beliefs and values, or can become a core belief or value. As a side note, this would be inclusive of repetitive thoughts and feelings whether they are positive or negative.

The Optimal Human Experience

Flow is a concept described by Csikszentmihalyi in the early 1990s which has been the subject of considerable research and study since that time. In the early work of Csikszentmihalyi, flow is defined as "the state in which people are so involved in an activity that nothing else seems to matter; the experience itself is so enjoyable that people will do it even at great cost, for the sheer sake of doing it" (Csikszentmihalyi, 1990, p. 4). This is the optimal experience, "when a person's body or mind is stretched to its limits in a voluntary effort to accomplish something difficult and worthwhile" (Csikszentmihalyi, 1990, p. 3).

Using Csikszentmihalyi's concept of flow, the eight conditions that combine to create the flow experience are: Clear goals; quick feedback; a balance between opportunity and capacity; deepened concentration; being in the present; being in control; an altered sense of time; and the loss of ego. As Csikszentmihalyi noted, "I have given the name 'flow' to this common experience, because so many people have used the analogy of being carried away by an outside force, of moving effortlessly with a current of energy, at the moments of highest enjoyment" (Csikszentmihalyi, 2003, p. 39).

In discussing the origins of flow, Csikszentmihalyi found elements of the flow experience in a number of religions—Christianity, Buddhism and Taoism, for example. He then quoted the anthropologist Mel Konner, who, when asked if every culture produced a religion, why every culture sought God, answered: "It's not God— they are seeking the rapture of life, to understand *what it means to be alive*" (Csikszentmihalyi, 2003, p. 60).

Each of us has experienced flow at times in our lives: playing a good tennis match, meeting a short deadline, or enjoying team camaraderie during an intense task. An individual or team is said to be in a state of flow when the activity at hand becomes so intense that the normal sense of time and space disappears, and all energy is invested in the task. In a team setting, individuals lose the sense of identity or separateness during the experience, then afterward emerge from the experience with a stronger sense of self. While involved in this flow state there is a sense of exhilaration and joy. As these optimal experiences are repeated, individuals develop a sense of experiencing their real reason for being, coupled with a strong feeling of being in control.

The concept of *autotelic work* is tied to the optimal experience of flow, a state where people are so involved with their work that nothing else seems to matter. Autotelic workers create their own experience of flow. They are often creative, curious, and lead vigorous lives, taking everything that comes along in their stride. They are "life-long learners" who enjoy everything they do, and, along the way, spread a bit of joy to those around them.

Although flow cannot be turned on and off, individuals and teams can develop the ability to experience flow and create environmental conditions that facilitate its onset. As developed and studied by Csikszentmihalyi (1990), the conditions required for a team flow experience are:

1. Tasks must have a good chance of being completed, yet not be too easy.

2. The team must be able to concentrate on what it is doing. Interruptions, distractions, or poor facilities prevent concentration.

3. The task should have clear goals, so that the team knows when it has succeeded.

4. Immediate feedback should be provided to the team so that it can react and adjust its actions (Csikszentmihalyi, 1990).

The phenomenon of flow results in individuals and teams giving their best capabilities to tasks at hand. Team members come away with feelings of accomplishment, joy, and well-being that positively influence their willingness to trust and openly communicate with other team members, enhancing collaboration and team performance. The bottom line for the organization is a high level of performance. The bottom line for the individual is personal growth and self-satisfaction.

Note that the description of flow as autotelic work is bounded; that is, with a specific task orientation, and specific boundary conditions cited to ensure success. Unfortunately, life in a CUCA environment rarely complies with boundary conditions. Change—planned or unplanned—is not tied neatly to a single event, nor can it be easily contained in one domain of action. Rather, change crosses physical, mental, emotional and spiritual differentiations to affect the very fabric of our lives.

****

TOOL 18-2: DISCOVERING FLOW

STEP (1): Find a location that you love and where you can have a few quiet moments alone. This may be indoors or outdoors, perhaps sitting on the beach, or on a stone in a field, or in the corner of a library.

STEP (2): Reflect on an activity in which you repeatedly engage around, which you have passion. This may be a physical or mental activity.

STEP (3): Using your creative imagination, slowly relive your perfect moment engaged in this activity. Let your body engage in active listening, moving and smiling as appropriate for reliving the experience. Relish the detail, enjoy the feelings.

STEP (4): Repeat as necessary. When you have achieved a "floating" feeling, losing track of time and in the moment, you are in the flow state.

****

As Csikszentmihalyi (1997, pp. 31-32) wrote, "It is the full involvement of flow, rather than happiness, that makes for excellence in life." Baird and Nadel argue that the "full involvement of flow" is, in and of itself, a state of natural happiness. Happiness is a state of mind or feeling that is characterized by inner peace, love and joy. The flow state first occurs as we are doing something we love doing; then it expands and merges into a fluid process. As Baird and Nadel (2010, p. 118) quote His Holiness the Dali Lama:

> As human beings we all want to be happy and free from misery … we have learned that the key to happiness is inner peace. The greatest obstacles to inner peace are disturbing emotions such as anger and attachment, fear and suspicion, while love, compassion, and a sense of universal responsibility are the sources of peace and happiness.

When we emerge from the flow experience, "your mind and body may be flooded with 'e-words': excitement, exhilaration, enthusiasm, and energy" (Baird & Nadel, 2010, p. 119). Happiness is addressed in Chapter 22/Part IV as a learning point along the path of life.

Final Thoughts

As can be seen, energy is a force, playing a key role in our thoughts, feelings and actions. The more energy moving through the energy centers and their related senses, the higher an individual's consciousness. The larger flow of life would include the thoughts, the emotions flowing with those thoughts, and actions related to those thoughts, of ever-increasing numbers of people, with the inner flow including the core beliefs and values of humanity.

Questions for Reflection:

Do your energy flows take your breath away or enable you to breathe easy?

Does information flow freely through your organization for optimal performance?

Chapter 19
Emotions as a Guidance System

SUBTOPICS: EMOTIONS AS ENERGY ... PRINCIPLES OF EMOTION ... COGNITIVE CONVEYORS ... LISTENING TO THE WHISPERS ... EMOTIONAL INTELLIGENCE ... THE WONDER OF LOVE ... INTO THE FLOW WITH PASSION ... FINAL THOUGHTS.

FIGURES: 19-1. EXAMPLES OF CONCEPTS THAT ARE COGNITIVE CONVEYORS.

TOOLS: 19-1. MOOD SHIFTING ... **19-2.** RELEASING EMOTIONS TECHNIQUE ... **19-3.** FOCUSING

Emotions are a critical element of personal, team and organizational performance. As an operational definition of emotion, we consider emotion as "a mental state that arises spontaneously rather than through conscious effort and is often accompanied by physiological changes; a feeling" (*American Heritage Dictionary*, 2006, p. 585). However, we add the caveat that the various peripheral characteristics of emotions noted in this chapter may also apply, depending upon the author, context, and content of application. For example, Pert (1997) speaks in broad terms, including the familiar human emotions of anger, fear, sadness, joy, and contentment right along with basic sensations like pleasure and pain, and drive states such as courage, hunger and thirst. Courage as a drive state was presented as a cognitive conveyor in Chapter 9/Part II. Pert focuses on the biochemical substrate of emotion. As she forwards, "Neuropeptides and their receptors thus join the brain, glands, and immune system in a network of communication between brain and body, probably representing the biochemical substrate of emotion" (Pert, 1997, p. 179).

On the other hand, Damasio (1999) separates emotions and feelings. As he describes, "The term feeling should be reserved for the private, mental experience of an emotion, while the term emotion should be used to designate the collection of responses, many of which are publicly observable" (p. 42). Thus, emotions are externally focused and feelings are internally focused.

Emotions as Energy

Our emotions are a building block of consciousness (Greenfield, 2000), with both emotions and feelings serving as a guidance system for survival and the pain and pleasure portals of personality. Indeed, emotional content is almost always present in verbal and non-verbal communication. As Plotkin (1994, p. 211) describes, "Normal human life is lived within a sea of experienced and expressed emotions." Reflect on a past experience where your emotions have taken over your thoughts, and perhaps your actions. We have all had this experience, which helps us to recognize just how powerful our emotional system can be!

Drawing on neuroscience learnings, we know that emotions play a strong role in learning. All incoming signals and information are immediately passed to the amygdala, where they are assessed for potential harm to the individual. The amygdala places a tag on the signal that gives it a level of emotional importance (Adolphs, 2004; Zull, 2002). If the incoming information is considered dangerous to the individual, the amygdala immediately starts the body's response, such as pulling a hand away from a hot stove. In parallel, but slower than the amygdala's quick response, the incoming information is processed and cognitively interpreted.

Another aspect of the emotional system is the role it plays in individual memory. Situations that have a high emotional impact are much easier to recall, sometimes remembered throughout life, and hard to lay aside even when we desire to do so. From a learning perspective, this means that (consciously or unconsciously) the learner is always evaluating the importance of incoming information, and this process helps the individual to remember the information (Christos, 2003).

This interplay of the physical and mental with the emotional is going on throughout the body. Pert's (1997) study of information-processing receptors on nerve cell membranes led her to discover the presence of neural receptors on most of the body's cells. This "established that the 'mind' was not focused in the head, but was *distributed via signal molecules to the whole body*" (Lipton, 2005, p. 132), with the mind, spirit, and emotions unified with the physical body as *part of a single intelligent system.*

As humans, we are prone to attribute various causes to our emotions and feelings. We say such things as: "He made me angry" or "I'm upset because of ..." or "That is frightening." However, these emotions and feelings are our own. To understand this concept, let's look at a few scenarios.

Scenario 1: You are the dad of a 17-year-old son who asks to use the family car on Friday night for a "hot" date. Agreeing, you give him a curfew of 12 Midnight. When Friday arrives, at half past Midnight he is not yet home. You are waiting in the front hall, saying to yourself, "When I know he's okay, I'm going to kill him!" The phone rings. "This is Mercy Hospital; I'm sorry. Your son, John Doe, was in an automobile accident. He died of massive head injuries." What happens to you? Your pulse speeds up, you are sweating, your head is pounding. You may very well have a stroke or heart attack. Two minutes pass, and the phone rings again. "This is Mercy Hospital. I'm sorry, wrong John Doe." And in walks your son, saying "Hey, dad, I ran out of gas, but I did everything you told me to ..." You may be there lying on the floor ... yet, NOTHING HAS HAPPENED. Your emotions and feelings were a result of your PERCEPTION of what had happened.

Scenario 2: You are a 23-year-old young woman who has just completed a Master's Degree in Marketing. You land an interview for the job of your dreams with the largest marketing firm in New York City! Seven grueling hours of interviews. They look at your layouts, they ask about your photographs, they have you do an instantaneous writing sample. (They do provide lunch, so you're hanging in there.) Then, finally, you are offered the job at twice the salary you ever expected! Floating on air, you exit the building and glide down the stairs to the street. It's dark, and you are parked 20 blocks away, quite close, actually, for New York! As you head toward your car, you note there are two large figures following you. You speed up; they speed up. You turn the corner; they turn the corner. You start to run, they run after you. Catching up to you, one of the figures grabs your elbow, bringing you to a halt. How do you feel? What thoughts and their corresponding emotions and feelings are coursing through your body? The man holding your elbow reaches out his other hand, which has an object in it, and says, "Excuse me, Miss, you dropped your wallet."

As can be seen from these scenarios, your emotions and feelings are very much a product of your personal beliefs, perceptions, thoughts, experiences, and even the newspapers you've read and the movies you've seen.

Fear is a catalyst for many other emotional responses. Using the example of fear, Walsch (2009) notes that different people are afraid of different things. He asks the question: So, what *does* produce the fear? Walsch (2009, p. 61) then responds,

> It's something inside you. It's your ideas and your memories and your projects and your concepts and your apprehensions and your understandings and your desires and your conditioning and more. And all of these things fall into one broad category. Thoughts. It is your *thoughts* that sponsor your fears, and nothing else. Thoughts sponsor *all* emotions.

Similarly, let's use stress as an example. Stress was introduced in Chapter 13, with low stress a potential accelerator of learning and high stress a blockage and quite dangerous to human systems. There are two possible responses to this danger: either *eliminate the cause* of stress, the situation at hand, or *change your perception* (thought) about the cause of stress. A cognitive approach [A SIMPLE THOUGHT TOOL] can help in this regard. For example, if you are in a job where you are continuously unhappy, you might have this conversation with yourself. *Why am I still in this job? Because the paycheck is regular and good, and I don't have another job to move into. Because there is some potential for advancement. Because I like the idea of this type of work. Because I am learning. Because ... because ... because ...* The idea here is that there ARE reasons why you have *not* left this job, regardless of your emotions/feelings *about* the job.

Fill in a two-column list, capturing on one side the reasons you are still in the job and on the other side the things you don't like about the job. Now look at this list closely. In your judgment, at least unconsciously, the positive elements currently outweigh the negative elements, *or you would choose to leave.* Acknowledging this— that currently staying in this job is a choice—you can shift your perception and, perhaps, develop a timeline or a list of actions you will take to move yourself into (1) a better position in the company, or (2) a better position to move to another company. While this shift of perception can help unblock emotions and move you back into the flow, simultaneously, appreciate your emotions! They are providing input, that is, letting you know that you need to stay open to the potential around you; in this case, the opportunity for a new job that is a closer fit to who you are and who you want to be.

<<<<<<<◇>>>>>>>

INSIGHT: **Our emotions are just that ... OURS. *We* determine how they make us feel and how we act accordingly.**

<<<<<<<◇>>>>>>>

The stress example, as well as the two scenarios presented above, deal with relative meaning, which is context sensitive and situation dependent. While emotional processing can—and regularly does—take place outside of conscious awareness, once aware of these emotional responses, humans have the potential to consciously observe, influence and shift their emotions. Recall the AUBFOE individual change model presented in Chapter 6/Part I.

Awareness often comes in the form of pain and, while this pain can be felt throughout the body, it is often felt as originating in the heart, the perceived center of emotions. Fortunately, thought has the potential to mitigate this pain. As Cooper (2005, p. 28) describes,

Many of life's events can damage a person emotionally. The mind can help the heart overcome its hurt and pain by creating new thought forms that allow a different heart reaction to otherwise traumatic events. In this way, the mind and the heart work together to enact a different perception of traumatic events, allowing love and compassion to remain intact even when one is under attack.

As a rule of thumb, it takes only 17 seconds of focused feeling to shift from one emotional state to another. How might you do this? You do this through your thoughts and actions. (See Tool 18-1 below). The body produces complex responses to emotional arousal. There is an electrochemical pathway that moves from the brain through the limbic system and then throughout the body utilizing adrenal glands and the autonomic nervous system. The firing of specific nerve cells forms and release amino acid neuropeptide chains which can activate or deactivate the biological process involved in both emotion and behavior. Pert (1997) calls these chains *the molecules of emotion.*

****

TOOL 19-1: Mood Shifting

Small and large perturbations have a way of working themselves into our lives, interfering with the flow. This is a simple tool that can serve you well. Your thoughts are quite powerful. By choosing our thoughts we can determine or adjust our emotional experience.

STEP (1): Each of us has moments in life that when we think about them it makes us feel good. We also have special memories that help remind us of who we are, and perhaps why we are here. Take a wallet-sized card and on one side write five things you are or have been a part of that you feel good about. On the other side write down five things you have done in your life to serve others. These can be as simple as a well-timed compliment to a loved one, or an act of kindness to a stranger.

STEP (2): Put that card in your wallet and carry it around with you.

STEP (3): Whenever a life perturbation occurs and your emotions tank, recognize your immediate emotional response and honor it, being sure to note any lessons learned. Then, pull out your card and read whichever side is most appropriate for the situation at hand. Spend several minutes (or as much time as needed) remembering and reflecting on the events or situations represented on your card.

STEP (4): When you feel your emotions positively shift, you are ready to address the issue at hand from a different viewpoint.

****

What is missing from Pert's description of the chemicals and molecules that activate the body's responses to emotional arousal is an explanation of *how* thought activates these chemical messages in the first place. Pert suggests an interesting phenomenon that offers a clue. Building on Pert's work, Lambrou and Pratt (2000, p. 52) contend,

> The receptor sites on a nerve cell vibrate at a certain frequency. However, when the neurotransmitter locks onto a receptor site, the frequency changes. Something is going on at the energetic, or vibratory, level. Our thesis is that the energy flowing in the meridians activates certain cells to trigger the manufacture of the neuropeptides.

This means that the energy of thought interacts with the meridian system, activating the electrochemical process and sending signals throughout the body.

Quantum theory can help us understand this relationship. Energy fields contain information. The more thought heading the same direction, the greater the potential impact of that thought. Relativity theory tells us that energy and matter are equivalent and interchangeable; energy can exist as either a wave or a particle. Further, we now know that the very act of observing a wave or particle can alter it. At the Quantum level, when things get smaller, then the observer has a greater influence (Lambrou & Pratt, 2000).

Tiller (2007), an engineering professor at Stanford University, spent 40 years experimenting with the power of intentional thought. Using a sensitive electrical capacitor, Tiller discovered that by focusing their intent, ordinary people could cause the capacitor to discharge. When the subjects focused their attention on the capacitor, setting their intention, the capacitor discharged during a few minutes. Early experiments involved changing the alkaline/acidity ratio of water. Further detail of Tiller's work is provided in Chapter 25/Part IV on Attention and Intention, and in the Addendum.

By understanding that emotions can be triggered by perceived external events, yet are simultaneously our creation and an act of will, we can set up situations where external events or internal thoughts provide stimuli to trigger desired feelings (LeDoux, 1996). We choose external stimuli regularly when we go to the movies or visit an amusement park, or even when we consume alcohol or stimulate our palate with a gourmet meal! Choosing internal stimuli, we can slip into a daydream of a favorite memory or imagine our perfect future. The bottom line is that with practice and conviction, we can *choose* to feel a certain way.

Principles of Emotion

The emotions we feel—or choose to feel—affect every part of our lives, personal and professional, whether alone or in a group. Ralston (1995, p. 16) identified eight principles of emotions that provide unique insights into the way people behave and why they behave that way. This is a good set that warrants repetition here. These principles are:

1. Emotional needs express themselves one way or another.

2. Anger is an expression of need.

3. Our feelings and needs are not wrong or bad.

4. Emotions are the gateway to vitality and feeling alive.

5. We can address emotional issues and still save face.

6. Immediate reactions to problems often disguise deeper feelings.

7. We must clarify individual needs before problem solving with others.

8. We need to express positive feelings and communicate negative ones.

If you've been around in life for a while, you no doubt have heard the expression, and probably felt, the emotional rollercoaster of life. This is the up and down ride between excitement and disappointment, emotional highs and lows. Humans seem to have a penchant for living from one extreme to another. One approach to balance forwarded by Willis (2012, p. 16) is to lower your expectations as to prevent disappointment. As he says,

> To free yourself from the emotional rollercoaster, have an expectation that events will be as they are going to be. Learn to accept things the way they are and do not expect events to be how you want them to be.

While this is certainly one approach to achieving a "calm, relaxing and balanced journey through our lives" (Willis, 2012, p. 16), it also reduces the emotional feelings of vitality and being alive. Further, as we have learned from neuroscience and, taking a consilience approach will be explored more fully in Chapter 23/Part IV, *our thoughts and feelings are very important to creating our reality*. Since thought form follows thought, setting intent (through expectations) is a powerful tool of self. When our thought is consistently supported by our emotions, it is like giving gas to our thought, which increases the force of our thought.

With this new frame of reference comes the understanding that events themselves, that is, things happening in the environment in which we live and, in our interactions, that that environment, *do not themselves have meaning*. It is our self, emerging from all the experiences of life, that *assigns meaning to events*. (See Chapter 5/Part I.) A power of emotions is their sensitivity to meaning, that is, to the meaning we have assigned to these types of things or events. Emotions exist to alert and protect individuals from harm, and to energize them to action when they have strong feelings or passions. However, *emotions are concerned with the meaning of the information and not the details*. This is because emotions bypass slower cognitive functions such as conscious thought. As detailed above, all incoming signals and information pass through the amygdala, where they are assessed for potential harm to the individual and tagged in terms of level of emotional importance (Adolphs, 2004; Zull, 2002). Thus, the body is responding before the incoming information is processed and cognitively interpreted, and prior to conscious awareness or thought.

<<<<<<<◇>>>>>>>

INSIGHT: **Emotions are concerned with the meaning of the information and not the details.**

<<<<<<<◇>>>>>>>

Sometimes it's difficult to value something that is part of everyday life until you don't have it anymore. When going through the hormonal changes that come with aging, one of the authors lost their emotions for a period of a year. While the mental faculties were still fully functioning, everything felt flat; there was less joy and excitement with the discovery of ideas, and less desire to take what was learned and write a book or share it with others. As the body adjusted to new chemical levels, emotions slowly returned, and even simple emotional responses to everyday activities, whether negative or positive, brought with them *the happiness of feelings*. As another example, when a family member died, one of the authors went through the five stages of loss detailed in Elizabeth Kubler-Ross's work on death and dying. Even as these strong emotions came forth, they were accompanied by laughter, what the author refers to as *joyous grieving*, for the deep feelings associated with the grieving process were a reminder of the love felt for this family member, and triggered gratitude for knowing and feeling that love so deeply. Thus, our emotions can, and if we choose do, add a richness to life, but are always in service to the mental faculties. How we express and respond to our emotions is a choice.

As the guidance system which punctuates the positive and negative aspects of our lives, our feelings and emotions need to be honored, and, as appropriate, considered in the making of our day-to-day decisions. Positive emotions such as love and joy make our lives more meaningful. While we may choose to hold on to strong negative emotions to purposefully create a force to propel us on a course of action, once they have been honored in terms of recognition and understanding, it is indeed a good idea to release emotions no longer needed. This will be discussed further in the following chapter dealing with stuck energy.

The Dalai Lama uses the term *emotional hygiene* to describe the necessity for each of us to bring destructive emotions under control before going out and acting in the world. Otherwise, these emotions can, and most likely will, cause harm to ourselves and others. This is a good practice to remember, and where perhaps the tool above can be of service. Goleman (2015) suggests that having calm, clarity and compassion as we act on the world will result in the greatest good. With reflection, no doubt we all agree.

****

TOOL 19-2: Releasing Emotions Technique

STEP (1): Recognize and name the emotions you are feeling, fully acknowledging their presence.

STEP (2): Put your arms around yourself and, rocking in a motion from left to right and back in a self-embrace, and with gratitude for these emotions, *say out loud* "I am having a human moment."

STEP (3): Ensuring that you have learned all you need to learn from their presence, thank your emotion for their presence and for this learning.

STEP (4): Using your creative imagination, choose to release these emotions, visualizing them floating away in a balloon, or imploding into the air, or sending them to a junk yard for potential reuse. Have fun with this. The only limit is your imagination.

STEP (5): When a negative emotion departs it leaves a clear space that needs filling. To fill this space, spend a few minutes thinking about some happy memories, or engage in an activity during which you feel joy.

NOTE: It's useful to create a small card (wallet-size) with happy thoughts. See TOOL 19-1. This card can be used to spur happy thoughts in the technique above, or can be used to raise your vibration anytime you feel an emotional low.

****

Cognitive Conveyors

In Chapter 9/Part II, we introduced the concept of cognitive conveyors. There are many words that represent concepts filled with a combination of thought, emotion and feelings, and while emotional arousal plays an important role in these concepts, affecting mental activity and having a physiological effect on the body, they are not identified directly as emotions. A subset of these words can be described as cognitive conveyors since they are very much in support of our thought. For example, consider the concepts of desire, drive, courage and intent, each representing different combinations of emotional and mental activity, with different levels of emotional content supporting mental thought and related physical action. See Figure 19-1. Conversely, there are also words that potentially represent cognitive impeders; an example is procrastination. There are also concepts, such as persuasion, that can be either a conveyor or impeder, dependent on the situation and context. Thus, again, we are reminded that it is how we use our feelings and how we use our emotions that makes a difference in our actions, which are, whether conscious or unconscious, a choice.

There are also conditions that *represent* emotional states but are not the emotions themselves. For example, claustrophobia is a condition that generally involves fear.

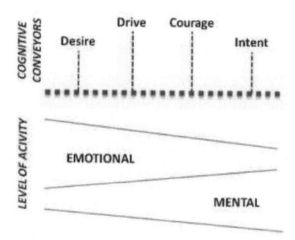

Figure 19-1. *Examples of concepts that are cognitive conveyors.*

Listening to the Whispers

People have a tendency to get caught up in life and not listen to their bodies. When this occurs, the body will eventually manifest pain or physical distress to catch our attention. In the 1960's, Professor Eugene Gendlin, a therapist and researcher at the University of Chicago, discovered a consistent difference between successful therapy clients and those who were unsuccessful. This difference could be identified in the client during the first or second sessions. The successful clients had a vague awareness of their bodies, a sense or feeling emerging from their bodies. As Cornell (1990) describes:

> [A]t some point in the session, the successful therapy clients would slow down their talk, become less articulate, and begin to grope for words to describe something that they were feeling at the moment. If you listened to the tapes, you would hear something like this: 'Hmmm. How would I describe this? It's right here. It's ... uh ... it's ... it's not exactly anger ... hmmm.' Often the clients would mention that they experienced this feeling in their bodies, saying things like, 'It's right here in my chest,' or 'I have this funny feeling in my stomach.'

From this research Gendlin (1978) developed an approach he called *Focusing* that became a self-help skill to use instead of therapy, to help make decisions and as a help with creativity. Cornell (1990, front cover) says that "Our bodies carry knowledge about how we are living our lives, what we need, what we value and belief, and what has hurt us emotionally and how to heal it." She sees focusing as offering exciting potential for change. "Focusing lets you form a trusting relationship with your body ... let's you listen to the whispers of your body before it has to shout."

****

TOOL 19-3: FOCUSING

We build on the work of Cornell (1990) to create a focusing process to share here.

STEP (1) Find a comfortable place to sit or lie where you will not be bothered. Now take three or four deep breaths, releasing your anxieties and any tenseness in your body as you release your breath. Feel your body become quiet.

STEP (2) Continue feeling your body. Take a tour of your body, letting your thoughts roam through your body. Invite something to be felt. *Ask:* "What wants my attention now?" Then listen to your body, *feel* your body.

STEP (3) When something catches your attention, focus on it. Say *hello* to it, then try to describe or name it. Putting it into words focuses it, and limits it. With interested curiosity get to know the feeling better. *Ask:* Is there an emotion connected with this feeling? When you name the emotion, *ask:* Is this the right word to describe it?

STEP (4) Gently, taking your time, invite the feeling to tell you more. *Ask:* Is this feeling connected to a memory or belief? Then, just put it aside or let it go. Don't deep dive into memory lane. As Cornell says, "There is no need to 'fix' or 'solve' the problem. *Acknowledging* [emphasis added] the message, really hearing it, is all that is needed to bring deep relief" (2009, p. 13).

STEP (5) Go back to sensing your body. *Ask*: Is this a good place to stop focusing for now? If the answer is "no", repeat STEPS (2) through (4). If the answer is "yes", thank your body for sharing this information, say you will be back, and slowly bring your focus back to the outside world and open your eyes.

HINT: It is not necessary to wait until your body catches your attention through pain or physical distress to use Focusing. All too often we only notice our bodies when something is wrong, yet our bodies are working day and night just for us. Take a few minutes every day to thank every cell for all they do for you; *it is all about you!* Check in with your body regularly.

****

Emotional Intelligence

Emotional intelligence has been extensively explored by Daniel Goleman (1995) in his seminal book. Emotional intelligence is the ability to sense, understand, and effectively apply the power and acumen of emotions as a source of human energy, information, connection, and influence. It includes self-control, zeal and persistence, and the ability to motivate oneself.

Goleman identifies four components of emotional intelligence at work: self-awareness; self-management; social awareness; and social skill. Since the publication of Goleman's first book, there has been much research in this area, and today EQ is recognized as a basic requirement for effective use of the intellect. As can be seen, emotional intelligence is both a personal tool of self and social engagement, managing ourselves and our relationships.

To understand emotional intelligence, we study how emotions affect behavior, influence decisions, motivate people to action, and impact their ability to interrelate. Emotions play a much larger role in our lives than previously understood, including a strong role in decision-making. For years it was widely held that rationality was the way of the executive. Now it is becoming clear that the full spectrum of what it is to be human—including the rational and the emotional parts of the mind—must be engaged to achieve the best performance in our personal lives and in our organizations.

Emphasizing the significance of emotions in learning, in 1997 the field of affective computing emerged out of MIT. Affective computing is described as computing that relates to, arises from or deliberately influences, emotions (Picard, 1997). Embedding the ability to recognize emotions into machines was driven by Picard's belief that putting emotions in machines would not only make them more human (thereby improving human-computer communication), but could lead to a more human decision-making process supporting decision-makers and learners. Further, "When we succeed, a feeling of pride might encourage us to keep on going and push ourselves even harder to reach even greater goals" (Neji & Ben Ammar, 2007).

Since emotions are contagious, it is this contagious nature that Neiji and Ben Ammar felt was potentially transferable and beneficial to the virtual world. Recognizing that the use of emotions to complement and indeed facilitate communication in collaborative virtual environments had been vastly under-explored, they developed a collaborative affective eLearning framework aimed at reintroducing emotional and social context to distance learning while offering a stimulating and integrated framework for affective conversation and collaboration. In essence, they were proposing an emotional framework for an intelligent emotional system.

<<<<<<<◇>>>>>>

INSIGHT: **The contagious nature of emotions can be both transferrable and beneficial to the virtual world.**

<<<<<<<◇>>>>>>

Simulations and visualization tools are widely used to study and explain complex systems in science and technology. While these systems are developed by expert teams with an in-depth understanding of the subject matter, all too often their tools and systems fail to emotionally address users and learners. One of the reasons for the "lack of emotion" or "lack of engagement" lies in the absence of micro control and game elements such as avatars, virtual buddies, levels, badges and achievements, widely known from competitive and social gameplays. People feel emotionally bonded when they have a high level of control and ownership over their virtual self. They feel safe and confident in the usage and find themselves emotionally "diving into their virtual reality", even to the point of failing to distinguish between their real self and their virtual self (Salen, 2008, Clark, 1998, Schwabe & Goth, 2005).

In 2009, Davidson and Goldberg observed that the ways we acquire and manage information had changed significantly over the past two decades, and that individuals, organizations and institutions needed to find new concepts and tools for personalized, flexible and mobile learning (Johnson et al., 2008). Smartphones and tablet computers are around everywhere today. They are used in schools, training centers and companies. This offered the opportunity for modern learning science to utilize technology to develop *intelligent emotional systems* that integrate "distributed cognition", "social competitive gameplay" and "game-based learning experiences", and entrepreneurs are fully engaging this opportunity.

For example, Quizzbizz, a small business founded by Maik Fuellman (2016) in Hong Kong, discovered that social mobile quiz and trivia games are a perfect tool to transfer explicit knowledge to students and this format can be an accepted *middle way* to bring the "World of learning and the World of gaming" closer together, without losing the focus on pedagogics and knowledge transfer. Since learning games were found to be a promising way to exchange information, build and share knowledge, and make learning interesting, interactive and fun (Admiraal et al., 2011, 2009; Gee, 2003), Fuellmann (2016) discovered that mobile micro learning quizzes and educational classroom games like Kahoot (www.getkahoot.com) or Socrative (www.socrative.com) foster students' emotional engagement by microcontrol, competitive gameplay, and high interactivity in class experiences. Both tools build on the concepts of *flow* (Csikszentmihalyi, 1997) and the *ARCS model of motivation* (Keller, 1987), which are often used to understand user experience and user involvement. From a pedagogic learner-centric approach, content and methodology are equally important to motivate students (Edelson et al. 1999).

As can be seen, the interplay of emotions and learning—reaching Csikszentmihalyi's (1990) zone of flow—is already upon us. Recent research shows that combining mobile micro learning with the methodology of inquiry-based learning (Savery, 2015) increases the emotional engagement of learners and improves memorization and knowledge retention. Mobile learning tools use relevant and individualized learning content provided by teachers or developed by students in class to engage learners in entertaining, short-lasting, interactive and competitive social gameplays.

In 2016 Quizzbizz held the first field tests of a gamified inquiry-based microlearning platform (*Uniquizz*) that combines entertaining trivia with relevant learning content resulted in significantly higher exam scores and positive feed-back from students and teachers. Students reported a high emotional involvement, better memorization and experience interactivity and fun while preparing for exams or when reflecting on and reviewing course materials and classes. The importance of the emotional experience tied to the mental experience can be discerned through the responses of four students pursuing Bachelor Degrees in Thailand:

From an International Business Student: *I found this course different because the teacher came with solid ideas such as question creation by each and every one and merging them into mobile apps such as Quizbizz, which was unique and **did not create a boring learning environment,** which was the first new learning method that I got a chance to experience.*

From a Knowledge Management Student: *"What I like is that the teacher lets students **create questions by themselves**. It makes me study the important things and focus on specific topics to understand them deeply. The Uniquizz application lets me **enjoy playing the course content rather than reading boring stuff**.*

From a Marketing Student: *Another thing I like about this course is the Uniquizz application; this is so useful for us to prepare for the final exam as it helps me remember the answers easily and fast. Normally I don't like to read to prepare for an exam as **it's so boring** and it takes a long time to remember what we have learned, but Uniquizz has shortened the time and **turned what was boring into fun.***

From an International Business Student: *I like the UNIQUIZZ application ... because it's extremely helpful, useful, **fun** and convenient to learn. I spent time on it before the exam for only 4 days, but can proudly rank no.1, with 6220 scores. It makes me remember the information faster that reading a book and I use it everywhere and **play** with my friends and classmates. It's coo. I have it with my phone everywhere.* (Quizzbizz, 2016)

These findings indicate that mobile micro learning within a learning trivia game fosters emotional bonding, increased motivation and is easily adapted by students (Fuellmann, 2016). They can better memorize relevant educational content and, through friendly competition and interaction, the gameplay improves communication and knowledge flows in and outside of the classroom. Clearly consideration of the emotional plane is an important part of the learning experience, whether virtual or face-to-face.

The Wonder of Love

Love first develops through consciousness, generally related by a growing child to the parent or caregiver. Later the concept takes on different meanings, and during puberty this feeling of strong affection becomes attached to the idea of romance and sexual desire. This strong affection also accompanies developing beliefs; for example, a growing connection to God. The highest form of this love—the love of God for man, and the love of man for God—is called agape. This universal, unconditional love that transcends all things is derived from the ancient Greek: ἀγάπη, agápē, which translates as gaping, as with wonder and expectation, the mouth wide open (Meriam-Webster, 2016).

Love and freedom are irrevocably connected. In the Ageless Wisdom tradition, freedom is described as the first part of God's mind, and love as the second part (MacFlouer, 1999). This is because without the freedom to choose, love cannot come into being. This concept is critical to our understanding of love. *Love grows. It cannot be created, manufactured, or purchased. You cannot will or demand love.* As Carey (1996, p. 39) reminds us,

> The choice to function on the love-centered motivational frequencies, **where you are designed to function** [emphasis added], is the only choice that brings freedom. It does not limit you to a predetermined script but offers a range of behavior that evokes your fullest potential.

Viktor Frankl, who endured three years at Auschwitz and other Nazi prisons, discovered the power of love in the midst of his suffering. The realization came as an image of his wife vividly arose in his mind. As he describes:

> A thought transfixed me: for the first time in my life I saw the truth as it is set into song by so many poets, proclaimed as the final wisdom by so many thinkers. The truth—that love is the ultimate and the highest goal to which man can aspire. Then I grasped the meaning of the greatest secret that human poetry and human thought and belief have to impart: *The salvation of man is through love and in love.* I understood ow a man who has nothing left in this world still may know bliss, be it only for a brief moment, in the contemplation of his beloved. In a position of utter desolation, when many cannot express himself in positive action, when his only achievement may consist in enduring his sufferings in the right way—an honorable way—in such a position man can, through loving contemplation of the image he carries of his beloved, achieve fulfillment. For the first time in my life I was able to understand the meaning of the words, 'The angels are lost in perpetual contemplation of an infinite glory'. (Frankl, 1963, pp. 58-59)

As a life of inflicted pain interrupted his connection, again and again Frankl was able to find his way back from the prisoner's existence to this place of love. He did not know whether his wife was alive or not, but he did know one thing, that "Love goes very far beyond the physical person of the beloved. It finds its deepest meaning in his spiritual being, his inner self. Whether or not he is actually present, whether or not he is still at all, ceases somehow to be of importance." (Frankl, 1963, p. 60)

Love is born of understanding another, truly knowing another, looking within at their motives, sentiments and values. Once you really know who someone is, love is contagious. In *Urantia* (1954, p. 1098), it is suggested that each day or week we achieve an understanding of one or more individuals.

If each mortal could only become a focus of dynamic affection, this benign virus of love would soon pervade the sentimental emotion-stream of humanity to such an extent that all civilization would be encompassed by love, and that would be the realization of the brotherhood of man.

Love, like knowledge, expands when it is given away. When combined with wisdom, good things happen. Wise giving, introduced in Chapter 22/Part IV as a learning point along the path of life, is the promotion of others to be giving, helping people find more ways to help others, which leads to beauty. Empathy comes into play in order to achieve wise giving. Empathy enables you to experience others in the sense of being them, with a whole new sense of reality emerging with the experience. Now you are beginning to understand them, and with that understanding comes compassion, then love. In Chapter 35/Part V, Conscious Compassion, we recognize that unconditional love is an attribute of the advanced human that emerges as we progress through the Intelligent Social Change Journey from sympathy to empathy to compassion and, ultimately, to unconditional love.

<<<<<<<<>>>>>>>

INSIGHT: **Empathy enables you to experience others in the sense of being them, with a whole new sense of reality emerging with the experience. With that understanding comes compassion.**

<<<<<<<<>>>>>>>

Recall that cooperation and collaboration are virtues of the physical plane. Along with gratitude, admiration and forgiveness, love is a hive emotion that supports cooperation, which leads to an edge in survival for that group. It is also the highest virtue on the emotional plane. Drawing on history, Seligman (2011, p. 144-45) explains:

A cooperative group will bring down a mastodon more readily than an asocial group. A cooperative group can form the 'turtle' in battle; a Roman offensive formation that sacrifices the men on the outer flanks, but easily defeats a group of selfish-only soldiers. A cooperative group can create agriculture, towns, technology, and music (singing, marching, and laughing tunes the group). To the extent that cooperation and altruism have a genetic basis, this entire group will pass on its genes more readily than a group that lacks cooperation and altruism.

Thus, there is the case made for the gradual improvement, through evolution, of the human race.

This has not gone unnoticed in the organization and management literature of this century. Andersen and Born (2008) specifically sees the phenomenon of love as explicitly cultivated in the work environment as increasingly common in the current age. Fleming and Sturdy (2009) introduced the idea of neo-normative control exhorting individuation and *being yourself*. Neo-management control, an emergent concept, posits that management through individual freedoms is a defining element of the 21st century workforce (Walker, 2011). The freedoms that are encouraged include those of self-expression and discretion (Cederström & Grassman, 2008; Fleming, 2009).

Sternberg's (1986) triangle of love theory has three components: intimacy (emotional investment and closeness), passion (excitement and arousal) and commitment (relationship over time). While Sternberg's model was applied to romantic love, Barsade and O'Neill (2014, p. 2) translate this into more general terms, the idea of "feelings of affection, compassion, caring, and tenderness for others."

e Cunha et al. (2016) related love to what they characterized as virtue-oriented communities, which is strongly tied to the leader's virtue anchored by a personal motivation toward "good" and informed by character strengths. (See "good character" in Chapter 34/Part V.) By acting in love, that is, by listening to employees, communicating openly, exhibiting compassion, etc., others are inspired to do the same (Barsade & Gibson, 2007; Chartrand & Lakin, 2013; Menges and Kilduff, 2015). Leading by example starts the process toward a culture of love, then the energy of love itself continues the process. As one responder in the e Cunha et al. (2016) research study described:

> … [Love] allows for an inner wealth, an insight, greater self-knowledge, self-confidence, and a great strength of character … a very strong self-awareness. So I think it is not immediate, it is not only by example … example leads people to think about love, to question themselves more, to be more aware. (e Cunha et al., 2016, p 8)

Argandoña (2011, p. 82) describes love as an organizational virtue. He defines this love as "a habit that facilitates decision-making … serves to evaluate actions … and moves the will to act in a particular way." That particular way *begins with ethics and is exhibited by honesty, kindness and care*. (See the example of care as an organizational value in Chapter 34/Part V.)

Into the Flow with Passion

The flow state, the focus of Chapter 18, is enabled by the strong emotion of passion. Passion is a feeling that Charles Belitz and Meg Lundstrom identify as one of nine attributes that create the power of flow. As Belitz and Lundstrom (1997, p. 57) contend:

> Flow is engendered by passion—passion for life, for knowledge, for a cause, for a relationship, for truth. Passion means caring deeply about something beyond ourselves. It means engaging with it at intense levels. It means letting go of self-protective caution to involve ourselves wholeheartedly with what we love.

This passion "opens us up to a larger picture." It is the intensity of flow, the intense desire to be "active and engaged in the course of events" and the intense drive to know truth, "to answer the basic questions of existence: why we're here, what we're supposed to be doing, what it all means. Not satisfied with surface explanations, we use every moment as an opportunity to break through to something new, to learn. We fully engage with what comes our way" (Belitz and Lundstrom, 1997, p. 57).

In a historical context, *passions* (in the plural) was used in the work of early Western philosophers to represent what we now call *emotions*. For example, early analysis of emotions using the term passions appears in dialogues of Plato and in Aristotle's *Rhetoric*; as well as in the Greek discussions of virtue and vice. As an aside, according to Lou Marinoff, ancient Greek philosophers had a propensity to indulge both their reason and passions alike, in the hopes of perfecting the former and outgrowing the latter (Marinoff, 2003). Some of this behavior can still be seen today.

Passions also appear in the moral theology of Thomas Aquinas and in Benedict Spinoza's *Ethics*; and in books of political theory, such as Niccolo Machiavelli's *The Prince* and Thomas Hobbes's *Leviathan* (Adler, 1992, p. 185). And, Rene Descartes' "six 'primitive' passions—wonder, love, hatred, desire, joy, and sadness—are not meaningless agitations of the animal spirits, but ingredients in the good life" (Frijda, 2000, p. 6).

David Hume insisted that, "What motivates us to right (and wrong) behavior . . . were our passions, and rather than being relegated to the margins of ethics and philosophy, the passions deserve central respect and consideration" (Frijda, 2000, p. 6). Hume also believed that *moral distinctions are derived from passion* rather than from reason. "Morals excite passions, and produce or prevent actions." By contrast, reason is "perfectly inert" and can never produce or prevent an action (Honderich, 1999, p. 110). The philosopher Georg Hegal affirmed, "Nothing great in the world has been accomplished without passion." In like manner, the term "passions" appears in many historic works of poetry and history (Adler, 1992, p. 185).

<<<<<<<◇>>>>>>>

INSIGHT: **Moral distinctions are derived from passion rather than from reason.**

<<<<<<<◇>>>>>>>

Although the use of the word *passion* to specifically represent a strong emotion or desire is first recorded around 1250 AD, "the generalized meaning of a strong liking, enthusiasm (as in a *passion for horses*) is first recorded in 1638" (Barnhart, 1988, p. 761). The *Oxford English Dictionary* (updated in 2002) cited 12 different perspectives on the concept of *passion*, first presenting the use of the term representing the suffering of pain, specifically the suffering connected to Jesus' Crucifixion in Christian theology.

Psychologist Nico Frijda saw passions as often extending to desires, thoughts, plans, and behaviors that persist over time. "They may lead to performing behaviors regardless of costs, external obstacles, and moral objections. These are the characteristics of passion in the more modern sense—the desires, behaviors, and thoughts that suggest urges with considerable force" (Frijda, 2000, p. 59). Thus, passions significantly contributed to achieving personal and organizational goals. As Peter Senge says, people's passions flow naturally into creating something that truly excites them. "The passion at the heart of every great undertaking comes from the deep longing of human beings to make a difference, to have an impact. **It comes from what you contribute rather than from what you get** [emphasis added]" (Senge, 1990, p. 62).

Further, in a discussion of people skills, Goleman cited focus and passion as important elements of achieving group flow. "The demands of meeting a great goal inherently provide focus; the rest of life can seem not just mundane, but trivial by comparison. For the duration, the details of life are on hold" (Goleman, 1998, p. 228). Passion, driving the intensity of flow, *elevates values and engages reality at all levels* in its search for "what it means to be alive" (Csikszentmihalyi, 2003, p. 60). This is also reflected in the spiritual context of passion, a spiritual freeflow as a strong vehicle for awakening (Gyatso, 1992; Walsh and Shapiro, 1983; Watts, 2002) and energy that helps people *speak from the heart*, drawing out other people and engaging them (Rockwell, 2002. p. 52).

Thus, both as an individual and as a collective, passion acts as emotional super-fuel, propelling us into the flow of life to think and act in a focused domain of knowledge. For a fulfilling life, we are asked to live our passion. (See Bennet, 2005, for an in-depth treatment of passion.)

Final Thoughts

Emotions are a gift to humanity which, when applied well, create great harmony and connect us in Oneness. However, when mismanaged or out of balance, emotions can create conflict, negativity and war. Once we become masters of our emotional system, love and passion weave their way through all elements of our lives, guiding us toward intelligent activity and becoming the co-creators of the life we choose to live.

Questions for Reflection:

Are you able to effectively listen to and translate your emotions when you are interacting with others?

How do you incorporate emotions in your strategic decision-making process?

Do your actions increase or decrease your passion and the passion of others?

Chapter 20
Stuck Energy:
Limiting and Accelerating

SUBTOPICS: Mental Models ... Stress ... Forgetting ... Letting Go ... Mental Chatter ... Webs of Energy ... Final Thoughts

FIGURES: 20-1. Learning Cycle for Threatening Events ... **20-2.** Webs of stuck energy accumulate between the physical and emotional planes, and between the emotional and mental planes.

TOOL: 20-1. Letting Go

If we didn't already believe it from the behavioral viewpoint, it is clear from what we've learned from neuroscience since the turn of the century that *the human mind/brain/body has amazing capacity and capabilities in terms of influencing the reality in which we co-evolve.* Whether referring to the concept of *Ki* introduced in Chapter 18, the scientifically measurable energetic fields of which we are a part, or the energetic information fields with which we interact every instant of our lives—including both thoughts and emotions—energy can be captured, slowed or stopped both intentionally and unintentionally, consciously and unconsciously. When that energy is retained in our system, whether physical, mental or emotional, it becomes stagnant, what we can describe as stuck, clogged, bounded, or gapped. When this occurs, it affects the energy flow within ourselves, as well as our interaction with the larger ecosystem of which we are a part. And it can have severe consequences.

What does it mean to have blocked or stuck energy? Blocked or stuck energy is in stasis, that is, a state of no change or a motionless state, often resulting from opposing forces that are balancing each other (*Encarta World English Dictionary*, 1999). As introduced in Chapter 3/Part I, Kurt Lewin (1946; 1997) demonstrates in his force field model that a situation will stay stuck as long as there is a balance of opposing forces. Changes can only come by upsetting this balance.

In the body, stuck energy might mean preventing fluids from flowing normally through their regular channels. Let's look at several obvious examples related to our physical bodies: breath, sustenance and blood. A blockage to the circulation of air throughout our system might be caused, for example, by asthma, bronchitis or emphysema, or food lodged in our airway, and lead to death. A blockage to food and water intake or output can cause system collapse. And we all know the potential consequences of a blood clot. Similarly, while we don't generally think of our thoughts and emotions in terms of energy, they are part of a powerful energy force that has very much to do with both living and dying, and the quality of those experiences.

<<<<<<<◇>>>>>>>

INSIGHT: **Our thoughts and emotions are part of a powerful energy force that has very much to do with both living and dying, and the quality of those experiences.**

<<<<<<<◇>>>>>>>

Our new worldview has ushered in the emerging field of vibrational medicine, a science that draws on both the latest scientific discoveries and ancient arts of healing. Vibrational medicine views the body as a "complex, integrated life-energy system that provides a vehicle for human consciousness as well as a temporary housing for the creative expression of the human soul." (Gerber, 2000, p. 4) Recall that consciousness is a state of awareness and a private, selective and continuously changing process, a sequential set of ideas, thoughts, images, feelings and perceptions along with an understanding of the connections and relationships among them and our self (see Chapter 5/Part I). Soul represents the animating principle of human life in terms of thought and action, specifically focused on its moral aspects, the emotional part of human nature, and higher development of the mental faculties (Bennet & Bennet, 2007c; Bennet et al., 2015a). From the philosophical aspect, soul is the vital, sensitive or rational principle in human beings (*Oxford English Dictionary*, 2002). And, as Csikszentmihalyi says, "an enduring vision in both work and life derives its power from soul—the energy a person or organization devotes to **purposes beyond itself** [emphasis added]" (Csikszentmihalyi, 2003, p. 19).

Vibrational medicine theory views illness as caused not only by toxins, germs and trauma, but by chronic dysfunctional emotional-energy patterns and the unhealthy ways that people relate to each other and themselves. In this new worldview, consciousness and emotions play key roles in determining who becomes sick and who stays well, and different forms of energy are being employed to collectively heal the body, mind and spirit.

Looking through this lens, negative thoughts disrupt the flow of *Ki* and bring about "feeling poorly". A blockage of *Ki* diminishes the vital function of organs and cells of the physical body, which brings about illness. Fortunately, various healing modalities that can assist in moving through blockages have been recorded for thousands of years. Energy healing concepts emerged in India and, later, appeared in Chinese, Egyptian, Greek, Roman and Tibetan cultures. For example, the Tibetans are said to have possessed a "deep understanding of the nature of spirit, energy and matter, using this knowledge to heal their bodies, harmonize their souls and lead their spirits to an experience of unity" (Baginski & Sharamon, 1985, p. 15).

A more recent and well-known form of holistic energy healing is Reiki, taken from the Japanese word *Ki* and involving the laying on of hands. Through Reiki, it is possible to clear our internal channels and open up the body to increased amounts of life energy for use in our own bodies, as well as to pass *Ki* on to others. This can happen in several ways.

> By flowing through the affected parts of the energy field and charging them with positive energy, Reiki raises the vibratory level in and around the physical body where the negative thoughts and feelings are attached. This causes the negative energy to break apart and fall away. In so doing, Reiki clears, straightens and heals the energy pathways, thus allowing healthy *Ki* to flow in a natural way. Sometimes the entire blocking energy is lifted up to a higher field of energy where it is processed. Other times, it is melted away or burned up … Once *Ki* is flowing naturally, the physical organs and tissues are then able to complete their healing process. (Rand, 1991, p. 1-10)

Reiki energy heals the whole person—physical, emotional, mental and spiritual. The physical part of the person is a dense body that can be perceived by sight and touch. The emotional, mental and spiritual parts of a person are nonphysical energy bodies comprised of *Ki*. These nonphysical bodies are intertwined with the health of the physical body. The Reiki principle is that healing cannot occur at the physical level alone, but must include all the vibrational energy bodies. Reiki healing, therefore, goes far beyond traditional Western medicine, getting to the emotional, mental and spiritual sources of dis-ease. "Most metaphysical healers believe that all physical pain has nonphysical roots in emotional trauma, negative mental patterns, or spiritual despair. To heal the dis-ease, these roots must be discovered and treated." (Stein, 1995, p. 18) Note that throughout this book we use the terms "planes", which is related to the use of "bodies" when talking about Reiki energy.

From a knowledge perspective (Bennet et al., 2015a), stuck energy means we cease to learn, and when we cease to learn, over time, we lose the capability to interact and deal with changes in our environment. As we now recognize, knowledge (the capacity to take effective action) is partial, imperfect and/or incomplete intelligence. This is because the effectiveness of knowledge is situation dependent and context sensitive, with knowledge shifting and changing in concert with our environment and the demands placed upon us, and new knowledge emerging from those interactions. When we cease to learn, we bound our knowledge to a model of the past while the future continuously presents differently. Examples are politicians who think they know what is best for their constituents without listening to them, or a professor who does a Ph.D. on a theory and keeps teaching that theory for 30 years, despite the fact that new research has emerged. Any theory can be considered but a short stopping point in a much larger journey, that is, the search for a higher level of truth (see Chapter 24/Part IV).

<<<<<<<◇>>>>>>>

INSIGHT: **When we cease to learn, we bound our knowledge to a model of the past while the future continuously presents differently.**

<<<<<<<◇>>>>>>>

From a knowledge perspective, being stuck can be a choice. For example, people can get stuck on mental models, being afraid to become too creative because they might have to take responsibility for their ideas and actions. Just as we say that with knowledge comes responsibility, **applied creativity and responsibility are in relationship.** While innovation can certainly equate to "success", however that may be defined by the innovator, it *always* equates to service, that is, processes and products others will use to make or do something better, generally to make their lives better in some way, and perhaps providing the opportunity for *them* to improve other's lives in some way. Innovation requires letting go of our ideas, sharing them, applying them, taking responsibility for them, and, as appropriate, expanding on them through iterative feedback loops.

<<<<<<<◇>>>>>>>

INSIGHT: **Innovation *always* equates to service, producing processes and products others will use to make or do something better, and perhaps providing the opportunity for *them* to improve other's lives in some way.**

<<<<<<<◇>>>>>>>

From the perspective of an intelligent complex adaptive system—as an individual or organization, stuck energy means we have closed our system off (Bennet & Bennet, 2004). The individual or organization no longer has permeable and porous boundaries, and has ceased to co-evolve with the very environment from which it gains sustenance. Closed systems can only focus on that which is within the system, reusing materials within, repeating the past over and over again, repeating mistakes, reducing consciousness and becoming less effective in a changing world, or just wearing out.

From a psychological point of view, when relying on past knowledge and experiences, this inward focus on self brings with it an inherent selfishness, often accompanied by egotism and entitlement. An example would be a religious fundamentalist who acknowledges no other belief set, actively condemning other beliefs and creating forces. In a global business environment where innovation is critical to survival, creative thought that is held within, not shared or applied, dissipates, that is, it is not only stuck energy but has the capacity to *reduce* an individual's level of consciousness. Further, ideas that are held onto decrease the diversity of the market and, as we are increasingly discovering, even a small shift in a concept offers the potential of rewards as the continued bisociation of ideas multiplies its value.

To help understand the concept of stuck energy more fully, we first explore this state from the viewpoint of mental models and stress. Then we take a quick look at memory with a focus on the concepts of forgetting and letting go, what that means from the perspective of the mind/brain, and asking the hard question: *Can humans really forget?* At the end of the chapter, we briefly touch on the roles of monkey chatter and webs of energy.

Mental Models

Recognizing that information is energy, an example of stuck energy is the retention and use of limiting mental models. Mental models guide our personal picture of reality. They are built up over time and through experience, and may represent our beliefs, assumptions, and ways of interpreting the outside world. As Senge describes,

> ...new insights fail to get put into practice because they conflict with deeply held internal images of how the world works, images that limit us to familiar ways of thinking and acting. (Senge, 1990, p. 174)

Mental models frequently serve as drivers for our actions as well as our interpretations. They are efficient in that they allow us to react quickly to changing conditions and make rapid decisions based upon our presupposed model. Concomitantly, they are limiting, and can be dangerous when inaccurate or misleading. Further, because of the current rapidly changing environment, many of our models quickly become outdated; yet we cling to them because they have worked in the past and bring with them the feeling of safety, circumventing the unknown.

To avoid stuck energy, there is the need to continuously review our perceptions and assumptions of the external world and question our mental models to ensure they are consistent with the current reality (Senge, 1990). While this is a process that occurs continuously in our subconscious using the preferences embedded in our personality, many of these preferences were developed early in our lives. However, despite being outdated, they may not come to our attention, that is, into our conscious awareness, until some thought or action causes us to question ourselves. To *expand our consciousness* and *ensure choice* we must periodically question ourselves as to our real (current) versus stated motives, goals, feelings and assumptions. For example, learning organizations manage their mental models through a process of surfacing, testing and improving their internal pictures of how the world works (Senge, 1990). This exercise helps us understand who we are, and provides the opportunity to change through conscious choice who we will be. As an example, the use of dialogue in a small group setting to normalize mental models with respected colleagues provides somewhat of a safeguard against the use of incomplete or erroneous mental models.

In *WorldShift 2012*, Laszlo (2009, p. 45) forwards that it is our personal responsibility to make a change in the way we live and think. This includes the need to forget some "old and long-cherished values and beliefs" as well as updating the ethics we live by and evolving our consciousness. Some values to forget include the value of getting, the paramount value of money, the undiscriminating valuation of technology, the worship of the latest and newest, the fetish of efficiency, and the value of classical patriotism. He also posits dangerous myths that need to be released. These include: the earth is inexhaustible, nature is a giant mechanism, life is a struggle where only the fittest survive, the market corrects economic gaps and injustices, the more you consume the better you are, and economic and political ends justify military means (Laszlo, 2009). The release of these former societal mental models enables emergence of an expanded global consciousness, expanding our present-day focus on mental consciousness to further embrace a subtle consciousness—archetypal, transindividual and intuitive—which can lead humanity into a new era (Wilber, 2000). This is the third phase of our change model, with the mental faculties in service to the intuitive (see the introduction to Part IV).

A subtle but powerful factor underlying mental models is the role of emotions in influencing our perception of reality. Emotions assign values to options or alternatives, often without our knowing it. There is growing evidence that fundamental ethical stances in life stem from underlying emotional capacities. These stances create the basic belief system, the values, and often the underlying assumptions that are used to see the world—our mental models. We further explore the role of emotions in our discussion of memory and the initial selection process below.

Stress

Stress was introduced in Chapter 13 in terms of its impact on learning and was also used as an example in Chapter 19 on emotions as a guidance system. This critical element of the human experience warrants additional focus in this chapter, with a focus on stuck energy. Depending on its level, stress can stop or slow natural energy flows throughout the body, and has been cited as the number one cause leading to death; yet, it is not solely a physical trauma. For example, four hours after a Harvard boat race the crew had a decline in cosinophil count (a stress blood measure). While the physical stress of the race might have caused this in the rowers, a similar decline was noted in the coxswains and coaches, whose stress was psychological (Thompson, 2000).

A second example is the study by Seymour Levine of Stanford University and Holger Ursin of the University of Olso, Norway. They examined the hormonal and behavioral responses of Norwegian paratroop trainees following repeated jumps off a

10-meter tower. There was a dramatic elevation of cortisol in the blood following the first jump, but in subsequent jumps the cortisol level in the blood was at basal levels. In addition, Levine and Ursin noted that fear levels as expressed by the participants were similarly significantly reduced after the initial jump (Levine & Ursin, 1991).

As Thompson (2000) describes,

The extent to which situations are stressful is determined by how the individual understands, interprets, sees, and feels about a situation. It is fundamentally a "cognitive" phenomenon depending more on how the individual construes the situation than on the nature of the situation itself. The key aspects are uncertainty and control: the less knowledge the individual has about a potentially harmful situation, the less control he or she feels can be exerted, the more stressful the situation is. Conversely, the more understanding and certainty the individual has about a situation the more he or she feels in control and the less stressful it is. (Thompson, 2000, p. 210).

Thompson (2000) summarizes, "We and other mammals appear to be driven by nature toward certainty" (p. 210). Further, he forwards that this may be the basis for the existence of various belief systems, since even if a person's understanding is wrong, "A person firmly committed to a belief system does in fact 'understand' the world and the nature of the controls that operate" (p. 210).

Despite its cause, there *are* a number of physical characteristics to the stress response. Adrenaline is released, the heart rate increases, blood pressure goes up, and blood-clotting elements increase in the bloodstream. As the body readies for movement (flight or fight), the senses are more alert, muscles tense, and palms become sweaty. **All of these processes stop the natural flow of energies throughout the body.** Simultaneously, "cortical memory systems retrieve any knowledge relevant to the emergency at hand, taking precedence over other strands of thought" (LeDoux, 1996, p. 39).

Interestingly, low stress can be good and is often termed arousal (Bennet et al., 2015b), that is, it can facilitate the flow of energy throughout the body. As noted in Chapter 13, in a learning situation, this focuses attention and could manifest as an excitement and eagerness to learn. However, if stress relates to fear, "the amygdala takes control and tends to miss details" (Zull, 2002, p. 141) and that same fear that causes a fight or flight response—specifically, the excessive levels of cortisol accompanying the response—can bring about negative long-term results (Zull, 2002, p. 141). As Byrnes (2001) observes,

Excessive levels of cortisol (a substance secreted by the adrenal glands during stress reactions) causes permanent damage to several regions of the brain, including the hippocampus (important for memory) and the locus ceruleus (important for selective attention). (p. 181)

While all this may make it sound like we are victims, we are not. For example, by measuring activity in the amygdala using the fMRI—an area active during times of distress, fear, anger, and anxiety—Davidson discovered that some people were able to *consciously change their level of response*. This is consistent with our previous discussion in Chapter 19 on learning to change our emotions through thought. Davidson discovered that, "individuals with greater activation in this area are better able, when they have the aspiration to relieve suffering, to change their brain and reduce the activation in the amygdala" (Begley, 2007, p. 233). The Dalai Lama's response to Davidson's discovery provides a good summary of Davidson's findings. "What seems to be very clear is that a purely mental process—for example, deliberately cultivating this aspiration—can have an effect that is observable in the brain level" (Begley, 2007, p. 233). Patterns in the mind *can and do* influence neurons in the brain, a reminder that **mind over matter is possible**, and therefore it is possible for an individual to consciously change his or her level of response to stress—affecting mental and emotional responses *and* the physical patterns associated with those responses.

Forgetting

The concept of forgetting builds on our introduction to memory in Chapter 18. In that regard, we will repeat a few concepts dealing with memory that will help move us into a discussion of forgetting. In both the conscious and unconscious mind, traumatic events—especially those charged with strong emotions—can cause blockages, impacting our thoughts, feelings and actions. Recall that the mind/brain is an associative patterner, continuously processing incoming information from the environment, specific to the situation and context at hand, and complexing it with internally-stored information. Of course, much of this is happening below our conscious awareness, that is, in our subconscious, orchestrated by and very much based upon the preferences and desires of our personality.

While the majority of our discussion on forgetting will be focused from the viewpoint of the mind/brain, we first address the element of consciously choosing to forget. In a study performed by The Scripps Research Institute, scientists identified a molecular biology process focused on active forgetting, which is most likely regulated. Through studying the memory function in fruit flies, found to be highly applicable to humans, it was discovered that "a small subset of dopamine neurons actively regulate the acquisition of memories and the forgetting of these memories after learning, using a pair of dopamine receptors in the brain" (Scripps Research Foundation, 2012). Dopamine, a neurotransmitter, plays an important role in the brain's reward and pleasure centers as well as memory, learning and cognition. The study suggests that, prior to being consolidated, new memories include an active dopamine-based forgetting mechanism, and that those new memories begin to erase unless they have some importance attached to them. Since forgetting is the fastest shortly after learning, that is, 15-20 seconds after a thought has presented itself in short-term memory, it appears that this may be part of the initial selection process orchestrated by the subconscious.

What would serve as indicators of importance or significance as part of this selection process? As with people, memories are not created equal, nor would we want them to be. Consistent with the introductory discussion of memory in Chapter 18, indicators for strong memories would include our conscious focus (repetition and rehearsal), our mental models (including values and beliefs and the strength of those values and beliefs), and the emotional tag attached to incoming information, perhaps a connection to a significant event in our lives. Memories and the emotional tags that gauge the importance of those memories, activated automatically without any conscious effort and become part of an individual's everyday life (LeDoux, 1996).

Recall that "tags" is a term indicating that the amygdala "tags" or puts some level of danger or importance on the incoming signal indicated by release of hormones throughout the body. This is consistent with our discussion of stress above. Memory is enhanced when emotions (such as fear or joy) are heightened (Christos, 2003). The *stronger the emotional tag*, the greater the strength of the memory connections and the easier to recall. Emotions have priority in our stream of consciousness and our memory. Through evolution, our brain has been wired such that the neuronal connections from the emotional systems to the cognitive systems are much stronger than the connections from the cognitive systems to the emotional systems. Thus,

> Emotions easily bump mundane events out of awareness, but nonemotional events (like thoughts) do not so easily displace emotions from the mental spotlight—wishing that anxiety or depression would go away is usually not enough. (LeDoux, 1996, p. 9)

The greater the power of the emotion that is associated with an experience, the more lasting the memory (Johnson, 2006). An example is what is called the "flashbulb memory" involving a very vivid memory connected with extremely emotional events such as the death of a close friend or a catastrophe like that experienced in New York on September 11 (Kluwe et al., 2003). However, this same event can cause the opposite response. As Taylor points out, "The exception is when the initial experience is so traumatic that dissociation occurs; under these circumstances, memories may be deeply buried or completely inaccessible to recall" (Taylor, 2006, p. 81). Note that these "deeply buried" or "completely inaccessible" traumatic events are still unconsciously affecting an individual's thoughts and actions, and as such are playing a role in blocking the free flow of energy.

The question becomes, **can/does the human mind really forget?** To "forget" has to do with the inability to remember: to leave behind unintentionally, to fail to mention, to disregard or to cease remembering (*American Heritage Dictionary*,

2011). Forgetting can be either spontaneous or a gradual process, and can involve apparent partial or total loss of a memory or modification of that memory. In his memory studies, Connerton (2008) forwards there are seven types of forgetting: repressive erasure, prescriptive forgetting, formation of new identity, structural amnesia, annulment, planned obsolescence and humiliated silence. Each of these descriptive terms well represent the state of each.

Perhaps the earliest work on the process of forgetting is the forgetting curve hypothesis forwarded by Hermann Ebbinghaus (1885). The forgetting curve shows that there is a decline in memory over time, purporting that half the memory of newly learned knowledge is forgotten in a matter of days or weeks unless it is consciously reviewed (Schacter, 2001). Ebbinghaus further hypothesized that the speed of forgetting was dependent on a number of factors, including the difficulty of materials, its meaningfulness to the individual, the way the materials were represented, and physiological factors such as sleep and stress. He concluded that these factors could be overcome through basic training in mnemonic techniques, which can produce over-learning and slow forgetting.

The trace decay theory of forgetting (Brown, 1958; Peterson & Peterson, 1959), says that memories in short term memory leave a trace in the brain that, if not rehearsed, automatically fades away in 15 to 30 seconds. In other words, according to this theory it is the length of time between a memory and the need to recall that memory that determines whether the information is retained or forgotten. There are, however, other theories, and recent neuroscience findings, that may help our understanding of the concept of forgetting, which will be interjected throughout this discussion.

Perhaps one of the best-known theories related to forgetting comes out of the field of psychology. Freud argued that quite often threatening or anxiety-provoking material cannot gain access to conscious awareness; in other words, it is repressed and gets stuck in the subconscious. There is considerable controversy regarding the idea of repression. For example, in looking at reports of recovered memories, Andrews et al. (1999) discovered that some of the recovered memories were false. Further, Lief & Fetkewicz (1995) found that people can be misled into believing events that didn't happen, and Ceci (1995) found that preschool children had difficulty distinguishing between real and fictitious events, which can continue into adulthood!

We now also understand that reliving events, whether in therapy or other conversation and especially when connected with deep emotion, embeds those memories deeper into long-term memory much like purposeful rehearsing, making them more impervious to any possible "forgetting" process. Ultimately, from the mind/brain perspective, *that which does not get attention eventually does go away* (use it or lose it). Thus, a good process for "forgetting" is *inattention*, and the very best way to avoid attending to some memory is to have a stronger, more significant memory replace it. This would infer stronger links than to similar stimuli in the older memory. For example, if there was a negative memory of coal in a stocking for Christmas, the very best way to overcome that effect is to have a positive memory of a reward for a good deed performed in a following Christmas stocking, perhaps acknowledging a reversal of behavior. However, this would prove quite difficult for deeply embedded memories with traumatic emotional tags, highly dependent on an individual's ability to develop positive events of greater significance to replace these older connections.

<<<<<<<◇>>>>>>

INSIGHT: **The very best way to avoid attending to some memory is to have a stronger, more significant memory replace it.**

<<<<<<<◇>>>>>>

Before touching on several more theories of forgetting, we'd like to quickly shift our frame of reference to provide an understanding of the role threatening or anxiety-provoking events play in our growth and expansion. Dependent on the unique characteristics of an individual, every event in life, no matter how traumatic, can provide some aspect of learning. For example, if you have learned nothing else, you have learned that you do not choose to have this event repeat itself. As you move further away from an event, and process the subjective memory in a variety of ways, you can begin to *reflect on it from a systems viewpoint* as a learning lesson. Then, over time, you can begin to appreciate the value of this lesson, and with that appreciation comes the realization that this lesson of the past has contributed to who you are today. You can potentially reach a point of gratitude, that is, being thankful for the learning experience. See Figure 20-1.

The word gratitude has Latin roots from *gratus*, meaning pleasing or thankful, and *gratia*, meaning favor or thanks, and in Spanish and French it translates as *gracia*. When used as a name, made popular by 17th-century Puritans, Gracia means "inspired by grace", with grace representing beauty, kindness and mercy. During this process the emotional tag becomes less and less prominent, diminishing altogether as the event is perceived as a positive learning experience, occupying a place in objective memory (follow track #2 in Figure 20-1.) As new learning lessons emerge and take center stage in terms of focus, the event may disappear entirely from memory, although the lesson as a pattern remains available as needed.

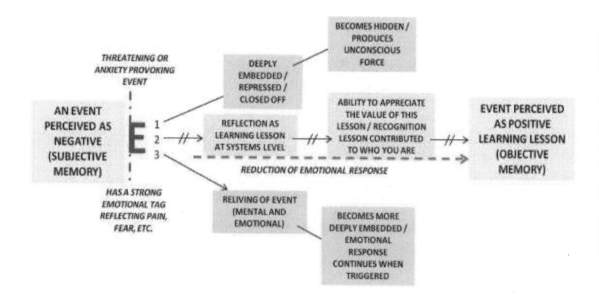

Figure 20-1. *Learning Cycle for Threatening Events.*

The paragraph above, of course, describes the ideal outcome for a threatening or anxiety-provoking event. And, indeed, when an individual takes ownership of this process, working through awareness, understanding, belief, and feeling good about it—and having enough knowledge and confidence to apply it—we have the ability to successfully do so. However, deep emotions can be difficult to deal with. For example, an event can be so deeply embedded (track #1 in Figure 19-1) that an individual is in a state of denial regarding the importance or impact of the event. Conversely, an individual could be so caught up in reliving the event over and over again that there isn't any space to separate from the event and reflect (track #3 in Figure 19-1).

Other theories of forgetting include Interference Theory, Consolidation, Retrieval Failure Theory, and State Dependent Cues. During the 20th century, Interference Theory—assuming that what is remembered can be disrupted by previous and future learning—was the dominant forgetting approach. Underwood and Postman (1960) described interference as (1) maximal when two different responses are associated with the same stimulus, (2) intermediate when two similar responses are associated with the same stimulus, and (3) minimal when two different stimuli are involved. Proactive interference is when what we know interferes with what we are learning (old memories disrupting new memories). Jacoby et al. (2001) found that this occurs when the incorrect response is connected to bias or habit. Retroactive interference is when we forget what we know when learning a new task (new learning disrupts old memories). For example, post-event questioning can alter the memory of events (Underwood & Postman, 1960).

Consolidation, or lack of consolidation, is focused on the biological processes of forgetting. Since a memory trace is an alteration of the brain substrate, some amount of time is required for changes in the nervous system to take place. This is the consolidation process, when neurons are modified as information is moved from short-term memory to long-term memory. This process can be impaired when there is damage to the hippocampus. For example, retrograde amnesia, resulting in the most recently formed memories being the most impaired, could be caused by epilepsy and aging (Manns et al., 2003).

Retrieval Failure Theory (including Cue-Dependent Forgetting and State-Dependent Cues) is the inability to access information stored in long-term memory. While the memory may still be there, it is not accessible because of the lack of triggering, that is, retrieval cues are not present. Retrieval cues can be external in terms of the context of the environment, or internal in terms of the state inside of us. Context, or external, cues might include characteristics of the situation or setting (weather, people present, etc.) or the way information is presented (conversation, singing, charts). Recall that all knowledge is situation-dependent and context-sensitive (Bennet et al, 2015a). This means that when a memory is encoded it is specific to a situation and context. Note that a single memory may be stored in a pattern that connects to a thousand or more neurons. While this is the strength of the associative patterning process of the human mind—enabling the bisociation of ideas which is the basis of creativity—it can also serve as a difficulty in the process of forgetting, with a variety of cues available to trigger a specific memory.

State-dependent retrieval occurs when the physical or psychological state of an individual is similar at retrieval to the state of the individual during encoding (Tulving & Pearlstone, 1966). For example, when in a relaxed comfortable environment, it is easier to recall and convey a joke previously heard in that same type of environment.

While we have discussed the ability to retrieve information in terms of a theory of forgetting, in the language of Knowledge Management, this would be described in terms of tacit, the inability of an individual to express knowledge. If knowledge can be pulled up and expressed, it is considered explicit. If an individual is unable to pull it up and express it, that knowledge is considered tacit in nature. Clearly this deals with an individual ability, and thus is context sensitive and situation dependent. Knowledge that is tacit is still in memory and, from an unconscious perspective, still impacting other knowledge (the capacity to take effective action) and potentially an individual's thoughts, feelings and actions. However, it is not remembered in terms of conscious awareness, and cannot be pulled up and expressed. Bennet et al. (2015a) point to a third area which they use the term "implicit" to describe. Historically, the term "implicit" has been interchangeable with the term "tacit", consistent with the description in the previous paragraph. The usefulness of the term in this new context is the recognition that a memory may be tacit in one situation, and triggered in another, that is, because our mind is an associative patterner and continuously creating knowledge for the moment at hand, tacit and explicit cannot be considered as absolute terms. See Appendix D, Engaging Tacit Knowledge.

Letting Go

Both learning and letting go—whether in terms of *freeing* or *filing away* (putting away on the bookshelf)— are the primary processes through which we change and grow. Since humans have limited processing capability and the mind is easily overloaded and clings to its past experience and knowledge, letting go becomes as important as learning to facilitate the free flow of energy and prevent blockages. In an article titled "Forgetting is Key to a Healthy Mind" appearing in the January 1, 2012, issue of *Scientific American Mind*, author Ingrid Wickelgren confirmed that letting go of memories supports a sound state of mind, a sharp intellect—and superior recall. In the context of this discussion we are referring to memories that are in consciousness awareness and subject to focus and choice.

Letting go or releasing is the art of being able to let go what was known and true in the past or to let go of concepts, beliefs and mental models that inhibit your growth and expansion. It is moving out of mind and thought into direct experience, allowing yourself to be that which you already are without bringing along events and perceptions of the past. As forwarded in the earlier discussion on mental models, being able to recognize the limitations and inappropriateness of past assumptions, beliefs, and knowledge is essential before creating new mental models and for understanding ourselves as we grow. It is one of the hardest acts of the human mind because it threatens our self-image and may shake even our core belief systems.

Note that "forgetting" and "letting go" are different concepts than that of "unlearning". As expressed above, new learning can, over time and especially when emotions are involved, replace old learning in terms of unused connections and neuronal firings (recall the concept of use it or lose it). However, it is difficult, if not impossible, to unlearn the truth of who you are. Even when this knowing is not at the conscious level, it lies beneath, ready to emerge in response to triggering and conscious choice.

****

TOOL 20-1: Letting Go

The Sedona Method, featured in the movie and book based on *The Secret*, is a technique developed for eliminating blocked energies that hold you back from being and doing what you choose. The method includes three ways to approach releasing: (1) by choosing to let go of the unwanted feelings; (2) by welcoming the feelings; and (3) by diving into the very core of the feeling. This unique and powerful technique consists of a series of simple questions that you ask yourself, which leads to expanding awareness of your feelings and enabling a choice to let them go. Details of the Sedona Method are included at www.sedona.com

Let us follow another scenario where a letting go sequence does *not* occur. You are a senior executive in a large engineering firm, and have been in the job for five years. The first year, it was new and exciting and you knew you could make a difference. And you did, with revenues soaring. The second year you put what you had learned in place, developing and stabilizing long-term processes. The third year you did much activity by rote, and just focused on challenges and opportunities. The fourth year the company was bought up by a larger conglomerate and their processes and approaches became standards of behavior right there beside the rote stuff that kept your (now department) running like clockwork. By the fifth year the paperwork had become nearly unbearable, with additional levels of review and approval, the necessity to only use "approved" products that came from other parts of the organization or their partners, and increased reporting and audit procedures. Somehow, the fun has dissipated, the work has become repetitive and boring, and there is no time for—or interest from management in—creative solutions. While you are financially thriving, your energy is stuck and you are stuck. The letting go that needs to occur here is choosing to leave the job; yet you remain. This is a choice.

In summary, the biggest barrier to learning and letting go arises from our own individual ability to develop invisible defenses against changing our beliefs or behaviors. These self-imposed mental defenses have been eloquently described by Chris Argyris (1990). The essence of his conclusion is that the mind creates built-in defense mechanisms to support belief systems and experience. These defense mechanisms are invisible to the individual and may be quite difficult to expose in a real-world situation. They are a widespread example of not knowing what we know, thus representing invisible barriers to change.

****

Mental Chatter

(a/k/a "monkey mind")

The human mind is in continuous motion, full of chatter: creating lists of what to do and what to buy, judging, remembering (and creating) fears, and imagining future scenarios. Zen Buddhists describe the human mind as filled with drunken monkeys who jump around and chatter continuously as they swing from tree to tree. When this chatter is accompanied by memories or feelings of negative emotions, it can make us unhappy or fearful or angry or restless, directly impacting our ability to focus, or even affecting or directing our behavior. While mental chatter is quite different than the idea of stuck energy, this chatter can also dampen, depress or misguide energy flows.

There is some similarity between mental chatter and dreams, that is, dream sequences and mental chatter often relate to random energy sequences occurring throughout the day, sequences that may or may not be attached to the energy of others. While mental chatter and dreams may be presenting these sequences in an attempt to cleanse the mind/brain, also embedded within these sequences may be thoughts and/or pictures emerging from within, subconscious messages demanding attention.

Fabrega (2016) cites ten ways to stop mental chatter. First, is knowing that it can be stopped, recognizing that we are the master of our thoughts. Second, is to begin the conversation with your monkey mind, listening, and seeing if there is something of note that your unconscious is trying to communicate. Is there something that needs doing? Is there some anxiety about the future? Is there some resentment from the past? Fabrega then provides tools to connect and correct mental chatter. These include meditation, reciting a mantra, engaging the mind, and deep breathing techniques.

Webs of Energy

MacFlouer (2004-16) says that there are webs of energy that accumulate between our various planes, that is, between our physical and emotional planes, and between our emotional and mental planes. These webs are created from retained energy in our various senses, primarily related to self-centeredness and selfishness as we have focused on developing our mental faculties without a spiritual counterbalance (see Chapter 4/Part I and Chapter 26/Part IV).

To understand this concept let's consider an analogy in our physical lives, specifically, the focus on materialism introduced in Chapter 10/Part II. Let's say we have a passion for art, and collect beautiful paintings, which bring us great joy. Only, the passion becomes an obsession, the collection expands, and everything and everyone else takes a backseat in life. Now, we become incredibly concerned regarding theft, so we set up various protection systems, perhaps hiring people to protect this art. As various other paintings are offered for sale, we bring pressure to bear to make sure that we can obtain them, and soon we are more obsessed with acquisition and ownership than the beauty of the paintings. "I must own this!" The joy we feel moves from appreciation of beauty to appreciation of ownership, which is ego-based. Thus, selfishness of thought and feelings brings with it negative energies that separate us from the flow of life, placing burdens upon ourselves. (See the discussion of balance in Chapter 32/Part V and beauty in Chapter 33/Part V.) This example involved both the physical and emotional planes.

These stuck energies settle in between our various planes (see Figure 19-2), creating a web that begins with our first selfish thoughts and acts and continues to become more intricate and heavier as we grow older and continue in this mode. These webs slow down the exchange of energy among our physical, emotional and mental senses. Recall from Chapter 4/Part I that all of our senses bring in tiny bits of information that are then amplified, catalogued and organized, with the personality identifying the things of interest to store initially driven by survival, pleasure and avoidance of pain, and hopefully eventually guided by the mature self. The webs of retained energy act as a force, shutting down part of our sensing capability, limiting connections and reducing consciousness. Interestingly, this is not necessarily negative as we progress through life. Forces offer opportunities for growth and expansion.

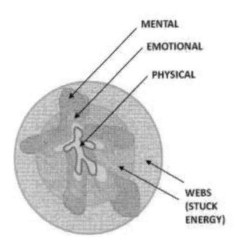

Figure 20-2. *Webs of stuck energy accumulate between the physical and emotional planes, and between the emotional and mental planes.*

How can this be valuable? As an example, consider a time when you needed to make a decision and there were many options available and a plethora of information bombarding you that had to be taken into consideration. It's quite easy to become overwhelmed in this environment. In slowing down the processing of incoming information among our senses, we have more time to reflect on issues at hand and, hopefully, through this reflection we choose to reduce our selfishness and make decisions and take actions that are geared toward the greater good, benefiting ourselves and others. Thus, the very web we have created through selfish thoughts and feelings can provide us the opportunity to reduce our selfishness and, as this continues to occur, the web eventually ceases to exist.

As a second example, consider the web between the emotional and mental planes, that is, slowing down the processing of incoming information among the senses with an emotional and mental focus. This means that our emotions cannot immediately control our mental thought, that is, our creative imagination does not trump our mental thinking, which can happen in highly charged events. Emotions are designed to support mental thought, to be used as a guidance system, not as a controlling mechanism (see Chapter 19 on emotions as a guidance system.) When the mental faculties of self are well developed, and as our consciousness expands, this web is no longer necessary. As a note, neither are emotions intended to trump the physical senses, which are required for a coordinated response to the world around you (MacFlouer, 2004-16).

Final Thoughts

We now recognize that stopped and stuck energy can be both positive and negative in learning and changing our experiences of life. The retention of limiting mental models is used as an example of stuck energy, and stress can both accelerate learning, or stop or slow natural energy flows throughout the body. The best process for "forgetting" is inattention by diverting the flow, and the very best way to avoid attending to some memory is to have a stronger, more significant memory replace it.

Questions for Reflection:

Recall a time when you were stuck … did this have a positive, effective focus or negative, destructive impact?

What enables you to let go when you are stuck?

Do your mental models keep you stuck or are you able to adapt your mental models with changing circumstances?

Chapter 21
Knowledge Capacities

SUBTOPICS: EXPLORING KNOWLEDGE CAPACITIES ... SOME QUICK EXAMPLES ... *LEARNING HOW TO LEARN ... SHIFTING FRAMES OF REFERENCE ... REVERSAL ... COMPREHENDING DIVERSITY ... ORCHESTRATING DRIVE ... SYMBOLIC REPRESENTATION ...* A WORKING EXAMPLE*: INSTINCTUAL HARNESSING ...* WHY IS INSTINCTUAL HARNESSING EFFECTIVE AS A KNOWLEDGE CAPACITY?

FIGURE: 21-1. WAYS HUMANS OPERATE IN THE WORLD.

TOOLS: 21-1. FOCUSED TRAIT TRANSFERENCE

In a changing, uncertain and complex environment where surprises emerge and must be quickly handled, capacity is more important than capability for sustainability over time. When you plan an outdoor event, you create an alternate plan for inclement weather. When you're raising a family, you try to put aside a bit for kid's learning experiences such as a school visit to the museum. When you study a domain of knowledge in college, you learn the theory right alongside pragmatic applications. This is why the case study approach was successful for so many years in higher education.

One of the authors, who taught nuclear physics for the U.S. Department of the Navy, recalls a story about a time when, in response to needed budget cuts, classes dealing with theoretical physics were on the chopping block. A short scenario quickly demonstrated the need for theory. Imagine a nuclear submarine with a full crew on board, deep under the North pole when the reactor fails. While there are a large number of possibilities for failure, this particular situation was not in the textbooks; it had never happened before. Do you want a nuclear officer well-trained in pragmatic responses, or do you need someone who also has the capacity to explore and understand the theory and deep relationships within the core which could have caused this failure? Both theory (capacity) and practice (pragmatic actions) are important and necessary in a CUCA environment.

As you can see from this example, knowledge itself is a capacity. Recall that we define knowledge as the capacity (potential or actual) to take effective action. Capacity is defined as the ability to receive, hold or absorb, a *potential for accomplishment* (*American Heritage Dictionary, 2006*). Thus, to think-know is a multi-asset, using knowledge from the past focused in the present offering potential for the future. Each learning experience builds on its predecessor by broadening the sources of knowledge creation and the capacity to create knowledge in different ways. For example, as an individual engages in more and more conversations across the Internet in search of meaning, thought connections across disciplines occur, causing an expansion of shallow knowledge. Knowledge begets knowledge. In a global interactive environment, the more that is understood, the more that can be created and understood.

We create knowledge every single day of our lives, with this knowledge serving the self and others with whom we interact as a bounding off point to bisociate ideas and trigger new thoughts. Expansion of shallow knowledge (the realm of social knowledge) is an area of strength for the next generation of knowledge workers. Through continuous connectivity and engagement in conversation and dialogue (a search for meaning), the Net Generation is developing a wide array of shallow knowledge. This knowledge (as a potential or actual capacity) prepares individuals for a changing and uncertain future by expanding areas of thought and conversation beyond a bounded functional and operational area of focus, supporting collaboration and knowledge sharing. Thus, new areas of interest are discovered, ideas expanded, and judgment and decisions made from a broader scale.

Capability is a subset of capacity, that is, a specific ability—a capacity to be used, treated or developed for a *specific purpose* (*American Heritage Dictionary*, 2006). Take the simple analogy of a bucket (capacity) which sits in the locker of a speedboat among various ropes and floats until needed for bailing water or holding your daily catch (capabilities).

The mind/brain/body is continuously changing. We now know that thoughts and feelings can nurture, develop and change the infrastructure of the mind/brain/body system. Quickly reviewing, recall that thoughts in the mind are patterns of neuronal firings, which in turn can change the physical structure of the brain. Simultaneously, the emotional tags connected to those thoughts affect the release of chemicals, which impact the neuronal junctions (synapses), which influence thoughts. This is at the core of the mind/brain/body system. This has only been understood the last decade. Eric Kandel (2006), who won the Nobel Prize in 2000, showed that when even simple information came into the brain it created a physical alteration of the *structure of neurons* that participate in the process. Thus, we are all continuously altering the patterns and structure of the connections in our brains. The conclusion is significant: thoughts change the physiological structure of our brains. This plasticity results from the connection between the mind (patterns in the brain) and the physical world (atoms and molecules of the brain).

Thus, we have the capacity—which can become a learned capability—to shape and influence our future thinking and behaviors through current thoughts and behaviors. Certainly, competencies and learning skills participate in this process. However, more often than not, we repeat over and over again the *way* we perceive the changes around us, exploring those changes through our mental models or from comfortable reference points. When this occurs the things around us are perceived and fixed from those reference points. For example, when you stand under a star-lit night sky, you are the center of the Universe in terms of point of reference.

Knowledge Capacities are sets of ideas and ways of acting that are more general in nature than competencies, more core to a way of thinking and being, that change our reference points and specifically support building capacity for sustainability in a changing, uncertain and complex environment. *They provide different ways for us to perceive and operate in the world around us.* The analogy here would be the building an infrastructure of sorts relating to the mind/brain (information, knowledge and the structure and connection strengths of neurons within the brain).

The building and expansion of relationship networks, the widening of interests and knowledge, and the opening of possibilities—undergirded by continuous change and uncertainty—all contributing to removing limits, real and perceived as well as self-imposed. These connections are opening the door for new ways of thinking and acting upon the world that are indeed participative and collaborative. As situations become more complex, the nature of learning, knowledge and action shifts. *Building knowledge capacity lays the groundwork for those shifts.*

Exploring Knowledge Capacities

Knowledge Capacities, developed from combining senses while co-evolving with a changing, uncertain and complex environment, brings us closer to the creative leap. Knowledge Capacities complement six different ways that humans operate in the world. These are looking and seeing, feeling and touching, perceiving and representing, knowing and sensing, hearing and listening, and acting and being. Each of these sets has two concepts introduced because while they are related, there is clarity added by coupling the concepts. Each area is briefly addressed below. See Figure 21-1.

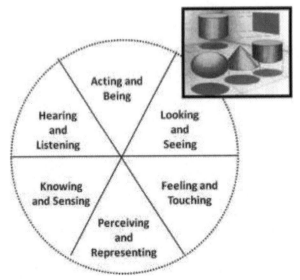

Figure 21-1. *Ways humans operate in the world.*

With our compliments (and apologies) to *Encarta World English Dictionary* (1999), we attach specific meanings to these six ways humans operate in the world, meanings that suggest ways of observing and processing the events that occur in our lives. Knowledge Capacities are all about expanding the way we see those events in order to raise our awareness and, in the case of problem solving and decision-making, offering new ideas and an expanded set of potential solutions.

Looking and Seeing: To direct attention toward something in order to consider it; to have a clear understanding of something. (*Example*: Shifting Frames of Reference, Reversal)

Feeling and Touching: The sensation felt when touching something; to have an effect or influence on somebody or something; to consider the response of others being touched. (*Example*: Emotional Intelligence)

Perceiving and Representing: To acquire information about the surrounding environment or situation; mentally interpreting information; an impression or attitude; ability to notice or discern. (*Examples*: Learning How to Learn, Comprehending Diversity and Symbolic Representation)

Knowing and Sensing: Showing intelligence; understanding something intuitively; detecting and identifying a change in something. (*Example*: Engaging Tacit Knowledge)

Hearing and Listening: To be informed of something, especially being told about it; making a conscious effort to hear, to concentrate on somebody or something; to pay attention and take it into account. (*Example*: Active Listening)

Acting and Being: to do something to change a situation; to serve a particular purpose; to provide information (identity, nature, attributes, position or value); to have presence, to live; to happen or take place; to have a particular quality or attribute. (*Examples*: Orchestrating Drive, Instinctual Harnessing)

Some Quick Examples

We first provide some short examples of Knowledge Capacities, specifically, Learning How to Learn (perceiving and representing); Shifting Frames of Reference (seeing and looking); Reversal (seeing and looking); Comprehending Diversity (perceiving and representing); Orchestrating Drive (acting and being); and Symbolic Representation (perceiving and representing).

Learning How to Learn (perceiving and representing)

Every individual is unique. Each person has a unique DNA, unique early development history, and adult life experiences and challenges different from all other humans. This uniqueness means that each of us learns differently and, to maximize that learning, we must understand ourselves, how we think and feel about specific subjects and situations, and how we best learn. For example, people who are more visual learners would prefer learning through books, movies or databases; those who are more auditory would prefer learning through stories and dialogue; those who are kinesthetic would prefer learning through hands-on approaches such as role-playing.

A first step is to observe ourselves as we learn and assess our efficacy in different learning situations, noting what works well and what doesn't work well. We can also try adding different techniques that aid learning such as journaling, creating songs and stories, or asking others (and ourselves) key questions, then trying to answer those questions, recognizing the importance of emotions and repetitiveness in remembering and understanding. For skills that require body movements, then similar body movements must be included in the learning process. For skills that require mental agility, then mental games or simulations might be involved. In other words, the best way to learn is to understand your preferences and ensure that the learning process is consistent with the skill or knowledge you want to learn.

Undoubtedly, *the most important factor in learning is the desire to learn*, to understand the meaning, ramifications and potential impact of ideas, situations or events (Bennet & Bennet, 2008d). In the present and future CUCA world, learning—that is, the creation and application of knowledge, the capacity to take effective action—is no longer just an advantage. It is a necessity. Because of their uniqueness, each knowledge worker must learn how they learn best; they cannot be taught by others. (The CUCA environment—increasing change, uncertainty and complexity and the anxiety resulting—was introduced in detail in Chapter 13.)

There is a relationship between your own learning style preferences and the way you share. Effective facilitation and communication require tailoring learning techniques to the preferred learning styles of your target audience. Applying multiple learning and communication styles enables you to reach target audiences with multiple preferences. Further, exposing multiple learning styles to the larger audience helps expand individual learning capacities, enriching their learning experience.

Shifting Frames of Reference (looking and seeing)

When we find ourselves in confusing situations, ambiguities or paradoxes where we don't know or understand what's happening, it is wise to recognize the limited mental capacity of a single viewpoint or frame of reference. Confusion, paradoxes and riddles are not made by external reality or the situation; they are created by our own limitations in thinking, language and perspective or viewpoint.

The patterns in the mind have strong associations built up through both experience and the developmental structure of the brain. For example, as children we learn to recognize the visual image of a "dog" and with experience associate that visual image with the word "dog". As our experience grows, we identify and learn to recognize attributes of the visual image of "dog" such as large, small, black, brown, head, tail, poodle, Akita, etc. The way we store those in the brain are as associations with the pattern known as "dog" to us, perhaps connected to the particular characteristics of a beloved childhood pet. Thus, when we think of a dog, we immediately associate other attributes to that thought.

Shifting Frames of Reference is the ability to see/perceive situations and their context through different lenses; for example, understanding an organization from the viewpoints of its executives, workforce, customers, banker, etc. The ability to shift frames of reference is enhanced by a diversity of experiences available to networked and interactive knowledge workers. Individuals who are subjected to a wide range of ideas and perspectives through social media are going to be much more attuned to difference, while at the same time becoming involved through dialogue. This participation with lots of people and interaction with differences helps develop a healthy self-image, and comfortable connections with different situations and people that build a feeling of "capability." Through these interactions' knowledge workers are actively doing things, which in and of themselves demonstrate their capability of interacting with the world. Through this broad set of reference experiences individuals can identify those disciplines or dimensions that they are excited about, and capable and competent to develop and grow from. This process can result in better decisions and choices that match their personal needs.

Frames of reference can be both expanding (as introduced above), and focusing and/or limiting, allowing the individual to go deeper in a bounded direction. Learning to consciously shift our frames of reference offers the self the opportunity to take a multidimensional approach in exploring the world around us. One approach is by looking at an issue from the viewpoint of different stakeholders. For example, if you are looking at an organization problem, you might ask the following questions: How would our customers see this problem? How would other employees see this problem? How would senior management see this problem? How would the bank see this problem? As another example, when exploring a system's issue, you might look at it from the inside out as well as the outside in, and then try to understand how you might see it differently from looking at it from the boundaries. Another example is learning to debate both sides of an issue. Still another approach is to look at an issue first as simple, then as complicated, then as complex and then as chaotic, each yielding a different potential decision set. A unique capability that develops as the self becomes proficient at shifting frames of reference is the ability to extend our visual and auditory sensing perception capabilities by analogy to other dimensions. For example, having the ability to "see" and "hear" some point in the future that is the result of a decision that is made today.

An excellent example of shifting frames of reference is the use of Dihedral Group Theory. Thought processes of entrepreneurs like Steve Jobs follow six distinct shifts in perspective which directly correspond to the six permutations of what is known in mathematics as a Dihedral (3) Group. Each of the six models changes the relationship of subject/verb/object, offering the opportunity to discover hidden connections and unique insights, giving rise to faster innovation and potentially more significant breakthroughs (McCabe, 2012). This meaning-making approach also helps individuals understand their personal focus, that is, where their awareness is centered.

Mathematician Tom McCabe's legendary work on algorithm complexity has led to an even more impactful mathematical breakthrough. He has discovered a connection between mathematical group theory and consciousness, directly connecting the mathematical group Dihedral order 6 with different perspectives of our thoughts. See Expanded Consciousness Institute: www.expanded-consciousness.com.

Reversal (looking and seeing)

One of the fun ways to shift our frame of reference is Reversal, that is, the ability to see/perceive situations and their context by turning something inside out, generally reversing the order of things, whether front and back, or top and bottom, or side to side. There are lots of ways to think about this. For example, during the big Acquisition Reform movement in the U.S. Department of the Navy, part of which was the shift to performance-based standards, there was the need to eliminate thousands of standards that had crept over the years into various contracting vehicles. Given one year and a pot of money to accomplish this task, the DON began down the same path as the other services, holding mini-trials with each standard, one-by-one, the defendant, such that it had to be "proved" that a standard was not needed. The task was an impossible one; there was always some contractor or some contracting officer who felt that each standard was absolutely essential. As the weeks went by, and maybe 5 or 6 standards had been eliminated out of several thousand needing to be addressed, it was clear this approach was doomed to failure. Embracing the Knowledge Capacity of Reversal, all of the standards were eliminated, and mini-trials were held for those around which contractors and contracting officers had enough energy to bring back to the board and support their reinstatement. This was a game changer; when all was said and done, a couple of hundred standards were important enough to invest the energy necessary to have them reinstated.

Comprehending Diversity (perceiving and representing)

From an internal perspective, quick responses require a diversity of responses from which to draw. Since there is not much time to effectively respond in a CUCA environment, it makes sense to explore and develop a variety of potential responses prior to their need. An example is the use of scenario building, a foresight methodology that has been well-developed and tested in government, business and education. Scenarios are a form of story that can be used to consider possible, plausible, probable and preferable outcomes. Possible outcomes (what might happen) are based on future knowledge; plausible outcomes (what could happen) are based on current knowledge; probable outcomes (what will most likely happen) are based on current trends; and preferable outcomes (what you want to happen) are based on value judgments. For a well-connected knowledge worker, building scenarios can be both fruitful and fun. When facing surprises, scenarios can help in understanding new situations or at least foster a faster response by comparing the surprise with a related scenario.

From an external perspective, Comprehending Diversity means developing a competency in identifying and comprehending a wide variety of situations. For example, if you know nothing about complexity you won't be able to differentiate a complex system from a complicated system, each of which requires different sets of decisions and actions to achieve goals.

A first step is to recognize what you are looking at: the existence of diversity, the situation, and its context. Key questions: Is it diverse? Does it have many aspects that are in play or that may come into play? A second step is to comprehend it. *Vericate,* that is, consulting a trusted ally, someone who understands the systems at play. Develop knowledge about a situation to comprehend it within the context of the situation. Move through the knowledge chain to develop knowledge about the diversity, that is, awareness, understanding, meaning, insight, intuition, judgment, creativity, and anticipating the outcome of your decisions and actions.

Orchestrating Drive (acting and being)

There are many wife's tales and beliefs about our personal energy. One is that we just have so much in a life, and we just sit down and die when it is spent. Another says the more you give away the more you have. Regardless of whether we refer to this energy as spark, subtle energy (metaphysics), prana (Hindu), chi (Chinese), libido (Freud), orgon energy (Reich), or any other of the numerous other descriptive terms, every individual possesses a life force or, as described by Henri Bergson, a French philosopher, the élan vital, a source of efficient causation and evolution in nature. What we have learned about this energy—both by observation, and confirmed more recently through neuroscience findings—is its relationship to feelings. As Candace Pert, a research professor of physiology and biophysics at Georgetown University Medical Center, describes, "… this mysterious energy is actually the free-flow of information carried by the biochemicals of emotion, the neuropeptides and their receptors" (Pert, 1997, p. 276).

While the expression of any strong emotion requires an energy output, the expression of negative emotions generally represents an expenditure of energy, and the expression of positive emotions generally represents a generator of energy. For example, consider the crowds following a close-tied football game. While all may be physically tired from the experience, those who supported the loosing team are generally depressed and drag home; those who supported the winning team are generally buoyant, and may well go out and celebrate.

By understanding—and using—the emotions as a personal guidance system and motivator, knowledge workers can orchestrate their energy output. For example, by interacting, working with, and writing about ideas that have personal resonance, a knowledge worker is generating energy while expending energy, thus extending their ability to contribute and influence.

Symbolic Representation (perceiving and representing)

Representations in terms of words and visuals are the tools of trade for facilitating common understanding. The mind/brain does not store exact replicas of past events or memories. Rather, it stores invariant representations that color the meaning or essence of incoming information (Hawkins, 2004). There is a hierarchy of information where hierarchy represents "an order of some complexity, in which the elements are distributed along the gradient of importance" (Kuntz, 1968, p. 162). This hierarchy of information is analogous to the physical design of the neocortex, "a sheet of cells the size of a dinner napkin as thick as six business cards, where the connections between various regions give the whole thing a hierarchical structure" (Hawkins, 2004, p. 109). There are six layers of hierarchical patterns in the architecture of the cortex. While only documented for the sense of vision, it appears that the patterns at the lowest level of the cortex are fast changing and spatially specific (highly situation dependent and context sensitive) while the patterns at the highest level are slow changing and spatially invariant (Hawkins, 2004). For example, values, theories, beliefs and assumptions created (over and over again) through past learning processes represent a higher level of invariant form, one that does not easily change, compared to lower level patterns (Bennet & Bennet, 2013).

Thus, once learned, the mind/brain can quickly associate with symbols which can represent large amounts of context yet be immediately understood and interpreted. For example, a cross or menorah carries with it all the myths it represents. "It is an outward sign of an inward belief" (James, 1996, p. 78). As self, symbols are everywhere we look. Mathematics is built on hypotheses and relationships, that is, patterns, assumptions and relationships. Letters represent sounds, notes represent tones, pictures represent thoughts and beliefs, shapes of signs on the highway represent the context of rules, and so on. We use symbols to organize our thoughts. For example, in human face-to-face interactions it has long been recognized that non-verbals and voicing (tone, emphasis) can play a larger role in communication than the words that are exchanged. New patterns are emerging in social media that represent and convey these aspects of communication, helping provide the context and "feeling" for what is being said. In electronic communication, these symbols, or emogi, are small icons used to express a concept or emotion. For example, whether on Twitter or eMail, ":)" immediately conveys a smiley face, so much so that when these keystrokes are entered in MSWord followed by a space, they are immediately translated into ☺. As social media has matured, these symbols have become patterns of patterns, well understood by practicing social networkers and quickly conveying the message they are sending. (Pattern thinking is discussed in Chapter 17.)

A Working Example: *Instinctual Harnessing*

To facilitate a deeper understanding the nature of Knowledge Capacities, we choose to focus on a single example, what is described as Instinctual Harnessing (Acting and Being), as supported and described in the work of Arthur Shelley (2007), *The Organizational Zoo: A Survival Guide to Work Place Behavior.*

Shelley begins his book with the appropriate dedication:

To all who have been preyed upon and survived: May your experiences continue to make you stronger, wiser and better at reading the behaviors of those above you in the food chain, and ... To those about to begin your career safari: Prepare well! Invest time with positive creatures and ensure conflicts happen in your territory on your terms.

And so, the building of capacity begins, the capacity to observe the characteristics and behaviors of the creatures in your personal "organizational zoo" and to build self-awareness of your own characteristics and behaviors. Because it provides a removed perspective, it is possible to dissociate from personal feelings and more objectively (and metaphorically) view the organization as a collection of creatures interacting in, and with, their environment (Shelley, 2007).

Shelley (2007, p. xiii) determined that perhaps humans had not evolved as far as we would like to think, and that we could learn from how nature responds. As he describes:

There are many lessons that we could learn from nature, which could apply very well to the business world. The natural balance that exists in nature is something rarely achieved in human systems ... nature usually rebalances herself. It is only when humans interfere that nature loses control and falls out of balance. Could we learn from nature how to better manage our systems?

From this starting point, the model expanded to (1) figure out who's who in the zoo, and (2) determine what to fight for and what to concede. Figuring out who *we* are in the zoo gives us a sense of belonging, an identity in relationship to the others we see in the zoo. As Shelley points out, identities and classification schemes representing patterns we put people in to make our lives easier. The mind is continuously—and mostly unconsciously—organizing and classifying people, and then using this schema for unconscious profile matching and passing judgment. And sometimes we are right and sometimes we are wrong. However, "having better defined character profiles and a wider set of profiles helps us to understand others more and interact better with them" (Shelley, 2007, p. xvi.).

<<<<<<<<>>>>>>>

INSIGHT: **We have the capacity to deliberately adapt our behavior to align with the situation at hand. The more we do this, the better we perform.**

<<<<<<<<>>>>>>>

Developing the capacity of Instinctual Harnessing goes beyond just knowing the capabilities, tendencies and behaviors of the characters in your zoo. It helps you understand moods, inconsistencies and vagaries, know their strengths and weakness, and know how to manage through these. It assists you in constructing strategies, relieving some of the stress by making this a game, and it assists you in your personal development and development of others.

In the traditional zoo, when in a survival mode, the characteristics that emerge in the zoo animals include aggression, leadership (lion style), hiding and/or camouflage, assertiveness, ubiquity, dependencies, endurance and accountability. When your zoo is flourishing, techniques that are employed include leadership (eagle style), motivation, maturity, productivity, pro-activity, collaboration, networking, control and awareness.

Shelley points out that there is a growing shift toward communities, which form a very different type of zoo. These tend to be more knowledge focused creatures who genuinely like helping others. As Shelley (2007, p. 119) describes:

The community is more of a well-balanced environment, maybe more like an open plains Zoo, but with no boundaries at all. Creatures can come and graze as they desire and interact as they please. They can come as often as they like and leave whenever they want, most unlike the corporate Zoo. Community Zoos satisfy the mind and spirit ....

Each zoo character—ordered from a to z—has a profile that includes characteristics, some behaviors relating to the character, the meaning of success to the character and a list of attributes often applied to the character and attributes not often applied to the character. There are many ways to use these profiles, including workshop games not requiring any special tools or preparation, enabling learning in a fun atmosphere. These include creature introduction, an attribute ice breaker, network diversity analysis, and business partner (or competitor) analysis. Metaphoric representation of behaviors provides a safe language for behavior conversations.

As the value of Instinctual Harnessing as a learning tool and management aide has become more widely recognized and used, Shelley has collected data and developed new approaches to use this Knowledge Capacity as an individual or as a group or organization. See www.organizationalzoo.com

****

TOOL 21-1: FOCUSED TRAIT TRANSFERRENCE

This short process provides a focal point for looking at specific animal traits that correlate to human traits, helping us to understand ourselves and others. Note that the human is a complex adaptive system with incredible diversity and individuation. In the list below we have identified and described seven diverse animals with the hopes that each individual will be able to identify with at least one attribute from each animal. Then, understanding the set as a whole and how they work together begins to honor the complexity of the human.

STEP (1): Print out the list below of seven different animals with short descriptions of traits that they represent (taken from several frameworks of thought). Read the descriptions for each animal. Because these are animals most likely familiar to you, perhaps you are aware of additional traits. Add these to the list.

STEP (2): Reflect for five minutes on the traits for each animal. *Ask*: Are these traits that I see in the people around me? Are any of these traits that I have or exhibit to others? Highlight the traits for each animal that you see in yourself.

STEP (3): Bring all the traits that you see in yourself together as a set. Identify the strength of each trait in terms of their value to you. *Ask*: Which ones are the strongest? How do these traits work together? How have these traits been valuable in the past? How do these traits impact my interactions with others? How do these traits impact my work? How can I use these traits to my benefit and the benefit of others with whom I interact? *or* How can I change these traits to add more benefit to myself and others?

STEP (4): Assess the value of this exercise. *Ask*: What have I learned about myself and my interactions with others?

THE LIST:

(1) *Elephants*. Symbolically, elephants represent **strength and power**, especially power of the libido. Their strong sense of smell represents higher forms of discrimination leading to **wisdom**. Elephants also show **great affection and loyalty** to each other and their families. In their behaviors are the ideals of true societies. (Andrews, 2005)

(2) *Mountain gorillas*. Mountain gorillas, **strong and powerful**, are generally **gentle and shy**. They are **highly social** and live in relatively **stable, cohesive groups**, with long-term bonds developing between the males and females. The dominant males mitigate conflicts within the group and protects the group from external threats.

(3) *House cats*. The cat represents the attribute of **independence** and a wide variety of traits such as **curiosity**, **cleverness**, unpredictability, unsociability and **healing**. Because they can see in the dark, they are often associated with mystery and magic. Shelley (2007) attributes the following to cats: individualist, agile, aloof, self-interested, vain, selfish, frustrating, and arrogant.

(4) *Songbirds*. This group of perching birds (*Passeriformes*) includes over 4,000 species of birds found around the world, all equipped with vocal organs that produce a diverse and elaborate bird song. Both physical and spiritual, sound is an expression of energy. For example, the canary reflects the **awakening** and stimulation of the throat and heart, which gives increased **ability to feel and to express feelings**. As Andrews (2005, p. 123) describes, "When the canary shows up as a totem, it is time to ask yourself what song you have been singing ... You may find that those things you say more lovingly will be felt more lovingly. Those things you say more sharply will cut more deeply. What you say is going to have a much greater impact, as the canary **awakens the power of sound, music, and voice** in you."

(5) *Horses*. Key concepts connected to the horse are travel, **freedom** and power. The horse's energy is expansive, historically serving people in agriculture, recreation, war and travel, enabling people to "explore and find freedom from the constraints of their own communities" (Andrews, 2005, p. 289). They signify **power** and **movement**, contributed to the rise of civilization, and have been poetically connected with the wind and foam of the sea.

(6) *Dogs*. The two words that immediately come to mind for dogs are **faithfulness** and **protection**. Other terms associated with the dog include companionship, nurturing and caring and guardianship. (Andrews, 2005). Shelley (2007) says that dogs, a highly versatile and enthusiastic group of creatures, are loyal followers, not leaders, with the behavior highly dependent upon their master (leader) and their environment. He attributes the following to dogs: **loyal**, **trusting**, energetic, **enthusiastic**, boisterous, gullible, reliable, predictable, **happy**, **playful**, protective (when directed), and trustworthy (mainly).

(7) *Rabbits*. Connected to fertility and new life and imbued with **ambition**, **finesses** and **virtue**, the rabbit brings with it the **sensitive** and **artistic** powers of the moon. Moving in hops and leaps, it is fleet of foot and active both day and night. Although associated with fear by some, the rabbit has wonderful defenses, clever at doubling back and making quick and rapid turns. (Andrews, 2005)

****

Why Is *Instinctual Harnessing* Effective as a Knowledge Capacity?

Whether our beliefs lean toward creation or evolution—or both or neither—there is general recognition that humans and animals share many attributes. From the creation viewpoint we can approach this relationship metaphorically. From the evolutionary viewpoint, Homo sapiens and Homo sapiens sapiens are classified as a branch of the Hominini, a taxonomical tribe belonging to the family of great apes (Groves, 2005). Gifted with larger and more complex brains, this tribe is characterized by erect posture, bipedal locomotion and manual dexterity (Global Mammal Assessment Team, 2008).

Common attributes found in humans and animals include culture, emotions, language, humor, tool use, memory, self-awareness, intelligence, farming and building. For example, animals that pass the self-awareness test include great apes, some gibbons, elephants, magpies and some whales. As another example, Mulcahy (2012) says the greatest builders are Nigerian termites. They build

... fantastically huge mounds with internal ventilation, heating, and cooling systems through specially designed tunnels so that the termites living inside enjoy a pleasant climate at all times. they even have self-contained nurseries, gardens, cellars, chimneys, expressways, and sanitation systems.

A common attribute in both animals and humans is the concept of instinct. What is instinct? Merriam-Webster (2016) sees instinct as a way of behaving, thinking or feeling that is not learned; a natural desire or tendency that makes you want to act in a particular way; something you know without learning it or thinking about it; a natural ability. Instinct is a complete pattern of behavior that is given to animals.

As introduced in Chapter 17, Sheldrake's (1989) hypothesis of formative creation proposes that memory is inherent in nature, suggesting that all natural things inherit a collective memory from previous populations of similar natural things. This would explain the passing down of instinct with an animal group from one generation to the next. Sheldrake describes this process as morphic resonance.

Identifying animal characteristics and behaviors that metaphorically parallel human characteristics and behaviors provides the opportunity to separate emotional baggage from past experiences. This past experience may have been with that individual or others perceived as similar with the focus on the good or bad characteristic, or good or bad behaviors, rather than a specific individual's actions. This separation, or looking from the outside in, provides the opportunity for mental engagement at least partially disconnected from specific past events and the emotions and feelings connected to those events.

Further, as a set and considering the diversity of attributes, there is the opportunity for learning through different frames of reference. While the attributes to each animal are rather succinct and somewhat related, the attributes of humans can be collectively pulled from *all of these animals* and combined to produce unique and individuated results. For example, diversity coupled with individuation provides tremendous flexibility, potentially resulting in the bisociation of often unassociated attributes and leading to expanded creativity. And we now know that when directed outwards and through cooperation and collaboration with others, learning and creativity lead to expanded self-awareness and consciousness.

Questions for Reflection:

Do I just focus on what I already know, or do I look for what I do not know?

Is my capacity greater than my current knowledge, and, if so, how do I fill the capacity gap?

Do I consciously shift my behavior in order to optimize future outcomes?

A Preview of Part IV: Co-Creating the Future

[Excerpt from Chapter 23]

Reality is essentially subjectively unknowable, existing as an image, perception, perspective or belief generated by an individual, a group or a society. Knowledge acquired from the external world comes through our senses, usually the result of physical, psychological and social interactions of our minds and bodies with an external world, or a perceived external world. Consciousness, because of its central role in our ontology, also plays a crucial part in shaping and filtering our epistemology. The physical characteristics of our brains, together with the emergence of language and higher-order consciousness, act as both filters and interpreters of the external world. However, no matter how much we know or think we know, the best we as evolutionary products of that world *can* know is a qualified reality, a reality limited by both our individual embodiment and our space-time location. Further limited by our genetic heritage, our developmental morphology, chance events and our external environment, the best we can hope for is a qualified understanding of ourselves and of our reality. "As mind pursues reality to its ultimate analysis, matter vanishes to the material senses but may still remain real to the mind." (*Urantia*, 1954, p. 1228)

Nevertheless, consciousness, supported by our unconscious mind/brain and bootstrapped through social collaboration, is the only resource available to observe, create and comprehend our existence. It is also the experiential lens through which we must look to interact with other beings and with the physical world. This lens is reminiscent of Plato's allegory of shadows in the cave.

According to Plato, all living beings in the sensible world are but imperfect copies of eternal forms residing in the world of Ideas…the world accessible to our senses is akin to the world of shadows experienced by the men in the cave. It is merely an imperfect manifestation of a perfect world—the world of Ideas, illuminated by the Sun of intelligibility. (Thuan, 2001, p. 300-301)

Another interpretation of a perfect world would be one in which everything in the Universe is exactly as it should be. What else could it be if we eliminate personal morality and accept the sentence as meaning that nature and the Universe work as they do, independent of but consistent with rocks and beetles and humans. Perhaps as Plato opined, it is only man that separates himself from nature and thereby creates the fuzziness and imperfections he then perceives. Does a true world of eternal and immutable ideas exist where mathematical relations and perfect geometrical structures reign supreme?

# # #

Appendix A: The Overarching ISCJ Model

The Intelligent Social Change Journey (ISCJ)

NOTE: Each model builds on the understanding gained from experiencing the previous phase

Phase 1: LEARNING FROM THE PAST
CHARACTERISTICS: Linear and Sequential; Repeatable; Engaging past learning; Starting from current state; Cause and effect relationships.

Phase 2: LEARNING IN THE PRESENT
CHARACTERISTICS: Recognition of patterns; Social interaction; Co-evolving with environment through continuous learning, quick response, robustness, flexibility, adaptability, alignment.

Phase 3: CO-CREATING OUR FUTURE
CHARACTERISTICS: Creative imagination; Recognition of global Oneness; Mental in service to the intuitive; Balancing senses; Bringing together past, present and future; Knowing; Beauty; Wisdom.

SOCIAL STATE (Depth of Connection)

SYMPATHY → EMPATHY → COMPASSION

MOVEMENT:

EXPANDED CONSCIOUSNESS

CONSCIOUSNESS is considered a state of awareness and a private, selective and continuously changing process, a sequential set of ideas, thoughts, images, feelings and perceptions and an understanding of the connections and relationships among them and our self.
(Open to the Spiritual)

REDUCTION OF FORCES (Engage forces by choice)

INCREASED INTELLIGENT ACTIVITY (Growth of wisdom)

INTELLIGENT ACTIVITY represents a perfect state of interaction where intent, purpose, direction, values and expected outcomes are clearly understood and communicated among all parties, reflecting wisdom and achieving a higher truth.

KNOWLEDGE (The capacity (potential or actual) to take effective action)

FORCES occur when one type of energy affects another type of energy in a way where they are moving in different directions. Bounded (inward focused) and/or limited knowledge creates forces.

NATURE:
- Product of the past
- Context sensitive, situation dependent
- Partial, incomplete

- Expanded knowledge sharing, social learning, cooperation, collaboration
- Questioning of why?
- Pursuit of truth

- Recognition that with knowledge comes responsibility.
- Conscious pursuit of larger truth
- Knowledge selectively used as a measure of effectiveness

REFLECTION:
- Review of interactions; feedback
- Determination of cause and effect (logic)
- (inward focus) Questioning decisions and actions: What did I intend? What really happened? Why were there differences? What would I do the same? What would I do differently?

- Deeper development of conceptual thinking (higher mental thought)
- Connecting power of diversity and individuation to whole
- (Moving toward outward focus)
- Recognition of different world views, the exploration of information from different perspectives
- Expanded knowledge capacities.

- Valuing of creative ideas; Asking larger questions: How does this idea serve humanity? Are there any negative consequences?
- (Outward focus); Openness to others ideas with humility; What if this idea is right? Are my beliefs or other mental models limiting my thought? Are hidden assumptions or feelings interfering with intelligent activity?

COGNITIVE SHIFTS:
- Recognition of importance of feedback
- Ability to recognize systems; impact of external forces
- Recognition and location of "me" in the larger picture (conscious awareness)
- Early pattern recognition and concept development

- Ability to recognize and apply patterns at all levels within a domain of knowledge to predict outcomes
- Growing understanding of complexity
- Increased connectedness of choices; recognition of direction you are heading; expanded meaning-making
- Expanded ability to associate ideas; increased creativity

- Sense and knowing of Oneness
- Development of both lower (logic) and upper (conceptual) mental faculties, which work in concert with the emotional guidance system
- Application of patterns across knowledge domains for greater good
- Recognition of self as a co-creator of reality
- Ability to engage in intelligent activity
- Developing the ability to tap into the intuitional plane at will

Taken from: Bennet, et al (2017). The Profundity and Bifurcation of Change, Parts I through V. Frost, WV: MQIPress.

Developed by Mountain Quest Institute. Contact [email] for permissions.

Appendix B: Five-Book Table of Contents

The Profundity and Bifurcation of Change
The Intelligent Social Change Journey

For Each:
Cover
Title Page
Quote from *The Kybalion*
Table of Contents
Tables and Figures
Appreciation

Preface

Introduction to the Intelligent Social Change Journey

Part I: LAYING THE GROUNDWORK

Part I Introduction

Chapter 1: Change is Natural
CHANGE AS A VERB...OUR CHANGING THOUGHTS...FINAL THOUGHT
Chapter 2: Knowledge to Action
KNOWLEDGE (INFORMING) AND KNOWLEDGE (PROCEEDING)...LEVELS OF KNOWLEDGE...FROM
KNOWLEDGE TO ACTION...THE NATURE OF KNOWLEDGE...LEVELS OF COMPREHENSION...FINAL
THOUGHTS
Chapter 3: Forces We Act Upon
AMPLITUDE, FREQUENCY AND DURATION...FROM THE VIEWPOINT OF THE INDIVIDUAL...CONTROL
AS FORCE...REDUCING FORCES...THE SELF AND FORCES...FROM THE SPIRITUAL
VIEWPOINT...STRATEGIC FORCES IN ORGANIZATIONS...THE CORRELATION OF FORCES...FINAL
THOUGHTS
Chapter 4: The Ever-Expanding Self
THE SUBJECT/OBJECT RELATIONSHIP...THE PERSONALITY...CHARACTERISTICS OF
PERSONALITY...DEVELOPMENT OF SELF...THE HEALTHY SELF...THE CONNECTED SELF...
INDIVIDUATION...THE POWER OF HUMILITY...FINAL THOUGHTS
Chapter 5: The Window of Consciousness
PROPERTIES OF CONSCIOUSNESS...THE THRESHOLD OF CONSCIOUSNESS...LEVELS OF
CONSCIOUSNESS...MEANING AND PURPOSE...CONSCIOUSNESS AS A QUANTUM FIELD...FLOW AS
THE OPTIMAL EXPERIENCE...CONSCIOUSLY ACCESSING THE UNCONSCIOUS...FINAL THOUGHTS
Chapter 6: The Individual Change Model

The Human as a Complex Adaptive System...The Environment and the Knowledge Worker...The Model...Applying the Model...Final Thoughts

Part II: LEARNING FROM THE PAST

Part II Introduction

Part III: LEARNING IN THE PRESENT

Part III Introduction

Part IV: CO-CREATING THE FUTURE

APPENDICES:
Appendix A: The Overarching ISCJ Model
Appendix B: The Table of Contents for All Parts
Appendix C: *An Infinite Story*
Appendix D: Engaging Tacit Knowledge
Appendix E: Knowing
Appendix F: Values for Creativity

ENDNOTES

REFERENCES

About Mountain Quest
About the Authors

TOOLS

Part I: Introduction
3-1. Force Field Analysis
4-1. Self Belief Assessment
4-2. Humility
5-1. Engaging Tacit Knowledge (See Appendix D.)

Part II: Learning From the Past
7-1. Personal Plane-ing Process
7-2. The Five Whys
9-1. Engaging Outside Worldviews
9-2. Practicing Mental Imagining
10-1. Grounding through Nature
10-2. Relationship Network Management
11-1. Co-Creating Conversations that Matter

Part III: Learning in the Present
13-1. Trust Mapping
14-1. Building Mental Sustainability
16-1. Integrating Time into the Self Experience
16-2. Scenario Building
17-1. Thinking Patterns
17-2. Storying: Capture (see Appendix G)
17-3. Storying: Sculpt (see Appendix G)
17-4. Storying: Tell (see Appendix G)
18-1. Connecting through the Heart

Appendix C: *An Infinite Story*

There is such joy to be had soaring through the skies above this glorious Earth, diving into the oceans and seas, shifting to a sunny afternoon float atop a passing cloud, perhaps connecting with this energy and entangling with that pattern for awhile. Instant after instant after instant, a continuous awareness of Nows filled with a love of Being. We of One are many, expressing our light in an array of colors, sometimes seen and captured in pictures taken by those souls journeying in human form. Have you ever seen us? Have you ever wondered who we are?

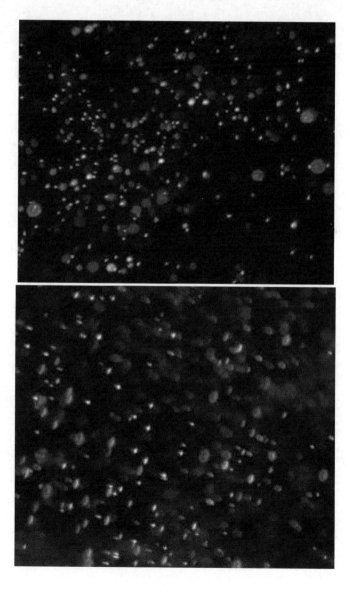

And then the Call goes out, a vibration of sound that comes from the heart of part of the One. What fun! In the instant we come together, a feeling of flowing breath riding the waves of life. And in that instant our light is stretched, moving out of the spherical form that is our natural setting and displaying the essence of a spectrum of color.

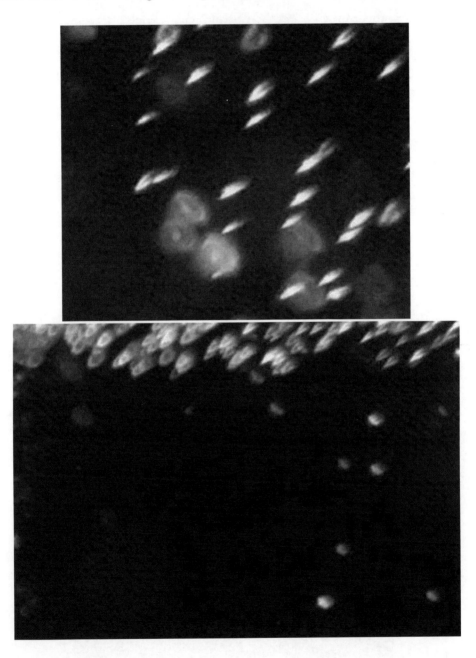

We expand as we connect with the mist in the air, moving as a collective, curving and shifting into form, sharing our energy, creating a pattern of Oneness.

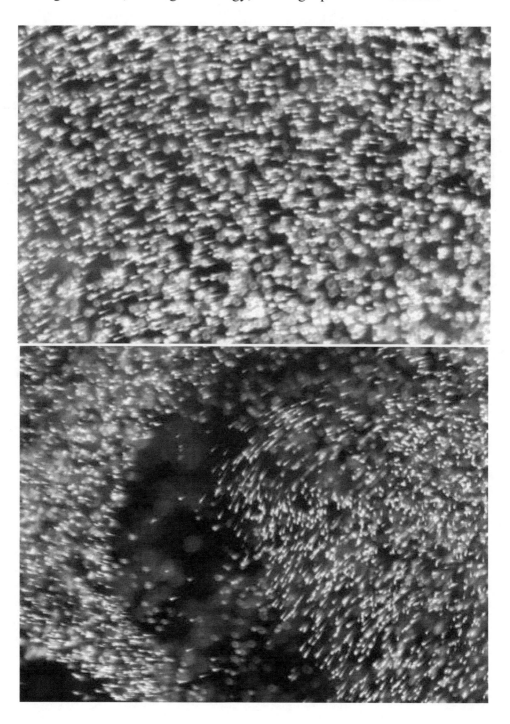

When we who respond to the Call are close in resonance, then oh the beautiful patterns we create! Some may perceive these as fractals. From one direction you will see an angle, and there is a split second when you can see our expansion. How gloriously bright the colors that present to the human eyes who choose to see us!

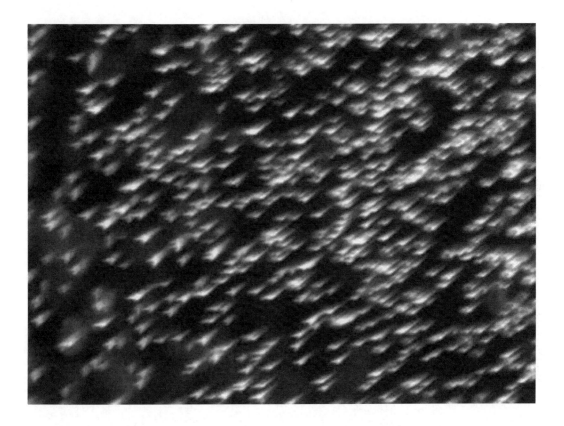

As we move closer and closer, we continue to expand, bringing in the water of the air to reassume comfortable spherical shapes producing faces within faces within form, with delight dissolving into the Oneness that we are.

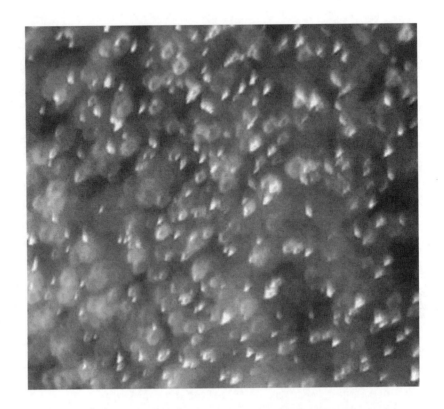

We *feel* the Joy of One as we create the *Myst* forms. We lighten into form, move into stillness, perhaps accenting the white of a full moon.

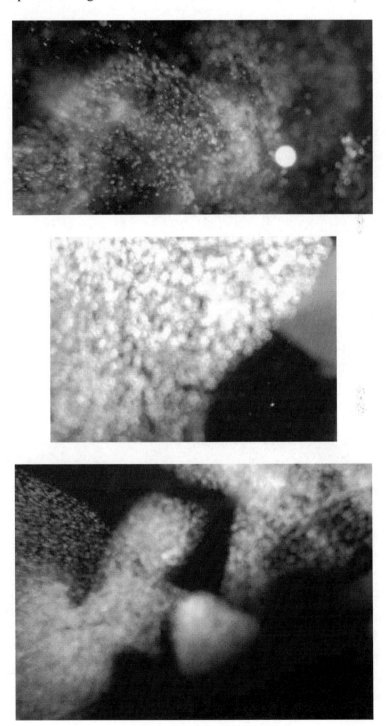

Oh, what beauty! Can you understand? We are individuated, yet one ... sharing our light, conveying a message, glowing in our delight! Can you see the faces? They represent our essence, the energy of us in a personalized fashion. And we love you.

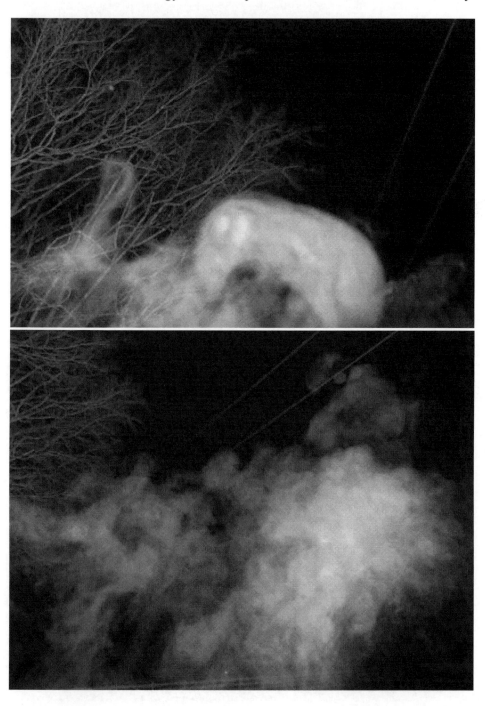

Now ...

we will share a secret. It is the same for all forms of life. There are inherent desires and possibilities moving us towards cooperation and collaboration, the Connectedness of love and joy and peace, Oneness.

Then, in an instant of ever-living Nows, the larger form releases. The circles of Orbs become skeletal, then dissipate, reducing into the spark of life that is so small, so large, so All.

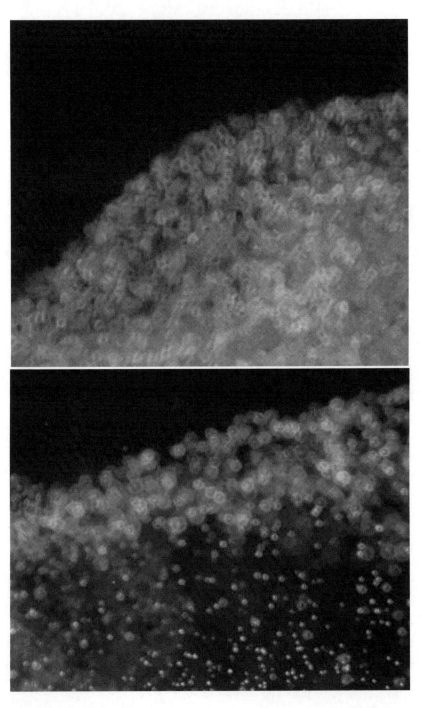

Do not be concerned. We do not really disappear. We are always here. When you are in joy, in the flash of a camera we will appear, and you will know us. You, too, are opening to the Call, and, even now, feeling the love that lights our way. We are One.

*[Excerpted from **Patterns in the Myst** (Bennet and Bennet, 2013)]*

Appendix D
Engaging Tacit Knowledge

[Detail for the Tool "Engaging Tacit Knowledge" introduced in chapter 5. Skip to the subtitle "Accessing Tacit Knowledge" below if you already understand the concepts of "knowledge", "tacit" and the four types of tacit knowledge: embodied, intuitive, affective and spiritual.]

SUBTOPICS: BACKGROUND ... THE TYPES OF TACIT KNOWLEDGE ... ACCESSING TACIT KNOWLEDGE ... SURFACING ... EMBEDDING ... SHARING ... INDUCING RESONANCE

FIGURE: D-1. CONTINUUM OF AWARENESS OF KNOWLEDGE SOURCE/CONTENT ... D-2. ACCESSING TACIT KNOWLEDGE

Background

Knowledge—the capacity (potential or actual) to take effective action—was introduced in Chapter 3. Our focus in this Part Is on that knowledge residing in the unconscious, that is, tacit knowledge (Item 1-E). Tacit knowledge is the descriptive term for those connections among thoughts that cannot be pulled up in words, a knowing of what decision to make or how to do something that cannot be clearly voiced in a manner such that another person could extract and re-create that knowledge (understanding, meaning, etc.). An individual may or may not know they have tacit knowledge in relationship to something or someone; but even when it is known, the individual is unable to put it into words or visuals that can convey that knowledge. We all know things, or know what to do, yet may be unable to articulate why we know them, why they are true, or even exactly what they are. To "convey" is to cause something to be known or understood or, in this usage, to transfer information from which the receiver is able to create knowledge.

As a point of contrast, explicit knowledge is information (patterns) and processes (patterns in time) that can be called up from memory and described accurately in words and/or visuals (representations) such that another person can comprehend the knowledge that is expressed through this exchange of information. This has historically been called declarative knowledge (Anderson, 1983). Implicit knowledge is a more complicated concept, and a term not unanimously agreed-upon in the literature. This is understandable since even simple dictionary definitions—which are generally unbiased and powerful indicators of collective preference and understanding—show a considerable overlap between the terms "implicit" and "tacit," making it difficult to differentiate the two. We propose that a useful interpretation of implicit knowledge is knowledge stored in memory of which the individual is not immediately aware which, while not readily accessible, may be pulled up when triggered (associated). Triggering can occur through questions, dialogue or reflective thought, or happen as a result of an external event. In other words, implicit knowledge is knowledge that the individual does not know they have, but is self-discoverable! However, once this knowledge is surfaced, the individual may or may not have the ability to adequately describe it such that another individual could create the same knowledge; and the "why and how" may remain tacit.

A number of published psychologists have used the term implicit interchangeably with our usage of tacit, that is, with implicit representing knowledge that once acquired can be shown to effect behavior but is not available for conscious retrieval (Reber, 1993; Kirsner et al, 1998). As described in the above discussion of implicit knowledge, what is forwarded here is that the concept of implicit knowledge serves as a middle ground between that which can be made explicit and that which cannot easily, if at all, be made explicit. By moving beyond the dualistic approach of explicit and tacit—that which can be declared versus that which can't be declared, and that which can be remembered versus that which can't be remembered—we posit implicit as representing the knowledge spectrum between explicit and tacit. While explicit refers to easily available, some knowledge requires a higher stimulus for association to occur but is not buried so deeply as to prevent access. This understanding opens the domain of implicit knowledge.

Tacit and explicit knowledge can be thought of as residing in "places," specifically, the unconscious and the conscious, respectively, although both are differentiated patterns spread throughout the neuronal system, that is, the volume of the brain and other parts of the central nervous system. On the other hand, implicit knowledge may reside in either the unconscious (prior to triggering, or tacit) or the conscious (when triggered, or explicit). Note there is no clean break between these three types of knowledge (tacit, implicit and explicit); rather, this is a continuum.

Calling them interactive components of cooperative processes, Reber agrees that there is no clear boundary between that which is explicit and that which is implicit (our tacit): "There is ... no reason for presuming that there exists a clean boundary between conscious and unconscious processes or a sharp division between implicit and explicit epistemic systems ..." (Reber, 1993, p. 23). Reber describes the urge to treat explicit and implicit (our tacit) as altogether different processes the "polarity fallacy" (Reber, 1993). Similarly, Matthews says that the unconscious and conscious processes are engaged in what he likes to call a "synergistic" relationship (Matthews, 1991). What this means is that the boundary between the conscious and the unconscious is somewhat porous and flexible.

Knowledge starts as tacit knowledge, that is, the initial movement of knowledge is from its origins within the Self (in the unconscious) to an outward expression (albeit driving effective action). What does that mean? Michael Polanyi, a professor of chemistry and the social sciences, wrote in The Tacit Dimension that, "We start from the fact that we can know more than we can tell" (Polanyi, 1967, p 108). He called this pre-logical phase of knowing tacit knowledge, that is, knowledge that cannot be articulated (Polanyi, 1958).

The Types of Tacit Knowledge

Tacit knowledge can be thought of in terms of four aspects: embodied, intuitive, affective and spiritual (Bennet & Bennet, 2008c). While all of these aspects are part of Self, each represents different sources of tacit knowledge whose applicability, reliability and efficacy may vary greatly depending on the individual, the situation and the knowledge needed to take effective action. They are represented in Figure D-1 along with explicit and implicit knowledge on the continuum of awareness.

Embodied tacit knowledge is also referred to as somatic knowledge. Both kinesthetic and sensory, it can be represented in neuronal patterns stored within the body. Kinesthetic is related to the movement of the body and, while important to every individual every day of our lives, it is a primary focus for athletes, artists, dancers, kids and assembly-line workers. A commonly used example of tacit knowledge is knowledge of riding a bicycle. Sensory, by definition, is related to the five human senses of form through which information enters the body (sight, smell, hearing, touch and taste). An example is the smell of burning rubber from your car brakes while driving or the smell of hay in a barn. These odors can convey knowledge of whether the car brakes may need replacing (get them checked immediately), or whether the hay is mildewing (dangerous to feed horses, but fine for cows). These responses would be overt, bringing to conscious awareness the need to take effective action and driving that action to occur.

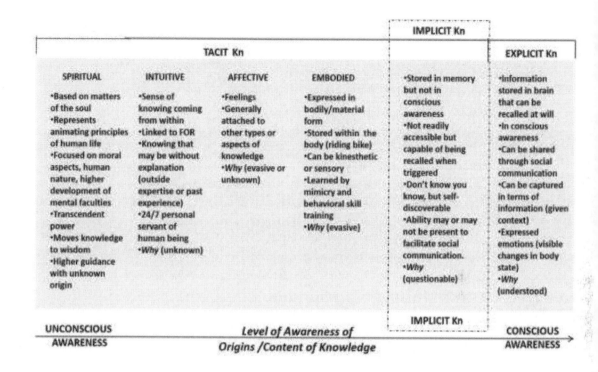

Figure D-1. *Continuum of awareness of knowledge source/content.*

Intuitive tacit knowledge is the sense of knowing coming from inside an individual that may influence decisions and actions; yet the decision-maker or actor cannot explain how or why the action taken is the right one. The unconscious works around the clock with a processing capability many times greater than that at the conscious level. This is why as the world grows more complex, decision-makers will depend more and more on their intuitive tacit knowledge, a combination of life lessons. But in order to use it, decision-makers must first be able to tap into their unconscious.

Affective tacit knowledge is connected to emotions and feelings, with emotions representing the external expression of some feelings. Feelings expressed as emotions become explicit (Damasio, 1994). Feelings that are not expressed—perhaps not even recognized—are those that fall into the area of affective tacit knowledge. Feelings as a form of knowledge have different characteristics than language or ideas, but they may lead to effective action because they can influence actions by their existence and connections with consciousness. When feelings come into conscious awareness, they can play an informing role in decision-making, providing insights in a non-linguistic manner and thereby influencing decisions and actions. For example, a feeling (such as fear or an upset stomach) may occur every time a particular action is started which could prevent the decision-maker from taking that action.

Spiritual tacit knowledge can be described in terms of knowledge based on matters of the soul. The soul represents the animating principles of human life in terms of thought and action, specifically focused on its moral aspects, the emotional part of human nature, and higher development of the mental faculties (Bennet & Bennet, 2007c). While there is a "knowing" related to spiritual knowledge similar to intuition, this knowing does not include the experiential base of intuition, and it may or may not have emotional tags. The current state of the evolution of our understanding of spiritual knowledge is such that there are insufficient words to relate its transcendent power, or to define the role it plays in relationship to other tacit knowledge. Nonetheless, this area represents a form of higher guidance with unknown origin. Spiritual knowledge may be the guiding purpose, vision and values behind the creation and application of tacit knowledge. It may also be the road to moving information to knowledge and knowledge to wisdom (Bennet & Bennet, 2008d). In the context of this book, spiritual tacit knowledge represents the source of higher learning, helping decision-makers create and implement knowledge that has greater meaning and value for the common good.

Whether embodied, affective, intuitive or spiritual, *tacit knowledge represents the bank account of the Self.* The larger our deposits, the greater the interest, and the more we are prepared for co-evolving in a changing, uncertain and complex environment.

Accessing Tacit Knowledge

There are many ways to bring our tacit resources into our consciousness. For example, we propose a four-fold action model with nominal curves for building what we call extraordinary consciousness, that is, expanding our consciousness through accessing tacit resources. The four approaches to accessing include surfacing, embedding, sharing and inducing resonance. (See Figure D-2 below.)

Surfacing Tacit Knowledge.

As individuals observe, experience, study and learn throughout life they generate a huge amount of information and knowledge that becomes stored in their unconscious mind. Surfacing tacit knowledge is focused on accessing the benefit of that which is tacit by moving knowledge from the unconscious to conscious awareness. Three ways that tacit knowledge can be surfaced are through external triggering, self-collaboration and nurturing.

The process of triggering is primarily externally driven with internal participation. For example, conversation, dialogue, questions, or an external situation with specific incoming information may trigger the surfacing of tacit knowledge needed to respond. Triggering is often the phenomenon that occurs in "sink or swim" situations, where an immediate decision must be made that will have significant consequences.

Although collaboration is generally thought about as interactions among individuals and/or groups, a type of collaboration that is less understood is the process of *individuals consciously collaborating with themselves*. What this means is the conscious mind learning to communicate with, listen to, and trust its own unconscious based on a relationship built over time between the self and the personality. With the self in charge, the selection process and semantic complexing of all the experiences, learning, thoughts and feelings throughout life is consistent with the focus and purpose of the self. One way to collaborate with your self is through creating an internal dialogue.

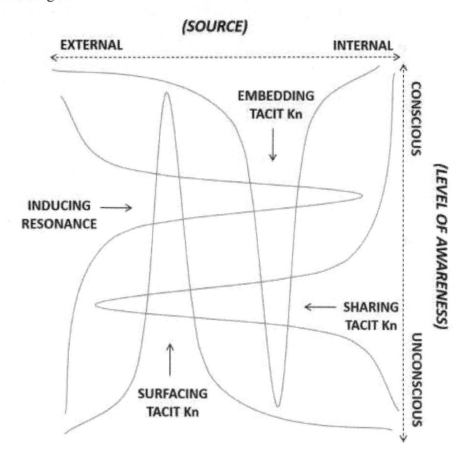

Figure D-2. *Accessing Tacit Knowledge.*

For example, accepting the authenticity of, and listening deeply to, a continuous stream of conscious thought while following the tenets of dialogue. Those tenets would include: withholding quick judgment, not demanding quick answers, and exploring underlying assumptions (Ellinor & Gerard, 1998, p. 26), *then* looking for collaborative meaning between what you consciously think and what you feel. A second approach is to ask yourself a lot of questions related to the task at hand. Even if you don't think you know the answers, reflect carefully on the questions, and be patient. Sleeping on a question will often yield an answer the following morning. Your unconscious mind processes information 24/7; it is not a figment of your imagination, or your enemy. To paraphrase the Nobel Laureate Neuroscientist Dr. Eric Kandel, your unconscious is a part of you. It works 24 hours a day processing incoming information on your behalf. So, when it tells you something via intuition, lucid dreaming, etc., you should listen carefully (but it may not always be right) (Kandel, 2006).

Although requiring time, openness and commitment, there are a number of approaches readily available for those who choose to nurture their sensitivity to tacit knowledge. These include (among others) meditation, inner tasking, lucid dreaming, and hemispheric synchronization. Meditation practices have the ability to quiet the conscious mind, thus allowing greater access to the unconscious (Rock, 2004). Inner tasking is a wide-spread and often used approach to engaging your unconscious. Tell yourself, as you fall asleep at night, to work on a problem or question. The next morning when you wake up, but before you get up, lie in bed and listen to your own, quiet, passive thoughts. Frequently, but not always, the answer will appear, although it must be written down quickly before it is lost from the conscious mind. Like meditation, the efficacy of this approach takes time and practice to develop (Bennet and Bennet, 2008e).

Lucid dreaming is a particularly powerful way to access tacit knowledge. The psychotherapist Kenneth Kelzer wrote of one of his lucid dreams:

> In this dream I experienced a lucidity that was so vastly different and beyond the range of anything I had previously encountered. At this point I prefer to apply the concept of the spectrum of consciousness to the lucid dream and assert that within the lucid state a person may have access to a spectrum or range of psychic energy that is so vast, so broad and so unique as to defy classification. (Kelzer, 1987)

Another way to achieve sensitivity to the unconscious is *through the use of sound*. For example, listening to a special song in your life can draw out deep feelings and memories buried in your unconscious. Sound and its relationship to humans has been studied by philosophers throughout recorded history; extensive treatments appear in the work of Plato, Kant and Nietzsche. Through the last century scientists have delved into studies focused on acoustics (the science of sound), psychoacoustics (the study of how our minds perceive sound) and musical psychoacoustics (the discipline that involves every aspect of musical perception and performance). As do all patterns in the mind, sound has the ability to change and shape the physiological structure of the brain.

For example, hemispheric synchronization (bringing both hemispheres of the brain into coherence) can be accomplished through the use of sound coupled with a binaural beat. (See Bullard and Bennet, 2013 or Bennet et al., 2015b for in-depth treatment of hemispheric synchronization.) Inter-hemispheric communication is the setting for brain-wave coherence which facilitates whole-brain cognition, assuming an elevated status in subjective experience (Ritchey, 2003). What can occur during hemispheric synchronization is a physiologically reduced state of arousal, quieting the body *while maintaining conscious awareness* (Mavromatis, 1991; Atwater, 2004; Fischer, 1971; West, 1980; Delmonte, 1984; Goleman, 1988; Jevning et al., 1992), thus providing a doorway into the unconscious. It is difficult to imagine the amount of learning and insights that might reside therein—and the expanded mental capabilities such access may provide—much less the depth and breadth of experience and emotion that has been hidden there, perhaps making such access a mixed blessing

Embedding Tacit Knowledge.

Every experience and conversation are *embedding* potential knowledge (information) in the unconscious as it is associated with previously stored information to create new patterns. Thinking about embedding as a process for improving our tacit knowledge can lead to new approaches to learning. Embedding is both externally and internally driven, with knowledge moving from the conscious to the unconscious through exposure or immersion, by accident or by choice. Examples include travel, regularly attending church on Sunday, or listening to opera and imitating what you've heard in the shower every day. Practice moves beyond exposure to include repeated participation in some skill or process, thus strengthening the patterns in the mind. For example, after many years of imitation (practice) look at what Paul Potts, an opera singer and winner of the *Britain's Got Talent* competition in 2007, accomplished!

Creating tacit knowledge occurs naturally through diverse experiences in the course of life as individuals become more proficient at some activity (such as public speaking) or cognitive competency (such as problem solving). When the scope of experience widens, the number of relevant neuronal patterns increases. As an individual becomes more proficient in a specific focus area through effortful practice, the pattern gradually becomes embedded in the unconscious, ergo it becomes tacit knowledge. When this happens, the reasons and context within which the knowledge was created often lose their connections with consciousness.

Embodied tacit knowledge requires new pattern embedding for change to occur. This might take the form of repetition in physical training or in mental thinking. For example, embodied tacit knowledge might be embedded through mimicry, practice, competence development or visual imagery coupled with practice. An example of this would be when an athlete training to become a pole vaulter reviews a video of his perfect pole vault to increase his athletic capability. This is a result of the fact that when the pole vaulter performs his perfect vault, the patterns going through his brain while he is doing it are the same patterns that go through his brain when he is watching himself do it. When he is watching the video, he is repeating the desired brain patterns and this repetition strengthens these patterns in unconscious memory. When "doing" the pole vault, he cannot think about his actions, nor try to control them. Doing so would degrade his performance because his conscious thoughts would interfere with his tacit ability.

In the late 1990's, neuroscience research identified what are referred to as mirror neurons. As Dobb's explains,

> These neurons are scattered throughout key parts of the brain—the premotor cortex and centers for language, empathy and pain—and fire not only as we perform a certain action, but also when we watch someone else perform that action. (Dobbs, 2007, p. 22)

Watching a video is a cognitive form of mimicry that transfers actions, behaviors and most likely other cultural norms. Thus, when we *see* something being enacted, our mind creates the same patterns that we would use to enact that "something" ourselves. As these patterns fade into long-term memory, they would represent tacit knowledge—both Knowledge (Informing) and Knowledge (Proceeding). While mirror neurons are a subject of current research, it would appear that they represent a mechanism for the transfer of tacit knowledge between individuals or throughout a culture. For more information on mirror neurons, see Gazzaniga, 2004.

Intuitive tacit knowledge can be nurtured and developed through exposure, learning, and practice. Knowledge (Informing) might be embedded through experience, contemplation, developing a case history for learning purposes, developing a sensitivity to your own intuition, and effortful practice. Effortful study moves beyond practice to include identifying challenges just beyond an individual's competence and focusing on meeting those challenges one at a time (Ericsson, 2006). The way people become experts involves the chunking of ideas and concepts and creating understanding through the development of significant patterns useful for solving problems and anticipating future behavior within their area of focus. In the study of chess players introduced earlier, it was concluded that "effortful practice" was the difference between people who played chess for many years while maintaining an average skill and those who became master players in shorter periods of time. The master players, or experts, examined the chessboard patterns over and over again, studying them, looking at nuances, trying small changes to perturb the outcome (sense and response), generally "playing with" and studying these *patterns* (Ross, 2006). In other words, they use *long-term working memory, pattern recognition and chunking* rather than logic as a means of understanding and decision-making. This indicates that by exerting mental effort and emotion while exploring complex situations, knowledge—often problem-solving expertise and what some call wisdom—becomes embedded in the unconscious mind. For additional information on the development of expertise see Ericsson (2006). An important insight from this discussion is the recognition that when facing complex problems which do not allow reasoning or cause and effect analysis because of their complexity, the solution will most likely lie in studying patterns and chunking those patterns to enable a tacit capacity to anticipate and develop solutions. For more on the reference to wisdom see Goldberg (2005).

Affective tacit knowledge requires nurturing and the development of emotional intelligence. Affective tacit knowledge might be embedded through digging deeply into a situation—building self-awareness and developing a sensitivity to your own emotions—and having intense emotional experiences. How much of an experience is kept as tacit knowledge depends upon the mode of incoming information and the emotional tag we (unconsciously) put on it. The stronger the emotion attached to the experience, the longer it will be remembered and the easier it will be to recall. Subtle patterns that occur during any experience may slip quietly into our unconscious and become affective tacit knowledge. For a good explanation of emotional intelligence see Goleman (1998).

Spiritual tacit knowledge can be facilitated by encouraging holistic representation of the individual and respect for a higher purpose. Spiritual tacit knowledge might be embedded through dialogue, learning from practice and reflection, and developing a sensitivity to your own spirit, living with it over time and exploring your feelings regarding the larger aspects of values, purpose and meaning. Any individual who, or organization which, demonstrates—and acts upon—their deep concerns for humanity and the planet is embedding spiritual tacit knowledge.

Sharing Tacit Knowledge

In our discussion above on surfacing tacit knowledge, it became clear that surfaced knowledge is new knowledge, a different shading of that which was in the unconscious. If knowledge can be described in words and visuals, then this would be by definition explicit; understanding can only be symbolized and to some extent conveyed through words. Yet the subject of this paragraph is sharing tacit knowledge. The key is that **it is not necessary to make knowledge explicit in order to share it**.

Sharing tacit knowledge occurs both consciously and unconsciously, although the knowledge shared remains tacit in nature. *There is no substitute for experience.* The power of this process has been recognized in organizations for years, and tapped into through the use of mentoring and shadowing programs to facilitate imitation and mimicry. More recently, it has become the focus of group learning, where communities and teams engage in dialogue focused on specific issues and experiences mentally and, over time, develop a common frame of reference, language and understanding that can create solutions to complex problems. The words that are exchanged serve as a tool of creative expression rather than limiting the scope of exchange.

The solution set agreed upon may retain "tacitness" in terms of understanding the complexity of the issues (where it is impossible to identify all the contributing factors much less a cause and effect relationship among them). Hence these solutions in terms of understanding would not be explainable in words and visuals to individuals outside the team or community. When this occurs, the team (having arrived at the "tacit" decision) will often create a rational, but limited, explanation for purposes of communication of why the decision makes sense.

Inducing Resonance.

Through exposure to diverse, and specifically opposing, concepts that are well-grounded, it is possible to create a resonance within the receiver's mind that amplifies the meaning of the incoming information, increasing its emotional content and receptivity. Inducing resonance is a result of external stimuli resonating with internal information to bring into conscious awareness. While it is words that trigger this resonance, it is the current of truth flowing under that linguistically centered thought that brings about connections. When this resonance occurs, the incoming information is consistent with the frame of reference and belief systems within the receiving individual. This resonance amplifies feelings connected to the incoming information, bringing about the emergence of deeper perceptions and validating the re-creation of externally-triggered knowledge in the receiver.

Further, this process results in the amplification and transformation of internal affective, embodied, intuitive or spiritual knowledge from tacit to implicit (or explicit). Since deep knowledge is now accessible at the conscious level, this process also creates a sense of ownership within the listener. The speakers are not telling the listener what to believe; rather, when the tacit knowledge of the receiver resonates with what the speaker is saying (and how it is said), a natural reinforcement and expansion of understanding occurs within the listener. This accelerates the creation of deeper tacit knowledge and a stronger affection associated with this area of focus.

An example of inducing resonance can be seen in the movie, *The Debaters*. We would even go so far as to say that the purpose of a debate is to transfer tacit knowledge. Well-researched and well-grounded external information is communicated (explicit knowledge) tied to emotional tags (explicitly expressed). The beauty of this process is that this occurs on *both sides* of a question such that the active listener who has an interest in the area of the debate is pulled into one side or another. An eloquent speaker will try to speak from the audience's frame of reference to tap into their intuition. Such a speaker will come across as confident, likeable and positive to transfer embodied tacit knowledge, and may well refer to higher order purpose, etc. to connect with the listener's spiritual tacit knowledge. An example can be seen in litigation, particularly in the closing arguments, where for opposing sides of an issue emotional tags are tied to a specific frame of reference regarding what has been presented.

[Excerpted from Bennet et al. (2015)]

Endnotes

13-1. There have been many research studies that have demonstrated perceived negative effects from multi-tasking. However, we as humans are multidimensional and, whether aware of it or not—conscious or unconscious—are multi-tasking throughout our lives. See Bennet et al., 2015b for an in-depth treatment of neuroscience findings related to experiential learning.

16-1. As a discipline, remote viewing utilizes scientific protocol to "access and provide accurate information through psychic means, bout a person, place, object or event, that is inaccessible through any normally accepted means, regardless of distance, shielding, or time" (McMoneagle, 2000, p. 220). It requires more than letting go, rather, an emptying such that an intimate connection can be made with another.

18-1. The KMTL Study is a 2005 research study that reached out to 34 Knowledge Management Thought Leaders located across four continents. The intent was to explore the aspects of KM that contributed to the passion expressed by these thought leaders.

References

Ackoff, R. L. and Emergy, F. E. (1972). *On Purposeful Systems*. London: Tavistock.

Adler, M. J. (1992). *The Great Ideas: A Lexicon of Western Thought*. New York: Scribner.

Admiraal, W., Huizenga, J., Akkierman, S. and ten Dam, G. (2011). "The Concept of Flow in Collaborative Game-Based Learning in Computers" in *Human Behavior*, 27 (3): 1185-1194. Retrieved 10/05/16 from http://dx.doi.org/10.1016/j.chb.2010.12.013

Adolfs, R. (2004). "Processing of Emotional and Social Information by the Human Amygdala" in Gazzaniga, M.S. (Ed.), *The Cognitive Neurosciences III*. Cambridge, MA: The Bradford Press.

Alberts, D. S. and Hayes, R. E. (2005). *Power to the Edge: Command, Control in the Information Age*. Washington, D.C.: Command & Control Research Program.

Allen, J. (2016). "Your Mental Attitude." Retrieved 11/30/16 from http://www.jamesallenlibrary.com/authors/james-allen/above-lifes-turmoil/your-mental-attitude

Amen, D. G. (2005). *Making a Good Brain Great*. New York: Harmony Books.

Andersen, N.A. and Born, A.W. (2008). "The Employee in the Sign of Love" in *Culture and Organization* 14(4): 325-343.

Anderson, J. A. and Allopenna, P. (2008). "A Brain-Like Computer for Cognitive Applications: The Ersatz Brain Project." Retrieved 08/10/16 from www.cog.brown.edu/Research/ErsatzBrainGroup/index.html

Andrews, T. (2005). *Animal Speak: The Spiritual & Magical Powers of Creatures Great & Small*. St. Paul, MN: Llewellyn Publications.

Andrews, B., Brewin, C. R., Ochera, J., Morton, J., Bekerian, D. A., Davies, G. M., et al. (1999). "Characteristics, Context and Consequences of Memory Recovery Among Adults in Therapy" in *British Journal of Psychiatry,* Vol 175, August: 141-146.

APQC (2002). "Retaining Valuable Knowledge: Proactive Strategies to Deal with a Shifting Workforce." A Consortium Learning Forum Best-Practice Report.

Argandoňa, A. (2011). "Beyond Contracts: Love in Firms" in *Journal of Business Ethics* 99 (1): 77-85.

Argyris, C. (1990). *Overcoming Organizational Defenses: Facilitating Organizational Learning*. Englewood Cliffs, NJ: Prentice Hall.

Argyris, C. and Schon, D. (1978). *Organizational Learning: A Theory of Action Perspective*. Reading, MA: Addison-Wesley.

Baddeley,A.D. (1997). *Human Memory: Theory and Practice* (Rev Ed). Hove: Psychology Press.

Baginski, B. and Sharamon, S. (1985). *Reiki: Universal Life Energy*. Mendocino, CA: Life Rhythm Publication.

Baird, J.D. and Nadel, L. (2010). *Happiness Genes: Unlock the Potential Hidden in Your DNA*. Franklin Lakes, NJ: New Page Books.

Barquin, R. C., Bennet, A., and Remez, S.G. (2001). *Knowledge Management : The Catalyst for Electronic Government*. Vienna, VA: Management Concepts.

Barnhart, R. K. and Steinmetz, S. (1988). *Chambers Dictionary of Etymology*. New York: Chambers.

Barsade, S. and Gibson, D. (2007). "Why Does Affect Matter in Organizations?" in *Academy of Management Perspectives* 21 (1), 36-59.

Barsade, S. and O'Neill, O.A. (2014). "What's Love Got to Do with It? A Longitudinal Study of the Culture of Companionate Love and Employee and Client Outcomes in a Long-term Care Setting" in *Administrative Science Quarterly* 59(4) (November), 551-598.

Bateson, G. (1979). *Mind and Nature: A Necessary Unity*. New York: Dutton.

Bateson, G. (1972). *Steps to an Ecology of the Mind*. New York: Ballantine.

Battram, A. (1996). *Navigating Complexity: The Essential Guide to Complexity Theory in Business and Management*. Sterling, VA: The Industrial Society.

Baxter, A.J., Scott, K.M., Vos, T. and Whiteford, H.A. (2013). "Global Prevalence of Anxiety Disorders: A Systematic Review and Meta-Regression" in *Psychological Medicine* Vol. 43, Issue 5 (May), 897-91

Begley, S., (2007). *Train Your Mind Change Your Brain: How a New Science Reveals Our Extraordinary Potential to Transform Ourselves*. New York: Ballantine Books.

Belitz, C. and Lundstrom, M. (1997). *The Power of Flow*. New York: Harmony Books.

Bennet, A. (2005). *Exploring Aspects of Knowledge Management that Contribute to the Passion Expressed by Its Thought Leaders*. Frost, WV: Self-published.

Bennet, A. and Bennet, D. (2013). *Decision-Making in The New Reality*. Frost, WV: MQIPress.

Bennet, A. and Bennet, D. (2008b). "The Decision-Making Process for Complex Situations in a Complex Environment" in Burstein, F. and Holsapple, C.W. (Eds.), *Handbook on Decision Support Systems 1*, 2-20. New York: Springer-Verlag.

Bennet, A. and Bennet, D. (2008c). "The Fallacy of Knowledge Reuse" in *Journal of Knowledge Management*, 12(5), 21-33.

Bennet, A. and Bennet, D. (2008d). "Moving from Knowledge to Wisdom, from Ordinary Consciousness to Extraordinary Consciousness" in *VINE: Journal of Information and Knowledge Systems*, Vol. 38, No. 1, 7-15.

Bennet, A. and Bennet, D. (2007b). *Knowledge Mobilization in the Social Sciences and Humanities: Moving from Research to Action*. MQIPress, Frost, WV.

Bennet, A. and Bennet, D. (2007c). "The Knowledge and Knowing of Spiritual Learning" in *VINE: The Journal of Information and Knowledge Management Systems*, 37 (2), 150-168.

Bennet, A. & Bennet, D. (2004). *Organizational Survival in the New World: The Intelligent Complex Adaptive System*. Boston, MA: Elsevier

Bennet, A., Bennet, D. and Avedisian, J. (2015a). *The Course of Knowledge: A 21st Century Theory*. Frost, WV: MQIPress.

Bennet, A., Bennet, D. and Lewis, J. (2015c). *Leading with the Future in Mind: Knowledge and Emergent Leadership*. Frost, WV: MQIPress.

Bennet, A., Bennet, D. and Lee, Shiang Long (2009). "Exploring the Military Contribution to KBD through Leadership and Values" in *Journal of Knowledge Management* , Vol. 14 No. 2, 314-330.

Bennet, D. (1997). *IPT Learning Campus: Gaining Acquisition Results through IPTs*. Alexandria: Bellwether Learning Center.

Bennet, D., Bennet, A. and Turner, R. (2015b). *Expanding the Self: The Intelligent Complex Adaptive Learning System*. Frost, WV: MQI Press.

Berman, Paul. 1981. *From compliance to learning: implementing legally-induced reform*. Stanford, CA: Institute for Research on Educational Finance and Governance, School of Education, Stanford University.

Bohlin, N. and Brenner, P. (1996). "The Learning Organization Journey: Assessing and Valuing Progress" in *The Systems Thinker*, Vol. 7, No. 5, 1-5.

Bownds, M. D. (1999). *The Biology of Mind: Origins and Structures of Mind, Brain, and Consciousness*. Bethesda, MD: Fitzgerald Science Press.

Braden, G. (2015). *Resilience from the Heart: The Power to thrive in Life's Extremes*. New York: Hay House, Inc.

Braden, G. (2014). *The Turning Point: Creating Resilience in a Time of Extremes*. New York: Hay House, Inc.

Brandenburger, A.M. and Nalebuff, B.J. (1997). *Co-opetition*. New York: Currency Doubleday.

Brown, John (1958). "Some Tests of the Decay Theory of Immediate Memory" in *Quarterly Journal of Experimental Psychology*, 10, 12-21.

Bullard, B. and Bennet, A. (2013). *REMEMBRANCE: Pathways to Expanded Learning with Music and Metamusic®*. Frost, WV: MQIPress.

Buonomano, D. V. and Merzenich, M. M. (1998). "Cortical Plasticity: From Synapses to Maps" in *Annual Review of Neuroscience, 21*, 149-186.

Burrell, G. and Morgan, G. (1979). *Sociological Paradigms and Organisational Analysis*. London: Heinemann.

Byrnes, J. P. (2001). *Minds, Brains, and Learning: Understanding the Psychological and Educational Relevance of Neuroscientific Research*. New York: The Guilford Press.

Campbell, D. (2014). *Music: Physician for Times to Come*. Wheaton, Ill: Quest Books.

Carey, K. (1996). *The Third Millennium: Living in the Posthistoric World*. New York: HarperCollins Publishers.

Carpenter, H. (2009). "Designing for innovation through competitive collaboration". Downloaded on 11/02/14 from http://www.cloudave.com/1036/designing-for-innovation-through-competitive-collaboration/

Carroll, S. (2016). *The Big Picture: On the Origins of Life, Meaning, and the Universe Itself*. New York: Dutton.

Ceci, S. J. (1995). "False Beliefs: Some Developmental and Clinical Considerations" in Schacter, D. L. (Ed.), *Memory Distortion: How Minds, Brains, and Societies Reconstruct the Past*. Cambridge, MA: Harvard University Press, 91-128.

Cederström, C. and Grassman, R. (2008). "The Masochistic Reflexive Turn" in *Ephemera* 8 (1): 41-57.

Chartrand, T.L. and Lakin, J.L. (2013). "The Antecedents and Consequences of Human Behavioral Mimicry" in *Annual Review of Psychology* 64, 285-308.

Christos, G. (2003). *Memory and Dreams: The Creative Human Mind*. New Brunswick, NJ: Rutgers University Press.

Church, D. (2006). *The Genie in Your Genes: Epigenetic Medicine and the New Biology of Intention*. Santa Rosa, CA: Elite Books.

Churchman, C.W. (1977). "A Philosophy for Complexity" in Linstone, H. A. and Simmonds, W.H.C., *Futures Research: New Directions*. Reading, MA: Addison-Wesley Publishing Company, Inc.

Clark, A. (1998). *Being There: Putting Brain, Body, and World Together Again*. Boston: MIT Press.

Coddington, M. (1978). *In Search of the Healing Energy*. New York, NY: Destiny Books.

Cohn, K.H. (2008). "Collaborative co-mentoring" downloaded on 03/15/08 from http://www.biomedsearch.com/article/lifelong-iterative-process-physician-retention/204857941.html

Coleman, D. (1997). *Groupware: Collaborative Strategies for Corporate LANs and Intranets*. New Jersey: Prentice Hall.

Coleman, J. (1973). *The Mathematics of Collective Action*. New York: Aldine.

Collinge, W. (1998). *Where Ancient Wisdom and Modern Science Meet ... Subtle Energy: Awakening to the Unseen forces in Our Lives*. New York: Warner Books.

Connerton, P. (2008). "Seven types of forgetting", 59-71. Retrieved 02/06/16 from http://mss.sagepub.com/content/1/1/59.short?rss=1&ssource=mfr

Cooper, L.R. (2005). *The Grand Vision: The Design and purpose of a Human Being*. Ft. Collins, CO: Planetary Heart.

Cooper, R. (2005). "Austinian Truth, Attitudes and Type Theory" in *Research on Language and Computation* 5: 333-362.

Cornell, A.W. (1990). *The Power of Focusing: A Practical Guide to Emotional Self-Healing.* New York: MJF Books.

Courteney, H. (2010). *Countdown to Coherence: A Spiritual Journey Toward a Scientific Theory of Everything.* London: Watkins Publishing.

Cowan, W. M. and Kandel, E. R. (2001). "A Brief History of Synapses and Synaptic Transmission" in Cowan, W. C., Sudhof, T. C. and Stevens, C. F. (Eds.), *Synapses.* Baltimore: Johns Hopkins Press.

Cozolino, L. J. (2006). *The Neuroscience of Human Relationships: Attachment and the Developing Social Brain.* New York: W.W. Norton.

Cozolino, L., and Sprokay, S. (2006). "Neuroscience and Adult Learning" in Johnson, S. and Taylor, T. (Eds.), *The Neuroscience of Adult Learning.* San Francisco: Jossey-Bass, 11-19.

Csikszentmihalyi, M. (2003). *Good Business: Leadership, Flow and the Making of Meaning.* New York: Viking.

Csikszentmihalyi, M. (1997). Finding *Flow: The Psychology of Engagement with Everyday Life.* The Mastermind Series. New York: Basic Books.

Csikszentmihalyi, M. (1990). *Flow: The Psychology of Optimal Experience.* New York: Harper Perennial.

Csikszentmihalyi, M. (1975). *Beyond Boredom and Anxiety: Experiencing Flow in Work and Play.* San Francisco: Jossey-Bass Publishing.

Cummings, R. (1922). *The Girl in the Golden Atom.* Nebraska: University of Nebraska Press.

Damasio, A. R. (1999). *The Feeling of What Happens: Body and Emotion in the Making of Consciousness.* New York: Harcourt Brace & Company.

Darwin, C. (1998). *The Descent of Man.* Amherst, NY: Prometheus Books.

Davidson, C. and Goldberg, D. (2009). *The Future of Learning Institutions in a Digital Age.* Boston: Massachusetts Institute of Technology.

de Chardin, P. Teilhard (1959). *The Phenomenon of Man.* St James Palace, London: Collins.

de Geus, A. (1997). *The Living Company.* Boston: Harvard Business School Press.

Denning, S. (2001). *The Springboard: How Storytelling Ignites Action in Knowledge-Era Organizations.* Boston: Butterworth Heinemann.

Devlin, K.J. and Lorden, G. (2007). *The Numbers Behind Numb3rs: Solving Crime with Mathematics.* New York: Penguin Group.

Dilts, R. (2003). *From Coach to Awakener.* Capitola, CA: Meta Publications.

Dunning, J. (2014). Discussion of consciousness via the Internet on December 13.

Ebbinghaus, H, (1885). "Memory: A Contribution to Experimental Psychology." Retrieved 07-15-2016 from http://nwkpsych.rutgers.edu/~jose/courses/578_mem_learn/2012/readings/Ebbinghaus_1885.pdf

e Cunha, M.P., Clegg, S.R., Costa, C., Leite, A.P., Rego, A., Simpson, A.V., de Sousa, M.O. and Sousa, M. (2016). "Gemeinschaft in the Midst of

Gesellschaft? Love as an Organizational Value" in *Journal of Management, Spirituality & Religion* (July), 1-19.

Edelman, G., and Tononi, G. (2000). *A Universe of Consciousness: How Matter Becomes Imagination*. New York: Basic Books.

Edelson, D.C., Gordin, D.N. and Pea, R.D. (1999). "Addressing the Challenges of Inquiry Based Learning Through Technology and Curriculum Design" in *The Journal of the Learning Sciences*, 8(3-4), 391-450.

Eden, D. (2008). *Energy Medicine: Balancing Your Body's Energies for Optimal Health, Joy, and Vitality*. New York: Penguin Group.

Ehrlich, P.R. and Raven, P.H. (1964). "Butterflies and Plants: A Study in Coevolution" in *Evolution* 18, 586-608.

Eigen, M. (1993). "Breathing and Identity" in Adam Phillips (Ed.), *The Electrified Tightrope*. Northvale, NJ: Jason Aronson.

Elmore, T. (2010). *More Predictions for Generation Y in the Workplace*. Retrieved 09/13 from: www.savetheirfuturenow.com/predictions

Encarta World English Dictionary (1999). New York: St Martin's Press.

Encyclopaedia Britannica (2016). Retrieved 06/29/16 from https://www.britannica.com/art/rhythm-music

Engle, R. W., Cantor, J. and Carullo, J. J. (1993). "Individual Differences in Working Memory and Comprehension: A test of Four Hypotheses" in *Journal of Experimental Psychology: Learning, Memory, and Cognition*, 19, 972-992.

Fabrega, M. (2016). "10 Ways to tame Your Monkey Mind and Stop Mental Chatter." Retrieved 02/23/16 from www.daringtolivefully.com/tame-your-monkey-mind

Fleming, P. (2009). *Authenticity and the Cultural Politics of Work: New Forms of Informal Control*. New York: Oxford University Press.

Forrester, J.W. (1971). "Counterintuitive Nature of Social Systems" in *Technology Review*. Cambridge, MA: MIT Press.

Forsythe, C. (2003). "Human-Machine Interface Possibilities: What if the Machine is a Human-Like Cognitive Entity?" Retrieved 02/08 from www.sandia.gov/cog.systems/Index.html

Frankl, V.E. (1939/1963). *Man's Search for Meaning: An Introduction of Logotherapy*. New York: Pocket Books.

Friedman, T. L. (2005). *The World is Flat: A Brief History of the Twenty-First Century*. New York: Farrar, Straus & Giroux.

Friedman, M. (1989). "Philosophical Anthropology, the Image of the Human, and Dialogue as Keys to the Integration of the Human Sciences" in *Humanistic Psychologist, 14*(1), 4-21.

Frijda, N. H. (2000). "The Psychologists' Point of View" in Lewis, M. and Haviland-Jones, J.M., *Handbook of Emotions* (2nd ed). New York: The Guilford Press, 59-74.

Fuellmann, M. (2016). "Micro-Learning and Emotional Engagement." Personal email from Maik Fuellmann (October 26).

Gebser, Jean (1985). *The Ever-Present Origin* (Noel Barstad with Algis Mickunas, Trans). Athens: Ohio University Press. (Original work published in German in 1949 and 1953).

Gee, J.P. (2003). "What Video Games Have to Teach Us About Learning and Literacy" in *ACM Computers in Entertainment*, 1, 1-4.

Gell-Mann, M. (1994). *The Quark and the Jaguar: Adventures in the Simple and the Complex*. NY: W.H.Freeman and Company.

Gendlin, E. (1981). *Focusing*. New York: Bantam.

Gerber, R., M.D. (2000). *Vibrational Medicine for the 21st Century. The Complete Guide to Energy Healing and Spiritual Transformation*. New York: Eagle Brook.

Gerth, H. & Mills, C. (Ed. and Trans.) (1946). From Max Weber: *Essays in Sociology*. New York: Oxford University Press.

Gerow, J. (1992). *Journal of Psychology: An Introduction*. New York: Harper Collins.

Gill, B. (1984). "The Manipulation of Time" in *The Phenomenon of CHANGE*. New York: Rizzoli for Cooper-Hewitt Museum, The Smithsonian institution's National Museum of Design.

Global Mammal Assessment Team (2008). "Homo Sapiens" on IUCN Red List of Threatened Species (Version 2013.2). International Union for Conservation of Nature. Retrieved 07/15/16 from http://www.iucnredlist.org/details/136584/0Chapter 19

Goldberg, E. (2005). *The Wisdom Paradox: How Your Mind Can Grow Stronger as Your Brain Grows Older*. New York: Gotham Books.

Goldringer, S. D. (1996). "Words and Voices: Episodic Traces in Spoken Word Identification and Recognition Memory" in *Journal of Experimental Psychology: Learning, Memory, and Cognition*, 22, 1166-1183.

Goleman, D. (2015). *A Force for Good: The Dalai Lama's Vision for Our World*. New York: Bantam Books.

Goleman, D. (1995). *Emotional Intelligence*. New York: Bantam Books.

Green, E., and Green, A. (1989). *Beyond Biofeedback*. New York: Knoll Publishing Co.

Greenfield, S. (2000). *The Private Life of the Brain: Emotions, Consciousness, and the Secret of the Self*. New York: John Wiley & Sons.

Groves, C.P. (2005). Wilson, D.E. and Reeder, D.M. (Eds.), *Mammal Species of the World: A Taxonomic and Geographic Reference* (3rd Ed.). Baltimore: Johns Hopkins University.

Gyatso, T. (The Fourteenth Dalai Lama) (1992). *The Meaning of Life: Buddhist Perspectives on Cause and Effect*. Boston: Wisdom Publications.

Hadar, G. (2009). "Reaching across Generational Lines" in *ei: Managing the Enterprise Information Network*.

Hawkins, J., with Blakeslee, S. (2004). *On Intelligence: How a New Understanding of the Brain Will Lead to the Creation of Truly Intelligent Machines*. New York: Times Books.

HeartMath (2016). "The Quick Coherence® Technique". Retrieved 12/05/16 from https://www.heartmath.org/resources/heartmath-tools/quick-coherence-technique-for-adults/

Heffner, C. L. (2014). "Chapter 6: Section 2: Memory and Forgetting." Retrieved 08/21/14 from http://allpsych.com/psychology101/memory/

Hicks, E. and Hicks, J. (2006). *The Law of Attraction: The Basics of the Teachings of Abraham*. Carlsbad, CA: Hay House, Inc.

Hillis, W.D. (1987), *The Connection Machine*, MIT Press, Cambridge, MA.

Hodgkin, R. (1991). "Michael Polanyi—Profit of Life, the Universe, and Everything" in *Times Higher Educational Supplement*, September 27, 15.

Hogarth, R. (1987). *Judgment and Choice*. New York: Wiley.

Honderich, T. (1999). *The Philosophers: Introducing Great Western Thinkers*. Oxford:
Oxford University Press.

Houston, J. (2000). *Jump Time: Shaping Your Future in a World of Radical Change*. New York: Penguin Putnam Inc.

Hutchins, R. M. (Ed.) (1952). *Great Books of the Western World*, Vol. 7—"The Dialogues of Plato" in *Encyclopaedia Britannica*, Chicago.

Impey, C. (Ed.) (2010). *Talking about Life: Conversations on Astrobiology*. New York: Cambridge University Press.

Inner World, Outer World (2012). Documentary by Daniel Schmidt. Creative Direction by Barbara Dimetto. REM Publishing Ltd. (Responsible Earth Media).

Ionesco, E. (1971). *Present Past, Past Present: A Personal Memoir*. New York: Grove Press.

Jacoby, L. L., Debner, J.A. and Hay, J. F. (2001). "Proactive Interference, Accessibility Bias, and Process Dissociations: Valid Subjective Reports of Memory" in *Journal of Experimental Psychology: Learning, Memory, and Cognition*, *27*, 686-700.

James, J. (1996). *Thinking in the Future Tense: A Workout for the Mind*. New York: Touchstone.

Jensen, E. (2006). *Enriching the Brain: How to Maximize Every Learners Potential*. San Francisco, CA: Jossey-Bass.

Jensen, E. (1998). *Teaching with the Brain in Mind*. Alexandria, VA: Association for Supervision and Curriculum Development.

The Jensen Group (1997). *Changing How We Work: The Search for a Simpler Way*. Northern Illinois University College of Business.

Johns, K. (2003). *Managing Generational Diversity in the Workforce*. Trends and Tidbits. Retrieved September 2013 from www.workindex.com

Johnson, R., Homik, S. and Salas, E. (2008). "An Empirical Examination of Factors Contributing to the Creation of Successful eLearning Environments" in *International Journal of Human-Computer Studies*, 66(5), 356-369.

Johnson, S. (2006). "The Neuroscience of the Mentor-Learner Relationship" in S. Johnson and Taylor, K. (Eds.), *The Neuroscience of Adult Learning: New Directions for Adult and Continuing Education*. San Francisco: Jossey-Bass, 63-70

Kahneman, D., P. Slovic and Tversky, A. (1982). *Judgment Under Uncertainty: Heuristics and Biases*. New York: Cambridge University Press.

Kandel, E. R. (2006). *In Search of Memory: The Emergence of a New Science of Mind*. New York: W.W. Norton & Company.

Kapeleris,J. (2012). "Collaboration: A Driver of Innovation". Retrieved 12/10/16 from http://johnkapeleris.com/blog/?s=Innovation+is+a+highly+interactive&op.x=28&op.y=13

Kluwe, R. H., Luer, G., and Rosler, F. (Eds.) (2003). *Principles of Learning and Memory*. Basel, Switzerland: Birkhauser Verlag.

Kropotkin, P. (1902). *Mutual Aid: A Factor of Evolution*. London: Heinemann. Retrieved on 01/26/15 from http://libcom.org/files/Peter%20Kropotkin-%20Mutual%20Aid;%20A%20Factor%20of%20Evolution.pdf

Kuhn, Thomas (1972). *The Structure of Scientific Revolution* (2nd ed.). Chicago: University of Chicago Press.

Kuntz, P G. (1968). *The Concept of Order*. Seattle, WA: University of Washington Press.

Kurzweil, R. (2005). *The Singularity is Near: When Humans Transcend Biology*. New York: Viking.

The Kybalion (1940/1912). *The Kybalion: A Study of Hermetic Philosophy of ancient Egypt and Greece.* Yogi Pub. Society.

Lambrou, P. and Pratt, G. (2000). *Acupressure for the Emotions: Instant Emotional Healing.* New York: Broadway Books.

Laming, D. (1992). "Analysis of Short-Term Retention: Models for Brown-Peterson Experiments" in *Journal of Experimental Psychology: Learning, Memory, and Cognition*, 18, 1342-1365.

Laszlo, E. (2009). *WorldShift 2012: Making Green Business, New Politics & Higher Consciousness Work Together*. Rochester, VT: Inner Traditions.

Lazarus, R. (Aug 1991). "Progress on a Cognitive-Motivational-Relational Theory of Emotion" in *American Psychologist*, Vol. 46, No. 8, 819-834.

Leadbeater, C.W. (8th printing) (1997). *The Chakras*. Wheaton, Ill: The Theosophical Publishing House.

LeDoux, J. (1996). *The Emotional Brain: The Mysterious Underpinnings of Emotional Life*. New York: Touchstone.

Lesch, M.F. and Pollatsek, A (1993). "Automatic Access of Semantic Information by Phonological Codes to Visual Word Recognition" in *Journal of Experimental Psychology: Learning, Memory and Cognition* 19, 285-294.

LeShan, Lawrence (1976). *Alternative Realities*. New York: Ballantine.

Lewicki, R.J., McAllister, D.J. and Bies, R.J. (1998). "Trust and Distruct: New Relationships and Realities" in *Academy of Management Review* 23(3), 438-459.

Lewin, K. (1946). "Force Field Analysis" in *The 1973 Annual Handbook for Group Facilitators*, 111-13.

Lewis, J. (2013). *The Explanation Age (3rd Edition)*. Charleston: Amazon Create Space.

Lewis, J. (2014). "ADIIEA: An Organizational Learning Model for Business Management and Innovation" in *The Electronic Journal of Knowledge Management*, v12-2, 98-107.

Lief, H. and Fetkewicz, J. (1995). "Retractors of False Memories: The Evolution of Pseudomemories" in *Journal of Psychiatry Law* 23,411–35.

Lipton, B. (2005). *The Biology of Belief: Unleashing the Power of Consciousness*. Carlsbad, CA: Hay House.

Lipton, B. and Bhaerman, S. (2009). *Spontaneous Evolution: Out Positive Future (And a Way to Get There from Here)*. Carlsbad, CA: Hay House.

Long, T.A. (1986). "Narrative Unity and Clinical Judgment" in *Theoretical Medicine* 7, 75-92.

Loveridge, D.J. (1977). "Shifting Foundations: Values and Futures" in Linstone, H.A. and Simmonds, W.H.C., *Futures Research: New Directions*. Reading, MA: Addison-Wesley Publishing Company, Inc.

MacFlouer, Niles (2004-16). *Why Life Is...* Weekly radio shows: BBSRadio.com (#1-#480) and KXAM (#1-#143). Retrieved from http://www.agelesswisdom.com/archives_of_radio_shows.htm

MacFlouer, N. (1999). *Life's Hidden Meaning*. Tempe, AZ: Ageless Wisdom Publishers.

Mandelbrot, B. (1983). *The Fractal Geometry of Nature*. New York: W.H. Freeman.

Manns, J.R., Hopkins, R.O., Reed, J.M., Kitchener, E.G., and Squire, L.R. (2003). "Recognition Memory and the Human Hippocampus" in *Neuron* 37, 171–180.

Marinoff, L. (2003). *The Big Questions: How Philosophy Can Change Your Life*. New York: Bloomsbury.

Martin, J. (2006). *The Meaning of the 21st Century: A Vital Blueprint for Ensuring Our Future*. New York, NY: Riverhead Books.

Mayer, R.E. (2009). *Multi-Media Learning* (2nd Ed.). New York: Cambridge University Press.

McMoneagle, J. (2017). email in AGC Open House Discussion Forum, January 15.

McMoneagle, J. (2000). *Remote Viewing Secrets: A Handbook*. Charlottesville, VA: Hampton Roads Publishing Company, Inc.

McHale, J. (1977). "Futures Problems or Problems in Futures Studies" in Linstone, H.A. and Simmonds, W.H.C. (Eds.), *Futures Research: New Directions*. Reading, MA: Addison-Wesley Publishing Company, Inc.

McWhinney, W. (1997). *Paths of Change: Strategic Choices for Organizations and Society*. Thousand Oaks, CA: SAGE Publications, Inc.

Menges, J.I. and Kilduff, M. (2015). "Group Emotions: Cutting the Gordian Knots Concerning terms, Levels of Analysis, ad Processes" in *Academy of Management Annals* 9 (1), 849-932.

"Mental Illness in America: More than a Quarter of Adults are Afflicted." (2008). *Scientific American Mind* (February/March 15).

Merriam, S. B., Caffarella, A. S. and Baumgartner, L. M. (2007). *Learning in Adulthood: A Comprehensive Guide*. San Francisco, CA: Jossey-Bass and Sons, Inc.

Quizzbizz (2016). "Findings and Surveys from Micro-Mobile Learning in South-East Asia". (Unpublished). For further information: www.quizzbizz.com or email maik.fuellmann@quizzbizz.com

Merry, U. (1995). *Coping with Uncertainty: Insights from the New Sciences of Chaos, Self-Organization and Complexity*. London: Praeger.

Meyer, C. and Davis, S. (2003). *It's Alive: The Coming Convergence of Information, Biology, and Business*. New York: Crown Business.

Michael, D. N. (1977). "Planning's Challenge to the Systems Approach" in Linstone, H.A. and Simmonds, W.H.C., *Futures Research: New Directions*. Reading, MA: Addison-Wesley Publishing Company, Inc.

Miller, G. A. (1956). "The Magical Number Seven, Plus or Minus Two: Some Limits on Our Capacity for Processing Information" in *Psychological Review, 63*, 81-96.

Minsky, M. (2006). *The Emotion Machine: Commonsense Thinking, Artificial Intelligence, and the Future of the Human Mind*. New York: Simon and Schuser.

Mitroff, I. I. (1977). "Shifting Foundations: On the Error of the Third Kind" in Linstone, H.A. and Simmonds, W.H.C., *Futures Research: New Directions*. Reading, MA: Addison-Wesley Publishing Company, Inc.

Morecroft, J. and Sterman, J. (eds.) (1994). *Modeling for Learning Organizations*. Portland: Productivity Press.

Mulcahy, K. (2012). "10 Human Attributes Found in Animals". Listverse (February 24). Downloaded 06/24/16 from http://listverse.com/2012/02/24/10-human-attributes-found-in-animals/

Mulford, P. (2007). *Thoughts Are Things*. New York: Barnes & Noble.

Naisbitt, J. (2006). *Mind set! Reset Your Thinking and See the Future*. New York: Collins.

Neji, M. and Ben Ammar, M. (2007). "Emotional eLearning System", presentation to the Fourth International Conference on eLearning for Knowledge-Based Society (November 18-19), Bangkok, Thailand.

Nonaka, I. and Takeuchi, H. (1995). *The Knowledge-Creating Company: How Japanese Companies Create the Dynamics of Innovation*. New York: Oxford University Press.

Northwrite 2013 (Competition website), downloaded on 01/26/15 from http://northwrite.co.nz/northwrite2013-collaborative-competition/

Oakeshott, M. (1933). *Experience and Its Modes*. Cambridge, UK: Cambridge University Press.

Panetta, L. (2013). *Worthy Fights: Memoir of Leadership in War & Peace*. New York: Penguin.

Pepper, Stephen C. (1942). *World Hypothesis: A Study of Evidence*. Berkeley: University of California Press.

Pert, C. B. (1997). *Molecules of Emotion: A Science Behind Mind-Body Medicine*. New York: Touchstone.

Peters, T. (1992). *Liberation Management*. New York: Alfred A. Knopf.

Peterson, L.R. and Peterson, M.J. (1959). "Short-term Retention of Individual Verbal Items" in *Journal of Experimental Psychology*, 58, 193-198.

Picard, R. W. (1997). *Affective Computing*. Cambridge, MA: MIT Press.

Plotkin, H. (1994). *Darwin Machines and the Nature of Knowledge*. Cambridge, MA: Harvard University Press.

Porter, D., Bennet, A., Turner, R., Wennergren, D. (2002). *The Power of Team: The Making of a CIO*. U.S. Department of the Navy, Washington, D.C.

Quizzbizz (2016). "Findings and Surveys from Micro-Mobile Learning in South-East Asia". (Unpublished). For further information: www.quizzbizz.com or email maik.fuellmann@quizzbizz.com

Ralston, F. (1995). *Hidden Dynamics: How Emotions Affect Business Performance & How You Can Harness Their Power for Positive Results*. New York: American Management Association.

Rand, W. L. (1991). *Reiki: The Healing Touch*. Southfield, MI: Vision Publications.

Ray-Band (2016). "#It Takes Courage". Retrieved 10/28/2016 from http://www.ray-ban.com/usa/courage

Reik, W., and Walter, J. (2001). "Genomic Imprinting: Parental Influence on the Genome" in *Nature Reviews Genetics, 2*, 21+.

Rockwell, I. (2002). *The Five Wisdom Energies: A Buddhist Way of Understanding Personalities, Emotions, and Relationships*. Boston: Shambhala.

Rooke, D. and Torbert, W. (1999). "The CEO's Role in Organizational Transformation." in *The Systems Thinker*, Vol. 10, No. 7, 1-5.

Rosenfield, I. (1988). *The Invention of Memory*. New York: Basic Books.

Ross, C.A. (2006). "Brain Self-Repair in Psychotherapy: Implications for Education" in Johnson, S. and Taylor, K., *The Neuroscience of Adult Learning: New Directions for Adult and Continuing Education*. San Francisco, CA: Jossey-Bass.

Ross, P. E. (2006b). "The Expert Mind" in *Scientific American*, (August), 64-71.

Sandia National Laboratories (2007). "Cognitive Science and Technology Program Becomes Sandia Initiative", news release (August 8).

Salen, K. (2008). *The Ecology of Games: Connecting Youth, Games, and Learning*. Boston: MIT Press.

Salk, J. (1973). *The Survival of the Wisest*. New York: Harper & Row.

Savery, J.R. (2015). "Overview of Problem-Based Learning: Definitions and Distinctions" in *Essential Readings in Problem-Based Learning: Exploring and Extending the Legacy of Howard S. Barrows*, 5-15.

Schacter, D. L. (1996). *Searching for Memory: The Brain, the Mind, and the Past*. New York: Basic Books.

Schank, R.E. (1990). *Tell Me a Story: Narrative and Intelligence*. Evanson, IL: Northwestern University Press.

Schrage, M. (1990). *Shared Minds: The New Technologies of Collaboration*. New York: Random House.

Schrödinger, E. (1983). *My View of the World*. Oxford, England: Ox Bow Publishers.

Schwartz, P. (2003). *Inevitable Surprises: Thinking Ahead in a Time of Turbulence*. New York: Penguin Group.

Scripps Research Institute (2012). "Scientists Identify Neurotransmitters that Lead to Forgetting" in *ScienceDaily* (May 9). Retrieved January 21, 2016, from www.sciencedaily.com/releases/2012/05/120509180113.htm

Seligman, M. E.P. (2011). *Flourish: A Visionary New Understanding of Happiness and Well-being*. New York: Free Press.

Senge, P. (2006). *The Fifth Discipline: The Art and Practice of the Learning Organization* (2nd ed.). New York: Doubleday Currency.

Senge, P.M. (2000). "The Puzzles and Paradoxes of How Living Companies Create Wealth: Why Single-Valued Objective Functions are not Quite Enough" in Beer, M and Nohria, N. (Eds.), *Breaking the Code of Change*. Boston: Harvard Business School Press, 59-81.

Senge, Peter (1990). *The Fifth Discipline*. New York: Doubleday.

Sheldrake, R. (1989). *The Presence of the Past: Morphic Resonance and the Habits of Nature*. New York: Vintage Books.

Shelley, A. (2016). *KNOWledge SUCCESSion: Sustain Performance and Capability Growth Through Strategic Knowledge Projects*.

Shelley, A. (2007). *Organizational Zoo: A Survival Guide to Work Place Behavior*. Fairfield, CT: Aslan Publishing.

Simmonds (1977). in Linstone, H.A. and Simmonds, W.H.C., *Futures Research: New Directions*. Reading, MA: Addison-Wesley Publishing Company, Inc.

Simon, H. (1982). *Models of Bounded Rationality*. Cambridge, MA: MIT Press.

Simon, H. (1979). "Rational Decision Making in Business Organizations" in *American Economic Review* 69: 493-513.

Simon, H. A. (1969). *The Science of the Artificial*. Cambridge, MA: The MIT Press.

Skyrme, D. (1999). *Knowledge Networking: Creating the Collaborative Enterprise*. Oxford: Butterworth Heinemann.

Smith, B. (2013). Personal conversation with Dr. Boyd Smith, Principal Faculty, School of Management, City University of Seattle. Also, founder of www.Everyoneslifestory.com

Smith, M.K. (2003). "Michael Polanyi and Tacit Knowledge" in *The Encyclopedia of Informal Education*, 2, www.infed.org/thinkers/Polanyi.htm

Sousa, D.A. (2006). *How the Brain Learns*. Thousand Oaks, CA: Corwin Press.

Squire, L.R. and Kandel, E.R. (1999). *Memory: From Mind to Molecules*. Scientific American Library. New York: W.H. Freeman & Co.

Stacey, R. (1996). *Complexity and Creativity in Organizations*. San Francisco: Berrett-Koehler Publishers.

Stein, D. (1995). *Essential Reiki: A Complete Guide to an Ancient Healing Art*. Freedom, CA: The Crossing Press, Inc.

Sterman, J.D. (1989). "Modeling Managerial Behavior: Misperceptions of feedback in a Dynamic Decision Making Experiment" in *Management Science* 35: 321-339.

Sternberg, R.J. (1986). "A Triangular Theory of Love" in *Psychological Review* 93 (2): 119-135

Stonier, T. (1997). *Information and Meaning: An Evolutionary Perspective*. London: Springer-Verlag.

Swomley, J. (2000). "Violence: Competition or Cooperation" in *Christian Ethics Today* 26, Vol. 6, No. 1.

Tapscott, D. (2009). *Grown up Digital*. McGraw Hill, New York.

Taylor, K. (2006). "Brain Function and Adult Learning: Implications for Practice" in Johnson, S. & Taylor, K. (Eds.), *The Neuroscience of Adult Learning: New Directions for Adult and Continuing Education*. San Francisco: Jossey-Bass, 71-86.

Teck, T.P. (SIA senior vice president for product services), retrieved on 01/26/15 from http://www.dnaindia.com/money/report-venture-with-tata-group-competitive-collaboration-sia-1994195

Thompson, R. F. (2000). *The Brain: A Neuroscience Primer*. New York: Worth.

Tiller, W. (2007). *Psychoenergetic Science: A Second Copernican-Scale Revolution*. DVD from www.illerfoundaion.com

Tsang, E. (2016). "Can Qi be Spiritual and Physical". Retrieved 10/07/16 from http://www.fengshuijinyan.com/E08_TCM_Articles/004%20Can%20Qi%20be%20spirit%20and%20physical-R.pdf

Tulving, E. (2005). "Episodic Memory and Autopoesis: Uniquely Human?" in Terrace, H.S. and Metcalfe, J. (Eds.), *The Missing Link in Cognition: Origins of Self-Reflective Consciousness*. Oxford: Oxford University Press.

Tulving, E. (2005). "Episodic Memory and Autopoesis: Uniquely Human?" in Terrace, H.S. and Metcalfe, J. (Eds.), *The Missing Link in Cognition: Origins of Self-Reflective Consciousness*. Oxford: Oxford University Press.

Underwood, B.J. and Postman, L. (1960). "Extraexperimental Sources of Inference in Forgetting" in *Psychol. Rev.* 67:73-95.

The Urantia Book (1955). Chicago: URANTIA Foundation.

Usatynski, T.J. (2008). *Instinctual Intelligence: The Primal Wisdom of the Nervous System and the Evolution of Human Nature*. Flying Cedar Press. Flyingcedar@msn.com

Vennix, J. (1996). *Group Model Building: Facilitating Team Learning Using System Dynamics*. New York: John Wiley & Sons.

Volk, T. (1995). *Metapatterns Across Space, Time, and Mind*. New York: Columbia University Press.

von Foerster, H. (1977). "Objects: tokens for (eigen-) behaviors" in Inheler, B., Gracia, R., and Voneche, J. (Eds.), *Hommage a Jean Piaget: Epistemologie Genetique et Eqilibration*. Delachaux et Niestel.

Wade, W. (2012). *Scenario Planning: A Field Guide to the Future*. Hoboken, NJ: John Wiley & Sons, Inc.

Wainwright, Stephen A. (1988). *Axis and Circumference: The Cylindrical Shape of Plants and Animals*. Cambridge: Harvard University Press.

Walker, A. (2011). "Creativity Loves Constraints: The Paradox of Google's Twenty Percent Time" in *Ephemera* 11, (4), 369-386.

Walsch, N.D. (2009). *When Everything Changes Change Everything: In a Time of Turmoil, a Pathway to Peace*. Ashland, OR: EmNin Books.

Walsh, R. and Shapiro, D. H. (1983). *Beyond Health and Normality: Explorations of Exceptional Psychological Well – Being*. New York: Van Nostrand Reinhold Company.

Watts, A. W. (2002). *ZEN: The Supreme Experience: The Newly Discovered Scripts*. London: Vega.

Watts, A. W. (1968). *The Wisdom of Insecurity*. New York: Vintage.

Webster's New World Dictionary of the American Language (1962). (College Edition).

Weeks, L. (20005). "The Story of You" in *The Washington Post*. Wednesday, April 26, C19.

Whitfield, P. and Ayensu, E.S. (1982). *Rhythms of Life*. London: Marshall

Wilber, K. (2000). *Integral Psychology: Consciousness, Spirit, Psychology, Therapy*. Boston: Shambhala Publications.

Wilber, K. (1993). *The Spectrum of Consciousness*. Wheaten, IL: Quest Books.

Wiig, K. (1993). *Knowledge Management Foundations—Thinking about Thinking—How People and Organizations Create, Represent, and Use Knowledge.* Arlington, TX: Schema Press.

Willis, A. (2012). *Achieving Balance.* Great Britain: Manicboy Publishing.

Wing, R.L. (Trans) (1986). *The Tao of Power: Lao Tzu's Classic Guide to Leadership, Influence, and Excellence.* New York: Doubleday.

Zull, J. E. (2002). *The Art of Changing the Brain: Enriching the Practice of Teaching by Exploring the Biology of Learning.* Sterling, VA: Stylus.

Index

About the Mountain Quest Institute

MQI is a research, retreat and learning center dedicated to helping individuals achieve personal and professional growth and organizations create and sustain high performance in a rapidly changing, uncertain, and increasingly complex world. Drs. David and Alex Bennet are co-founders of MQI. They may be contacted at alex@mountainquestinstitute.com

Current research is focused on Human and Organizational Systems, Change, Complexity, Sustainability, Knowledge, Learning, Consciousness, and the nexus of Science and Spirituality. MQI has three questions: The Quest for Knowledge, The Quest for Consciousness, and The Quest for Meaning. **MQI is scientific, humanistic and spiritual and finds no contradiction in this combination**. See www.mountainquestinstitute.com

MQI is the birthplace of Organizational Survival in the New World: The Intelligent Complex Adaptive System (Elsevier, 2004), a new theory of the firm that turns the living system metaphor into a reality for organizations. Based on research in complexity and neuroscience—and incorporating networking theory and knowledge management—this book is filled with new ideas married to practical advice, all embedded within a thorough description of the new organization in terms of structure, culture, strategy, leadership, knowledge workers and integrative competencies.

Mountain Quest Institute, situated four hours from Washington, D.C. in the Monongahela Forest of the Allegheny Mountains, is part of the Mountain Quest complex which includes a Retreat Center, Inn, and the old Farm House, Outbuildings and mountain trails and farmland. See www.mountainquestinn.com The Retreat Center is designed to provide full learning experiences, including hosting training, workshops, retreats and business meetings for professional and executive groups of 25 people or less. The Center includes a 26,000 volume research library, a conference room, community center, computer room, 12 themed bedrooms, a workout and hot tub area, and a four-story tower with a glass ceiling for enjoying the magnificent view of the valley during the day and the stars at night. Situated on a 430 acres farm, there is a labyrinth, creeks, four miles of mountain trails, and horses, Longhorn cattle, Llamas and a myriad of wild neighbors. Other neighbors include the Snowshoe Ski Resort, the National Radio Astronomy Observatory and the CASS Railroad.

About the Organizational Zoo Ambassadors Network

The Organizational Zoo Ambassadors Network (OZAN) is an international group of professionals interested in using The Organizational Zoo concepts as part of their capability development programs. Zoo Ambassadors have been trained in the application of OZAN Tools and approaches. They freely share their experiences through an international network which interacts primarily through a wiki supplemented by occasional face to face events and some on-line learning modules. See http://www.organizationalzoo.com/ambassadors/

About Quantra Leadership Academy

Quantra Leadership Academy (aka QLA Consulting) is a **transformational leadership and personal development training company run by** Dr. Theresa Bullard**. QLA is dedicated to helping individuals and organizations innovate their way of thinking to achieve breakthrough results.** There is one question that lies at the foundation of QLA: *What is your potential?* When you tap into your potential, greatness happens, you experience breakthroughs, "Ah-ha" moments occur, and you get into "The Zone" of peak performance. It is our passion to help you access your full potential, sustain what you achieve, and be able to refuel whenever you want. When you get to the point where you can do this on demand that is when you become a self-transforming agent of change. QLA shows you how to get there and gives you tools to accelerate your progress. By blending science, consciousness studies, and mental alchemy, or the art and science of transforming your mindset, we help you **reach your potential** and become more successful in essential areas of your work and life. *To help you* **access more of your potential,** *we offer a progression of transformative tools and trainings that integrate quantum principles, cutting-edge methods, and ancient wisdom for using your mind more creatively and effectively.* For more info: www.QLAconsulting.com

About the Authors

Dr. Alex Bennet, a Professor at the Bangkok University Institute for Knowledge and Innovation Management, is internationally recognized as an expert in knowledge management and an agent for organizational change. Prior to founding the Mountain Quest Institute, she served as the Chief Knowledge Officer and Deputy Chief Information Officer for Enterprise Integration for the U.S. Department of the Navy, and was co-chair of the Federal Knowledge Management Working Group. Dr. Bennet is the recipient of the Distinguished and Superior Public Service Awards from the U.S. government for her work in the Federal Sector. She is a Delta Epsilon Sigma and Golden Key National Honor Society graduate with a Ph.D. in Human and Organizational Systems; degrees in Management for Organizational Effectiveness, Human Development, English and Marketing; and certificates in Total Quality Management, System Dynamics and Defense Acquisition Management. Alex believes in the multidimensionality of humanity as we move out of infancy into full consciousness.

Dr. David Bennet's experience spans many years of service in the Military, Civil Service and Private Industry, including fundamental research in underwater acoustics and nuclear physics, frequent design and facilitation of organizational interventions, and serving as technical director of two major DoD Acquisition programs. Prior to founding the Mountain Quest Institute, Dr. Bennet was CEO, then Chairman of the Board and Chief Knowledge Officer of a professional services firm located in Alexandria, Virginia. He is a Phi Beta Kappa, Sigma Pi Sigma, and Suma Cum Laude graduate of the University of Texas, and holds degrees in Mathematics, Physics, Nuclear Physics, Liberal Arts, Human and Organizational Development, and a Ph.D. in Human Development focused on Neuroscience and adult learning. He is currently researching the nexus of Science, the Humanities and Spirituality.

Dr. Arthur Shelley is a capability development and knowledge strategy consultant with over 30 years professional experience. He has held a variety of professional roles including managing international projects in Australia, Europe, Asia and USA and has facilitated professional development program with organisations as diverse as NASA, Cirque du Soleil, World Bank, government agencies and corporates. He has facilitated courses in Masters programs on Executive Consulting, Leadership, Knowledge Management, Applied Research Practice and Entrepreneurship in face to face, blended and on-line modes. Arthur is the author of three books: *KNOWledge SUCCESSion (2017) Being a Successful Knowledge Leader (2009)*; *The Organizational Zoo, A Survival Guide to Workplace Behavior (2007)*. In 2014 he was awarded with an Australian Office of Learning and Teaching citation for "Outstanding contributions to student learning outcomes". Arthur is a regular invited speaker and workshop facilitator at international conferences to discuss his writing or to share experiences as the former Global Knowledge Director for Cadbury Schweppes. He is founder of The Organizational Zoo Ambassadors Network (a professional peer mentoring group), creator of the RMIT University MBA mentoring program and co-facilitator of the Melbourne KM Leadership Forum. Arthur has a PhD in Project Management, a Master of Science in Microbiology/Biochemistry, a Graduate Certificate in Tertiary Learning and Teaching and a Bachelor of Science. Arthur may be reached at arthur.shelley@rmit.edu.au

Dr. Theresa Bullard combines a Ph.D. in Physics with a life-long path of embracing the new paradigm of Science and Consciousness. Her passion and ability to bridge these worlds are her strengths and distinguish her as an exceptional teacher, speaker, leader and change-agent. Theresa is the founder of QLA Consulting Inc., President of the Board of Directors of Mysterium Center, an International Instructor with the Modern Mystery School, and co-founder of the Universal Kabbalah Network. She has over 15 years of experience in science research, international speaking, and transformational training. Author of *The Game Changers: Social Alchemists in the 21st Century*, along with several guided meditation albums and audio tools for accessing Quantum conscious states, her mission is to help individuals and organizations thrive in a changing world. Theresa may be contacted at Theresa@quantumleapalchemy.com

Dr. John Lewis is a speaker, business consultant, and part-time professor on the topics of organizational learning, thought leadership, and knowledge & innovation management. John is a proven leader with business results, and was acknowledged by Gartner with an industry "Best Practice" paper for an innovative knowledge management implementation. He is a co-founder at The CoHero Institute, creating collaborative leadership in learning organizations. John holds a Doctoral degree in Educational Psychology from the University of Southern California, with a dissertation focus on mental models and decision making, and is the author of *The Explanation Age*, which Kirkus Reviews described as "An iconoclast's blueprint for a new era of innovation." John may be contacted at John@ExplanationAge.com

Other Books by These Authors

Possibilities that are YOU! by Alex Bennet

This series of short books, which are published under *Conscious Look Books*, are conversational in nature, taking full advantage of your lived experience to share what can sometimes be difficult concepts to grab onto. But, **YOU ARE READY!** We live in a world that is tearing itself apart, where people are out of control, rebelling from years of real and perceived abuse and suppression of thought. Yet, this chaos offers us as a humanity the opportunity to make a giant leap forward. *By opening ourselves to ourselves, we are able to fully explore who we are and who we can become.* With that exploration comes a glimmer of hope as we begin to reclaim the power of each and every mind developed by the lived human experience!

These books share 22 large concepts from *The Profundity and Bifurcation of Change*. Each book includes seven ideas offered for the student of life experience to help you become the co-creator you are. Available in soft cover from Amazon.

Titles:

All Things in Balance
The Art of Thought Adjusting
Associative Patterning and Attracting
Beyond Action
The Bifurcation
Connections as Patterns
Conscious Compassion
The Creative Leap
The Emerging Self
The Emoting Guidance System
Engaging Forces
The ERC's of Intuition
Grounding
The Humanness of Humility
Intention and Attention
Knowing
Living Virtues for Today
ME as Co-Creator
Seeking Wisdom
Staying on the Path
Transcendent Beauty
Truth in Context

A 23rd little book titled **The Intelligent Social Change Journey** *provides the theoretical foundation for the* **Possibilities that are YOU! series.** Also available in soft cover from Amazon

Other Books by MQI Press (<ins>www.MQIPress.net</ins>)

MQIPress is a wholly-owned subsidiary of Mountain Quest Institute, LLC, located at 303 Mountain Quest Lane, Marlinton, West Virginia 24954, USA. (304) 799-7267

Other Bennet eBooks available from in PDF format from MQIPress (US 304-799-7267 or <ins>alex@mountainquestinstitute.com</ins>) and Kindle format from Amazon.

The Course of Knowledge: A 21st Century Theory
by Alex Bennet and David Bennet with Joyce Avedisian (2015)

Knowledge is at the core of what it is to be human, the substance which informs our thoughts and determines the course of our actions. Our growing focus on, and understanding of, knowledge and its consequent actions is changing our relationship with the world. Because **knowledge determines the quality of every single decision we make**, it is critical to learn about and understand what knowledge is. **From a 21st century viewpoint,** we explore a theory of knowledge that is both pragmatic and biological. Pragmatic in that it is based on taking effective action, and biological because it is created by humans via patterns of neuronal connections in the mind/brain.

In this book we explore *the course of knowledge*. Just as a winding stream in the bowls of the mountains curves and dips through ravines and high valleys, so, too, with knowledge. In a continuous journey towards intelligent activity, context-sensitive and situation-dependent knowledge, imperfect and incomplete, experientially engages a changing landscape in a continuous cycle of learning and expanding. *We are in a continuous cycle of knowledge creation such that every moment offers the opportunity for the emergence of new and exciting ideas, all waiting to be put in service to an interconnected world.* Learn more about this **exciting human capacity**! AVAILABLE FROM AMAZON in <ins>Kindle Format</ins>. AVAILABLE FROM <ins>MQIPress</ins> in PDF.

Expanding the Self: The Intelligent Complex Adaptive Learning System
by David Bennet, Alex Bennet and Robert Turner (2015)

We live in unprecedented times; indeed, turbulent times that can arguably be defined as ushering humanity into a new Golden Age, offering the opportunity to embrace new ways of learning and living in a globally and collaboratively entangled connectedness (Bennet & Bennet, 2007). In this shifting and dynamic environment, life demands accelerated cycles of learning experiences. Fortunately, we as a humanity have begun to look within ourselves to better understand the way our mind/brain operates, the amazing qualities of the body that power our thoughts and feelings, and the reciprocal loops as those thoughts and feelings change our physical structure. This emerging knowledge begs us to relook and rethink what we know about learning, providing a new starting point to expand toward the future.

This book is a treasure for those interested in how recent findings in neuroscience impact learning. The result of this work is an expanding experiential learning model called the Intelligent Complex Adaptive Learning System, adding the fifth mode of social engagement to Kolb's concrete experience, reflective observation, abstract conceptualization and active experimentation, with the five modes undergirded by the power of Self. A significant conclusion is that should they desire, adults have much more control over their learning than they may realize. AVAILABLE FROM AMAZON in <u>Kindle Format</u>. AVAILALBE FROM <u>MQIPress</u> in PDF.

Decision-Making in The New Reality: Complexity, Knowledge and Knowing
by Alex Bennet and David Bennet (2013)
We live in a world that offers many possible futures. The ever-expanding complexity of information and knowledge provide many choices for decision-makers, and we are all making decisions every single day! As the problems and messes of the world become more complex, our decision consequences are more and more difficult to anticipate, and our decision-making processes must change to keep up with this world complexification. This book takes a consilience approach to explore decision-making in The New Reality, fully engaging systems and complexity theory, knowledge research, and recent neuroscience findings. It also presents methodologies for decision-makers to tap into their unconscious, accessing tacit knowledge resources and increasingly relying on the sense of knowing that is available to each of us.

Almost every day new energies are erupting around the world: new thoughts, new feelings, new knowing, all contributing to new situations that require new decisions and actions from each and every one of us. Indeed, with the rise of the Net Generation and social media, a global consciousness may well be emerging. As individuals and organizations, we are realizing that there are larger resources available to us, and that, as complex adaptive systems linked to a flowing fount of knowing, we can bring these resources to bear to achieve our ever-expanding vision of the future. Are we up to the challenge? AVAILABLE FROM AMAZON in <u>Kindle Format</u>. AVAILABLE FROM <u>MQIPress</u> in PDF.

Leading with the Future in Mind: Knowledge and Emergent Leadership
by Alex Bennet and David Bennet with John Lewis (2015)
We exist in a new reality, a global world where the individuated power of the mind/brain offers possibilities beyond our imagination. It is within this framework that thought leading emerges, and when married to our collaborative nature, makes the impossible an everyday occurrence. *Leading with the Future in Mind*, building on profound insights unleashed by recent findings in neuroscience, provides a new view that converges leadership, knowledge and learning for individual and organizational advancement.

This book provides a research-based *tour de force* for the future of leadership. Moving from the leadership of the past, for the few at the top, using authority as the explanation, we now find leadership emerging from all levels of the organization, with knowledge as the explanation. The future will be owned by the organizations that can master the relationships between knowledge and leadership. Being familiar with the role of a knowledge worker is not the same as understanding the role of a knowledge leader. As the key ingredient, collaboration is much more than "getting along"; it embraces and engages. Wrapped in the mantle of collaboration and engaging our full resources—physical, mental, emotional and spiritual—we open the door to possibilities. We are dreaming the future together. AVAILABLE FROM AMAZON in <u>Kindle Format</u>. AVAILABLE FROM <u>MQIPress</u> in PDF.

Other books available from the authors and on Amazon..

The Game Changers: Social Alchemists in the 21ˢᵗ Century

by Theresa Bullard, Ph.D. (2013), available in hard and soft formats from Amazon.
Just about everywhere we look right now change is afoot. What is all this change about? Why now? And how do we best adapt? Many have called this time a "quickening", where the speed with which we must think, respond, and take action is accelerating. Systems are breaking down, people are rising up, and there is uncertainty of what tomorrow will bring. This book is dedicated to times such as these, times of great transformation. It can be seen as a companion guide on how to navigate the tumultuous tides of change. It aims to put such current events into a possible context within the evolutionary and alchemical process that humanity is going through. In it, author, physicist, and change-agent, Theresa Bullard, Ph.D., discusses emerging new paradigms, world events, future trends, and ancient wisdom that help reveal a bigger picture of what is happening. She offers insights and solutions to empower you, the reader, to become a more conscious participant in these exciting times of change. With this knowledge you will be more equipped to harness the *opportunities* that such times present you with.
AVAILABLE FROM AMAZON in Kindle Format ... Paperback

The Organizational Zoo: A Survival Guide to Work Place Behavior

by Arthur Shelley (2006), available in hard and soft formats from Amazon.
Organizational Zoo is a fresh approach to organizational culture development, a witty and thought-provoking book that makes ideal reading for students and management. When you think of your organization as containing ants, bees, chameleons, and other creatures on through the alphabet, your work world becomes more manageable. Discover the secret strengths and weaknesses of each distinct animal so that you can communicate more productively—or manipulate more cunningly. Your choice!
AVAILABLE FROM AMAZON in Paperback

The Explanation Age

by John Lewis (2013) (3rd Ed.), available in hard and soft formats from Amazon.
The technological quest of the last several decades has been to create the information age, with ubiquitous and immediate access to information. With this goal arguably accomplished, even from our mobile phones, this thought-provoking book describes the next quest and provides a blueprint for how to get there. When all organizational knowledge is framed as answers to our fundamental questions, we find ubiquitous and visual access to knowledge related to who, where, how, etc., yet the explanations are still buried within the prose. The question of "why" is arguably the most important question, yet it is currently the least supported. This is why business process methodologies feel like "box-checking" instead of "sense-making." This is why lessons learned are not actually learned. And this is why the consequential options and choices are captured better within a chess game than within the important decisions faced by organizations and society. With implications for business, education, policy making, and artificial intelligence, Dr. Lewis provides a visualization of explanations which promotes organizational sense-making and collaboration. AVAILABLE FROM AMAZON in Paperback

KNOWledge SUCCESSion: Sustained Capability Growth Through Strategic Projects

by Arthur Shelley (2016), available in hard and soft formats from Amazon.
KNOWledge SUCCESSion is intended for executives and developing professionals who face the challenges of delivering business benefits for today, whilst building the capabilities required for an increasingly changing future. The book is structured to build from foundational requirements towards connecting the highly interdependent aspects of success in an emerging complex world. A wide range of concepts are brought together in a logical framework to enable readers of different disciplines to understand how they either create barriers or can be harvested to generate synergistic opportunities. The framework builds a way to make sense of the connections and provides novel paths to take advantage of the potential synergies that arise through aligning the concepts into a portfolio of strategic projects. AVAILABLE FROM AMAZON. Kindle Format ... Paperback

Knowledge Mobilization in the Social Sciences and Humanities: Moving from Research to Action

by Alex Bennet and David Bennet (2007), available in hard and soft formats from Amazon.
This book takes the reader from the University lab to the playgrounds of communities. It shows how to integrate, move and use knowledge, an action journey within an identified action space that is called knowledge mobilization. Whether knowledge is mobilized through an individual, organization, community or nation, it becomes a powerful asset creating a synergy and focus that brings forth the best of action and values. Individuals and teams who can envision, feel, create and apply this power are the true leaders of tomorrow. When we can mobilize knowledge for the greater good humanity will have left the information age and entered the age of knowledge, ultimately leading to compassion and—hopefully—wisdom. AVAILABLE FROM AMAZON. Kindle Format ... Paperback
AVAILABLE FROM MQIPress in PDF and Softback.

Being a Successful Knowledge Leader: What Knowledge Practitioners Need to Know to Make a Difference.

by Arthur Shelley (2009). AVAILABLE FROM AMAZON. Paperback
Being a Successful Knowledge Leader explores the challenges of leading a program of knowledge-informed change initiatives to generate sustained performance improvement. The book explores how to embed knowledge flows into strategic development cycles to align organizational development with changing environmental conditions. The high rate of change interferes with the growth of organizational knowledge because what is relevant only generates a competitive advantage for a short time. Also, the people who possess this knowledge are more mobile than previously. Combined, these factors can have a detrimental impact on performance and need to be mitigated against to ensure capabilities are built rather than diluted overtime. The characteristics for success that a knowledge

leader needs to possess are explored from a unique perspective to stimulate creative thinking around how to develop and maintain these in emergent times.

Organizational Survival in the New World: The Intelligent Complex Adaptive System
   by Alex Bennet and David Bennet (Elsevier, 2004), available in hard and soft formats from Amazon.
In this book David and Alex Bennet propose a new model for organizations that enables them to react more quickly and fluidly to today's fast-changing, dynamic business environment: The Intelligent Complex Adaptive System (ICAS). ICAS is a new organic model of the firm based on recent research in complexity and neuroscience, and incorporating networking theory and knowledge management, and turns the living system metaphor into a reality for organizations. This book synthesizes new thinking about organizational structure from the fields listed above into ICAS, a new systems model for the successful organization of the future designed to help leaders and managers of knowledge organizations succeed in a non-linear, complex, fast-changing and turbulent environment. Technology enables connectivity, and the ICAS model takes advantage of that connectivity by fostering the development of dynamic, effective and trusting relationships in a new organizational structure. AVAILABLE FROM AMAZON in Kindle Format ... Hardback ... Paperback

Other MQIPress books available in PDF format at www.MQIPress.net (US 304-799-7267 or alex@mountainquestinstitute.com) and Kindle format from Amazon.

REMEMBRANCE: Pathways to Expanded Learning with Music and Metamusic®
   by Barbara Bullard and Alex Bennet (2013)
Take a journey of discovery into the last great frontier—the human mind/brain, an instrument of amazing flexibility and plasticity. This eBook is written for brain users who are intent on mining more of the golden possibilities that lie inherent in each of our unique brains. Begin by discovering the role positive attitudes play in learning, and the power of self affirmations and visualizations. Then explore the use of brain wave entrainment mixed with designer music called Metamusic® to achieve enhanced learning states. Join students of all ages who are creating magical learning outcomes using music and Metamusic.® AVAILABLE FROM AMAZON in Kindle Format.

The Journey into the Myst (Vol. 1 of The Myst Series)
   by Alex Bennet and David Bennet (2012)
 What we are about to tell you would have been quite unbelievable to me before this journey began. It is not a story of the reality either of us has known for well over our 60 and 70 years of age, but rather, the reality of dreams and fairytales." This is the true story of a sequence of events that happened at Mountain Quest Institute, situated in a high valley of the Allegheny Mountains of West Virginia. The story begins with a miracle, expanding into the capture and cataloging of thousands of pictures of

electromagnetic spheres widely known as "orbs." This joyous experience became an exploration into the unknown with the emergence of what the author's fondly call the Myst, the forming and shaping of non-random patterns such as human faces, angels and animals. As this phenomenon unfolds, you will discover how the Drs. Alex and David Bennet began to observe and interact with the Myst. This book shares the beginning of an extraordinary *Journey into the Myst*. AVAILABLE FROM AMAZON in Kindle Format. AVAILABLE FROM MQIPress in PDF.

Patterns in the Myst (Vol. 2 of The Myst Series)
by Alex Bennet and David Bennet (2013)
The Journey into the Myst was just the beginning for Drs. Alex and David Bennet. Volume II of the Myst Series brings Science into the Spiritual experience, bringing to bear what the Bennets have learned through their research and educational experiences in physics, neuroscience, human systems, knowledge management and human development. Embracing the paralogical, patterns in the Myst are observed, felt, interpreted, analyzed and compared in terms of their physical make-up, non-randomness, intelligent sources and potential implications. Along the way, the Bennets were provided amazing pictures reflecting the forming of the Myst. The Bennets shift to introspection in the third volume of the series to explore the continuing impact of the Myst experience on the human psyche. AVAILABLE FROM AMAZON in Kindle Format. AVAILABLE FROM MQIPress in PDF.

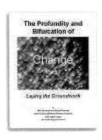

The Profundity and Bifurcation of Change *Part I: Laying the Groundwork* by Alex Bennet and David Bennet with Arthur Shelley, Theresa Bullard and John Lewis

This book lays the groundwork for the **Intelligent Social Change Journey** (ISCJ), a developmental journey of the body, mind and heart, moving from the heaviness of cause-and-effect linear extrapolations, to the fluidity of co-evolving with our environment, to the lightness of breathing our thought and feelings into reality. Grounded in development of our mental faculties, these are phase changes, each building on and expanding previous learning in our movement toward intelligent activity. As we lay the groundwork, we move through the concepts of change, knowledge, forces, self and consciousness. Then, recognizing that we are holistic beings, we provide a baseline model for individual change from within.

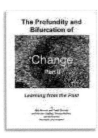

The Profundity and Bifurcation of Change *Part II:*

Learning from the Past by Alex Bennet and David Bennet with Arthur Shelley, Theresa Bullard and John Lewis

Phase 1 of the Intelligent Social Change Journey (ISCJ) is focused on the linear cause-and-effect relationships of logical thinking. Knowledge, situation dependent and context sensitive, is a product of the past. **Phase 1 assumes that for every effect there is an originating cause.** This is where we as a humanity, and as individuals, begin to develop our mental faculties. In this book we explore cause and effect, scan a kaleidoscope of change models, and review the modalities of change. Since change is easier and more fluid when we are grounded, we explore three interpretations of grounding. In preparation for expanding our consciousness, a readiness assessment and sample change agent's strategy are included. (Release 01/15/17)

The Profundity and Bifurcation of Change *Part III:*

Learning in the Present by Alex Bennet and David Bennet with Arthur Shelley, Theresa Bullard and John Lewis

As the world becomes increasingly complex, Phase 2 of the Intelligent Social Change Journey (ISCJ) is focused on **co-evolving with the environment**. This requires a deepening connection to others, moving into empathy. While the NOW is the focus, there is an increasing ability to put together patterns from the past and think conceptually, as well as extrapolate future behaviors. Thus, we look closely at the relationship of time and space, and pattern thinking. We look at the human body as a complex energetic system, exploring the role of emotions as a guidance system, and what happens when we have stuck energy. This book also introduces Knowledge Capacities, different ways of thinking that build capacity for sustainability.

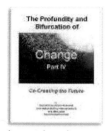

The Profundity and Bifurcation of Change Part IV: Co-Creating the Future by Alex Bennet and David Bennet with Arthur Shelley, Theresa Bullard and John Lewis

As we move into Phase 3 of the Intelligent Social Change Journey (ISCJ), **we fully embrace our role as co-creator**. We recognize the power of thought and the role of attention and intention in our ever-expanding search for a higher level of truth. Whether we choose to engage it or not, we explore mental discipline as a tool toward expanded consciousness. In preparing ourselves for the creative leap, there are ever-deepening connections with others. We now understand that the mental faculties are in service to the intuitional, preparing us to, and expanding our ability to, act in and on the world, living with conscious compassion and tapping into the intuitional at will.

The Profundity and Bifurcation of Change Part V: Living the Future by Alex Bennet and David Bennet with Arthur Shelley, Theresa Bullard, John Lewis and Donna Panucci

We embrace the ancient art and science of Alchemy to **explore the larger shift underway for humanity** and how we can consciously and intentionally speed up evolution to enhance outcomes. In this conversation, we look at balancing and sensing, the harmony of beauty, and virtues for living the future. Conscious compassion, a virtue, is introduced as a state of being connected to morality and good character, inclusive of giving selfless service. We are now ready to refocus our attention on knowledge and consciousness, exploring the new roles these play in our advancement. And all of this—all of our expanding and growth as we move through the Intelligent Social Change journey—is giving a wide freedom of choice as we approach the bifurcation. What will we manifest?

Available in Softback from <u>www.amazon.com</u>

Available in Kindle format from <u>www.amazon.com</u>

Available in PDF format from <u>www.MQIPress.net</u>

Made in the USA
Middletown, DE
03 June 2023

31830636R00161